A DIFFERENT PATH

"I have a disability, yes that's true, but all that means is I may have to take a slightly different path than you."

CONTENTS

The Story	4
A Different Path	14
The Question	24
Education, Fit For Purpose?	32
How Can I Believe In God?	49
Disability Hate Crime	61
Our World	77
Redefined Politically	78
Am I A Stereotypical Disabled Person?	88
A Minority Within A Minority	97
The Housing Crisis	106
What Is Normal?	116
The Disability Card	126
COVID-19: The least of my worries	141
Mental Health	152
Postcode Lottery	165
The Employment Scam	176
Actions Speak Louder Than Words	187

Forgiveness, The Key To True Happiness	202
Are We Completely Independent?	212
Social Media, The Enemy Of Society	224
Are We Unreliable?	235
Health Comes First	260
I Messed Up Big Time	273
The Comments	284
A letter	294
References	302

Introduction
The Story

Hey!

I'm not sure how I intend to do it. I have a lot to say in a short space! Firstly, I've made many mistakes over the years; some didn't affect me, others have made my life hell. Never in a million years did I think I'd write this book. Ten years ago, I wouldn't have believed I'd be publishing a book! During what I thought would be one of the toughest years of my life, I started writing about society and disability. This book was originally meant to be my story from primary school to now. I asked a very close friend to do a photo shoot for the book and cover. Thank you Toby for helping me with this crazy project and for driving to London and back!

I shared my original title with a friend who's a children's author. After reading the first draft of the first chapter she told me to scrap the name and call it A Different Path. I'm so glad I listened to you, Angie! The book was neglected for a few years for no reason at all. I just didn't feel like writing. Later in the book, you will find out about my Christian faith. I have not always found it easy to follow god but I have over the past two years become stronger in my faith.

I believe the break was God's way of saying this is not the finished book. Four years later, we were in lockdown due to Covid-19. This was the most difficult year of my life to date. You will find out why later. I re-read my first draft and cringed immediately. I deleted it, not just into my trashcan, but completed it so that I would never come across it again. In the event someone is able to hack into iCloud and find the original copy of the book, please keep it to yourself, do not share it with anyone else and preferably burn it so that nobody must have to read a book that can be written by a two-year-old.

If I could I would get onto my knees and beg but once I'm on my knees there is no way of getting back up into my wheelchair. After reading that garbage, I decided to scrap the idea of writing a book and focus on writing for myself. I found my love of writing. For the first time, it became a relaxing and somewhat therapeutic time instead of being a chore which it had felt like in the past, especially in education. I started writing about my journey so far, finding my faith and my battle to feel accepted in society. This was not meant to be seen by anyone and it was my way to release emotions. In those four years, I tried to run my own business but ended up being in debt. I decided to give up on life and spent 90% of my time scrolling on social media and YouTube while the state paid me due to my disability.

I was not happy but was not willing to change. I had lost two of my closest friends due to actions I regret to this day. To this day I am still paying off the debt that I owed back in 2018. I had a lot to say and thoughts running through my head. You are so busy during the day that you don't have time for negative thoughts. However, as soon as you lie down at night your brain starts to think about everything you have been trying to ignore. Nights were horrible for me. I could not sleep because negative, damaging and upsetting thoughts would come into my head. It feels like we are in an unprecedented time at the moment. However, it also feels like we say this every year and it doesn't seem to make a difference. There is a lot of uncertainty and anxiety at the moment.

The Western world seems to be becoming more and more tribal, forcing its brand of politics and ideology on countries in the South. This has caused conflict for decades and yet we still ask why there is so much hatred in this world. I do not condone in the least the actions of extremists. Their actions have unfortunately led to the rise of hate crime as people lose trust and judge a book by its cover. People see the colour of your skin and instantly think you are going to bomb their city. I promised myself I wouldn't make this book all political and we are only on page five and I am already talking about world politics ha! To be honest I am surprised I got this far. I thought I would have mentioned it at least four times in the first sentence. Right, let's move on quickly. While yes there is a lot of negativity in today's society we also have a lot of things to be grateful for. I am not here to be Mr. Positive and tell you to Always Look on the Bright Side of Life.

However, there have been things that have been a positive shift in the right direction. BSL is now a recognised language, we have more people with disabilities in the media, every newly built building has to be accessible and finally, after decades of campaigning, we now have children with disabilities attending mainstream schools rather than mental institutions as they had in the 1950s and 60's. Paralympic sports and Paralympic athletes are getting the recognition they deserve. I'm not saying for one moment that we don't have a long way to go. As my old basketball team's manager would always remind me, Rome was not built in a day. Rome has yet to be completed. There is still work to be done. This is a very relevant life analogy for me. We are not flawless, we can always improve, we are a work in progress.

We are always learning and experiencing situations that challenge us and ultimately make us stronger and better. I feel like it has become forbidden to change your opinion and if you do it is branded as insincere and trying to follow the crowd. We have become so cynical of politicians that if they do a U-Turn on a policy then we have permission to shred them to pieces just because they have had second thoughts and have spoken and heard what the public want and need. I've been accused of introducing my faith into every conversation. This is very rare as I'm not one to shout and scream about my faith. In this book, I will be talking about my faith, the challenges and how ultimately everything I have done and experienced is because of God. These trials and challenges are a test to see if we can still worship the king of kings and Lord of Lords despite not wanting to. This is especially true when we feel like our walls are crumbling. Now I understand that most of you reading this will not have a relationship with God. I understand that for some in the disability community religion is a no-go area.

I wouldn't be true to myself if I didn't share my faith. I am not about to preach at you or force you to believe in God just because I do. I mention it because I want you to understand how my faith and Christian upbringing have shaped me to be who I am. When I first had this idea to write the book I Was not going to mention my faith at all. It has only been in the past couple of months that I realised that I would not be true to myself if I didn't. Fun fact, while I write each chapter I am listening to worship music. Even when I have forsaken god I have still blasted worship songs through my speakers. Even when I stopped going to church I still blasted worship music through my speakers.

Some of my closest friends are atheists. They refuse to even consider the possibility of there being a god. They can't get their heads around the fact that there is hurt and suffering on this earth but there is a god that is kind, loving and everlasting. A god that sent his son to die for us, to forgive us for our sins. I get why so many people are angry and blame God for their suffering and in all honesty I was like that once. It's easier to blame someone than to take ownership and responsibility for our own actions. If we are completely honest with each other and ourselves we have all questioned why me at some point in our lives. I still ask that from time to time. That question is a prayer, a prayer to ask God to show me what he has planned for me. A prayer for guidance so that I am able to follow him and understand my purpose in life.

It is difficult to trust God when you are one of the 7000 disabled people being attacked due to your disability. You are also told you are not able to work as your employer will not make any reasonable adjustments. It is difficult to trust God when you feel neglected by society and excluded from everything. It is challenging to believe in a god of love and kindness when all you can see is the glass half empty. What I have learnt over the past decade is that everything that has made my life more stressful has nothing to do with God but with my own actions. I have caused myself pressure sores, I have neglected my health, and I chose to sit at home watching YouTube rather than building my experiences and qualifications.

I was the one who put myself in debt. I chose to lie to people and destroy lifelong friendships. I knew what I was doing and there was nobody else to blame for the consequences. Yes, I am fed up with the doctor's appointments and the waiting list to receive the support I need. However, again, that is not because of God but the system we are in. I am tired and fed up of being angry at God. I am tired of just being angry generally. I got into the mindset that I could only negatively view the world. I couldn't positively see people, so I judged them without much thought. However, I was the one who excluded myself from society. I judged society just because a minority of people did not like me being a part of society. I recently read a book called God on Mute by Pete Greig. At the beginning of the book, he adds a quote written during WW2, on the wall of a cellar, by a Jew in the Cologne concentration camp.

> I believe in the sun even when it is not shining.
> I believe in love even when I cannot feel it.
> I believe in God even when he is silent.

This is a very powerful statement and one that has challenged my own journey and faith. As I read this I was reminded of one of my favourite verses in the Bible. Hebrews 11:1 explains, "Faith is the confidence in what we hope for and the assurance of what we do not see." Why is this so significant to me? Throughout school I was never one of the cool kids, I wasn't on the school football team. I was so caught up with my issues and believed the world revolved around me I never looked at the bigger picture. I tricked myself into believing that I was a failure and that nobody saw me as a person. Too much time was spent thinking about times when people treated me like I was a waste of space. I convinced myself that everyone felt the same way. That's when my anxiety and depression started. If you feel like the world hates you and you don't feel accepted, you'll start thinking about committing suicide. That was me in 2011. Self harm was a daily part of my life, I thought about ways to kill myself. I would often lie awake thinking how much the world hated me.

This was as well as trying to complete my GCSE's. As per usual I put way too much pressure on myself to pass all my exams. If I didn't achieve the grade that I needed to get into sixth form I would punish myself and convinced myself I was worthless and I had nothing going for me. Fast forward to summer 2013, I had completed all my GCSE's and I had agreed with my consultant to have a major operation to detether my spinal cord. I was in hospital for two weeks and I had to lie down for the majority of the time. Before I continue, I would like to thank all those who came to visit me while I was there. Towards the end of my time in hospital I received my GCSE results. My mum drove to my school and collected the A4 brown envelope.

Throughout Year 11, I completed several exams early and received the results. I was never strong in Maths and I didn't progress until the end of year 10. My predicted grade was a G. Yes, I know the whole grading system has changed and even saying that makes me feel old. I stayed after school doing mock exams and having 1:1 sessions to get my grades up. My goal was a C, the highest grade I could achieve in the foundation exam. The day I got my results, I was feeling sick, anxious and I had already convinced myself I had failed.

My teacher came round with brown envelopes. I opened the envelope and without looking at the results, I showed my teaching assistant the results. I thought if I saw her reaction first, I could work out what my expectations should be. Yeah, that failed! I turned the paper around and scanned the information. The atmosphere in the room was strange. Some students were elated with their results, while others burst out crying. There were only five people in the class who achieved the highest grade. The thought of me having to resit the exam was not something I wanted to think about. Fortunately, this was not something I had to think about.

As soon as I saw the grade, a huge smile appeared on my face. Somehow with God's help and guidance and the support of my teachers I achieved the grade that I was told was impossible for me to achieve. As I lay in my hospital bed with my parents at my side I opened the envelope. The current education system is an epic fail. I talk more about that later, the current system is focused more on the academic and less on how students learn best. Though these subjects are relevant, the way they are taught does not fit the 21st century. Just a side note, I didn't always think certain subjects were that crucial. It turns out that all the subjects are relevant on a day-to-day basis. I wish I listened more in my Food Tech lessons, If I had I probably would be eating and cooking a lot better. If I had spent more time taking photos and gathering evidence as instructed by my teacher, then my final projects in photography would have been pieces I could be proud of. It was not that I was not capable of achieving the grades I desired, I just did not have the willingness to spend time revising.

I never found a way to revise but also enjoy it enough to retain the information. I have come to realise that the information that I have retained is because of the way I have learned about the information. This is something I still struggle with today. There are routines and pieces of information I don't seem to remember. It is not that I am not able to remember, it is that I am not making the effort to pay attention. These routines are boring to me but they are also routines that billions of people do every day. Hygiene has never been top of my list but I know it should be. I just seem to always find a distraction which usually is Youtube or Netflix or talking to people on FaceTime. I know what I need to do but I just choose not to do them because in my head I am thinking what is the point.

I have not valued my self-worth. I have to do better and I will do better. I am not proud of the way I live. I am not proud of the way I look after myself. I am not happy with the way I am playing the cards that I have been dealt. I am tired of the way I am living but I don't know how to get out of this cycle. I am ready for change but I don't have the mental capacity to change on my own. I can't do this alone as I seem to always give up after two weeks. I know I can change because I have changed other routines and I am still carrying on with those routines today. I know I can but there doesn't seem to be any motivation. As a kid I used to see people like Ade Adepitan and Tanni Grey-Thompson on TV and think that they had it all together.

I thought that they didn't have the same struggles as me. It was not until I got older and started to join Facebook groups that I realised I was not alone. I realised that others struggled with motivation especially if they felt that the system had failed them. The difference between me and Ade or Tanni is they have the motivation to jump over those hurdles and to get on with life no matter what. I want that same motivation, that same drive but I don't...yet! Today is Sunday so maybe this week will be different. Start fresh. I hope and pray that as you read this book you will become more aware of the journey that millions of people are on around the world. The journey we take in trying to feel accepted in a world that is not always willing to accept us for who we are.

We are all broken and we need to realise that. Once we have made that connection, maybe the world will be a better place. A world that doesn't care about the way we look or act. A world that is about community and loving each other. A world where we look after each other no matter what nation they are from or what language they speak. Maybe I am hoping for too much. We need to be realistic instead of moving full steam ahead. We will have to take small baby steps as Rome was not built in a day. We need to work this out together, share ideas, listen to each other's views and experiences and we have to do this without shouting at each other. We can respect others without necessarily agreeing with them.

We cannot judge someone's actions without walking in their shoes. I need to warn you about some things in the book. You are about to read something that has not been written just by me. I have had the privilege and honour to meet people along the way and their stories are worth telling. Their stories of when they were attacked just for living their life. Their names have been changed. To those who contributed to the book thank you. Your stories and your passion for change have inspired me. I hope that by sharing these stories people will wake up and smell the coffee. Oh one last thing before you sit back and start reading the first chapter while you sip your coffee. Thank you for buying this book, It has been a crazy journey trying to get this all on to paper.

"YOU'RE NOT DISABLED BY THE DISABILITY YOU HAVE,
YOU ARE ABLE BY THE ABILITIES YOU HAVE."

CHAPTER 1
A Different Path

"There is no greater disability in society than the inability to see a person as more."

I just came across an amazing quote that perfectly captures how some parts of society perceive me. It's by Robert M. Hensel, who was born in a small town in New York in 1969. Hensel, who has Spina Bifida, believed that we should focus on people's abilities rather than their disabilities. In 2000, he successfully advocated for Oswego County to designate October 1st - 7th as beyond limitations week. Isn't that incredible? In 2004 he realised that society was still concentrating more on his disability and less on his many abilities. He wanted to change that perspective. He, therefore, decided that the only way to get people to change their minds was to set a world record.

He, therefore, decided to attempt to do the longest continuous wheelie. He not only completed the task by setting a new world record of 6.178 miles, but he still holds the title to this day! When being interviewed, Hensel said, "I have a disability, yes that's true, but all that means is I may have to take a slightly different path than you". This got me thinking; It's interesting that even before we are born, we have already been given labels. For me, Male, British, Son, Nephew, Brother. Harmless right? Lets' add disabled and physically impaired into the mix. I am just stating the obvious. These labels that we are given even before birth start the foundations of our personality, the characteristics that make us who we are. For many disabled people, the labels given to us are hostile and, unfortunately, overpower the other positive labels we were born with. The label disability has become a negative label that then diminishes our abilities. Our one disability becomes more important than the many abilities that we have.

It becomes a massive barrier that gets in the way of our dreams and goals for our future. My name is Simeon Wakely, and six months before I was born, I was diagnosed with Spina Bifida, Hydrocephalus, and later Scoliosis. Spina Bifida is a disability that people are born with. As the name suggests, it's to do with the spine. There was a gap at the bottom of my spine when I was born. The doctors had to do an operation when I was 48 hours old to close the gap. Due to this, the nerves that send messages from my brain to the muscles in my legs are damaged. As a result, I am paralysed from my waist down. I have a manual chair that helps me get around everywhere, so my chair has become my legs.

Hydrocephalus is a disability that sometimes gets mistaken as a disability that comes with Spina Bifida. It doesn't! Hydrocephalus is when Cerebrospinal fluid (CSF) builds up and surrounds the brain. For someone without Hydrocephalus, the CSF can be absorbed into their bloodstream. However, for someone with Hydrocephalus, the fluid needs to be transported using a shunt that helps the fluid flow into their stomach. Scoliosis is a pain in the back. No, seriously, it is! Scoliosis is where the spine curves to the side. It can affect people of any age, from babies to adults, but most often starts in children aged 10 to 15. Scoliosis can be improved with treatment, but it is not usually a sign of anything serious. Treatment is not always needed if it's mild.

Treatment for scoliosis depends on your age, how severe the curve is, and whether it's likely to worsen with time. A brace may be considered an alternative to surgery if you're not well enough to undergo an operation. This may sound negative, and yes, it can be at times. However, I am glad and proud to have been born with a disability. I understand how that sentence may come across but let me explain what I mean. All I know is what it's like to be in a wheelchair. I don't miss walking because I have never had the experience of walking. If I were an "able-bodied" person, I would probably have turned a blind eye to the issues that disabled people face daily. I would not hold the same values as I do. Don't get me wrong,

I get fed up with all the doctor's appointments I need to attend, but they are only a tiny part of my life. Likewise, my disability is only a small part of my life. So, Should we be looking at the label of disability so negatively? Is society to blame for this label turning into a negative thing? Or are disabled people partly to blame? In another recent report, 67% of the public openly shared that they are embarrassed to talk to and socialise with disabled people. When hearing that statistic, I was shocked; I knew it would be high but not higher than 50%. I'm fed up with people pointing fingers and putting the blame on other people. It is my responsibility as a disabled person to change this. It is our responsibility as a minority community to make a change. We need to show that we are proud to be called disabled. We need to show that life is sometimes challenging but not impossible.

So we are not ashamed of discussing our disability and are open to conversations. When I was in secondary school, and people asked me questions, I took offence very quickly and did not want to participate. It was my responsibility at school to show that people did not need to talk to the teaching assistant or my parents rather than me. My responsibility was to help my friends understand that despite having this label shadowing me, It does not mean I could not meet up on the weekend. But I chose not to. I decided to stay in my little world and just let things happen. I was recently talking to a friend of mine about society's mindset. Today, people rapidly judge each other on their appearances, how they dress or walk, or the amount of make-up they put on. I'm not just talking about disability now; I'm talking about everyone. Whenever the word disability is mentioned in a conversation, the first thing that comes into people's heads is the sentence, "They CAN'T do something." I am a wheelchair user. Does that mean I am bed bound or cannot communicate for myself? No! I can't believe I will be quoting this person, but Richard Hammond said a fascinating statement on the Amazon Prime Series "The Grand Tour". He said, "Able-bodied people like to think that everything that could be done to make life easier and convenient for disabled people has been done. But when you find yourself in that position, you realise it hasn't." And he has a point!

It was humbling to hear this from someone who has a following that might not engage in disability issues and who might turn a blind eye to disability issues with no fault. This is why my point earlier is so essential for me to remember. Society is ignorant when it comes to disability. This is not their fault; they don't use a wheelchair daily or need to take 19 different types of medication to keep them alive for another day. They don't need to visit the hospital every two weeks for various appointments. So I think we need to be more open with people to eliminate political correctness. No more outstanding example is with kids. When you're four years old, you love asking questions.

"Why is the sky blue? Why is the grass green?". When I'm in town, and it's a Saturday, and all the families are out enjoying their days of school and work, I hear now, and again kids asking their parents why I am in a wheelchair. Now, the parents go bright red and tell their kids to shut up, try to distract them, or pretend they did not hear the question. Now, firstly I should stop, turn to the kid and explain. I should because if we start having conversations about disability, it all begins with a question. Even though my brain is telling me, "Stop and talk to the child", my body seems to ignore my brain. I seem to be still pushing away from the child. Also, it is wrong of the parent to do what they did. Adults seem to think, "For goodness sake, what has just happened? What is that poor boy going to think? Why did my child ask that question? It had to be my child." There are a couple of things wrong with that statement. Firstly, I may be short for my age, but I am not a boy. I am a 24-year-old man. Secondly, It is an entirely valid question for them to ask. Most likely, they will see the wheelchair as a buggy or a pushchair, so why would a 24-year-old man still be in a pushchair? When we tell our kids to be quiet when they ask questions, they will be more reluctant to ask questions. They will join the 67% of society who are ashamed or even shy of socialising with disabled people just in case they offend us. People always say, "We need to start educating the next generation", but I think it doesn't start with them. It begins with changing the views and opinions of their parents.

They need to lead by example. Children copy and look up to their parents. Suppose they see their parents feeling awkward and embarrassed to ask questions or talk about disability issues. In that case, their child will grow up feeling uncomfortable and ashamed to ask questions. You need to ask questions to understand what life is like for people society perceives as disabled. It's crazy to say this, but the lack of questions is because we are British. It is not polite to ask personal questions like "why are you in a wheelchair?" It is the same as being in a lift with strangers! Nobody talks, but if you go to the US, everyone talks to each other in the elevator, which is how it is. Nobody cares about political correctness or never talking to strangers. It is as if we have moved forward in some areas but are still stuck in the 1800s in others things.

When I talk to students about my experiences growing up with Spina Bifida, I make sure I leave enough time to allow them to ask questions. Now, I have found that if I went into a primary school, I would be asked questions like "How do you go to bed?" Or "Will you ever walk?" These questions might seem obvious, and I could say a one-worded answer, but what would that do? It would show that I do not want to talk and give short answers to try and move on with the conversation. It means that the child will grow up, remember that one experience, and think that disabled people like to be left alone. It goes back to the point that I made earlier. I am responsible for showing that a stereotypical disabled person is not your average disabled person. Our responsibility is to live our lives to our full potential. Some might argue that we should not care about other people's opinions. Yes, that is true; the flip side is that employers will say no to disabled people for no valid reason. It means shops and cafes will not get ramps, lifts, or accessible toilets. There is a compelling argument for the label being positive. It can spark social concern and aid advocacy efforts. For people with a recognised disability, advocacy groups have an opportunity to identify the problem and lobby for it on behalf of the individuals.

In other words, Labelling creates cohesive communication for advocacy groups. It may make the majority without disabilities more tolerant of the minority with disabilities. Labelling allows the person without the disability to research the condition and make them more tolerant of the person with the disability. This is so because people are labelled based on their educational or medical diagnosis. It makes it easier for legislators to understand the need for laws protecting the rights of individuals with disabilities. In cases where applicable, Labelling allows legislators to see the discrimination that persons with disabilities face, thus, making legislators develop laws to protect persons with disabilities.

Labelling has led to the development of specialised teaching methods, assessment approaches, and behavioural interventions that are useful for teachers of all students. By Labelling, educators can research the disabilities and identify or develop specialised methods to teach students with varied disabilities. An obvious pro of labelling a child with special needs in the classroom is that teachers can use this information to help the child learn using their limitations as a guide. By labelling a child, they will receive extra services that they may not have been able to obtain otherwise. For example, the child may be able to receive instruction in a learning support room at a pace that works for them.

In this book there will be different paths leading to the same destination. These paths all have potholes and broken paving stones. Terminology has become possibly out of control. We have become so invested in making sure we use the right labels we forget the person's true identity as a human being. Rose Kivi, author of "How the 'Learning Disabled'" once said:

> "They can receive frequent repetition and instruction in a much smaller setting with other students just like them,"

Kivi says that by labelling the child as "learning disabled," these students can get help to remediate their specific problems.

> "Receiving instruction based on what students need is crucial in helping them excel and be successful in the future,"

The teachers and staff are better equipped to teach the child in a way that ensures learning by knowing the specific learning disability of each student. However, there are also issues with labelling students who have conditions. Firstly, Low Self-Esteem among the students. Many laws protect the rights of students with disabilities, including access to services and helping to ensure these students are not discriminated against.

> "Students identifying as students with disabilities may doubt themselves, feel that they are not as smart as others, and create a sense of learned helplessness,"

First, these students may feel that they cannot do well in school or are not wise. Furthermore, there is the issue of diminished expectations from both parents and teachers. In some cases, parents and educators may unintentionally underestimate the abilities of children with special needs. This could lead to lowered academic expectations, as they may assume that these students cannot meet the same standards as their peers. If the teachers and parents don't believe in the child, then the child won't believe in himself either. Newsome says:

> "Lower expectations set up the student for failure,"

Finally, Peer Issues. Fellow students can be mean and make fun of students with special needs because they are different. "This may lead to the student having difficulty making friends and makes them vulnerable to bullying or another mistreatment," adds Newsome. Teachers and parents must help these students to build a positive self-image and boost their self-esteem by helping them develop healthy relationships with others and to recognise their strengths. In 2010 W.L. Heward said:

> "Labelling is required to be included in special education. Under current law, to receive special education services, a child must be identified as having a disability"

So here's to educating so many ignorant minds. I suggest they are disabled, rejecting our place as part of humanity. We have so much to impart, unbound amounts to give, but lots of them believe that we have no point in living. We embrace them as they are. So, why not welcome us? For being just how we are, they need the blinkers off. Despite the intelligence man's pride, disability issues remain low on the shelf. Awareness is something a lot of them need.

If only we could eradicate their ignorance and greed. A little chip on my shoulder, though you may have guessed, in the style of many of us, it generally stays suppressed. Ironically, so many have no care, believing we should be in homes shut away from all out there. If they took just a moment to think it through, they too might end up disabled; how would they cope? What would they do? In a world just like us with disability issues to bear, I'll bet they'd all start crying, finding so much so unfair.

So in a desire to spread knowledge of the discrimination we all have to face, I try to write words with the wish that ultimately, we're treated as we should be. Too many people are entirely ignorant of disability issues. They do not accept us as normal human beings with so much to offer to society. They need to get the blinkers off, smell the coffee, stop stereotyping us and get a grip on how much we have to give. It might take time, it will not happen overnight, and it might not happen in our lifetime, but it will for your kids and their kids. In the following 365 pages, I hope whoever reads this realises we are all human. We all make mistakes, but we all participate in life.

CHAPTER 2
The Question

"If I were to say 'why me god?' About the bad things, then I should say, 'why me, god?' About all the good things in my life" – Arthur Ashe

I've only asked, "why me?" around 148,920 times in my life! For any mathematicians out there, you will be able to work out that 17 times a day. For me, the question has never changed, but the recipient of the question has. That question was directed to God between the ages of 4-15. Why on earth would he give me a life with so many limitations? He is, of course, meant to be a god of love and kindness and yet is putting me in a wheelchair showing me love? Not in a million years, so God, why do I have to live this life? If you can heal the sick, then heal me!

However, as I get older, I realise I am asking the question to the wrong person. Yikes! I was angry and didn't know how to project my feelings to others. So, as usual, I blame the one person there for me. The lyrics "I was lost, but now I'm found. I was blind, but now I see" come to mind. So, who is the question meant for? Have they replied? Have I got any more apparent answers to why me? I realised my question was directed to 4 sectors; Public Transport, Health, Building regulators and councils.

Richard Hammond said a fascinating statement on the Amazon Prime Series "The Grand Tour".

> "Able-bodied people like to think that everything that could be done to make life easier and convenient for disabled people has been done. But when you find yourself in that position, you realise it hasn't."

Today's society has disabled me, not God, not Jesus, just humanity! If every building had a ramp or lift, if every platform were the same height, I wouldn't struggle to get on and off the train. If every car park had more than five disabled bays, it would mean I could go out without anxiety. It would mean I could spend the millions of pounds the government gives me due to my disability. When I have spoken in different schools about life with a disability, I always share the five main hurdles I need to overcome to live a "normal" life. There I go again about being normal. What is normal? More on that later! As a wheelchair user, I have to think before I Act.

I can't just say, "Let's just jump in the car and go away for the weekend", because I need to think about making sure the room is wheelchair accessible. I live in Bath, a beautiful Georgian city with incredible architecture and 95% listed! Unfortunately, the infrastructure cannot be changed when a building is listed. Now I would understand if it was churches or historic buildings such as the Roman baths. However, most churches and even historic buildings are now pretty much accessible. I'm talking about retail shops like HMV or Costa, with three massive steps leading into the cafe. I recently went to Exeter with my Dad for 24 hours. I love just going around the city, visiting shops and visiting the cathedral. I was pleasantly surprised that an 18th-century Cathedral was fully accessible, yet a bookstore with three floors had no lift. Figure that one out!

The only explanation I can come up with is that a cathedral is a place of worship. Therefore they can't stop people from attending services. A few years ago, I met a friend after leaving school. Now, for those who know me, I'm always running late. I'm trying to improve, but it's still a problem today! I'm already five years late writing this book. However, on this occasion, I was early, and I mean 45 minutes early! So, I decided that to pass the time; I would go into a store that is not wheelchair accessible and talk with the manager. I was running on adrenaline, probably too cocky even for me. Anyway, I went to the front cashier and asked for the manager. After a few moments, a tall, muscular guy walks toward me and bends down. Some people you know will not be friendly, giving you blunt answers and trying to send you on your way as soon as possible.

This was him! I explained that I understood that the building is probably listed, but there must be a way to access the top and bottom floors! If a church built in the 18th century can do it, surely the store could fit a lift in. Thinking the answer will be the same line: "We would love to, but we are not able to due to planning permission." His response was different. An answer that, even for me, I was not expecting.

"I don't have £35,000 in my pocket to fit a lift in."

Yep, nothing to do with building regulations, just a manager who didn't want to spend money on a lift. He probably is right about not having £35,000 in his pocket. However, the company last year made a profit of £17 million. Yes, the company is now close to administration but still makes a profit of £17 million. That is enough to add 45,000+ lifts and ramps and still have £14 million left over. The story isn't yet over! He suggested asking a staff member to go and get the products I wanted. This was very kind of him to offer…not! What if I wanted just to browse? What if I saw a product that wasn't on my list?

That would be impossible! But like every suggestion, I tried to prove that plan would not work. A few months down the line and I had just started college. A friend of mine wanted to go into the store. I asked him to get me a few DVDs for me to look at. After 5-10 minutes of waiting on the middle floor, he returned with 15 DVDs. We laid them all on the bed, ensuring we were in the way. The manager saw us and rushed into the office to ensure he didn't interact with us. Now, this was a stunt; I didn't want any DVDs. I just wanted to prove that if I were to get someone to get a few DVDs for me, It would not be practical at all, and I would be in the way of every customer. Since then, I have not yet been back to that store. The manager might have changed, and their outlook on these issues might have changed. There have been numerous occasions where I have been in similar situations.

To be honest, I have lost count of the number of times I have been to shops, offices, and cafe's to find there is no lift or ramp or even a disabled bathroom. On other occasions, I find that there is access to the building, but then you're screwed after that as there are two flights of stairs, no lift, or the escalator is out of order, and there are no meeting rooms on the ground floor! My other issue with public places is that the company uses the disabled bathroom as a store cupboard! They tick the box for being accessible but then fill the facilities with so much junk that there is no room for anyone to stand, let alone someone in a wheelchair! As you can probably tell, this angers me. I was doing a talk at a school a few years ago. I wanted to talk about the barriers that society has created for people who use a wheelchair.

I tried to find photos of disabled bathrooms that were not accessible. Most pictures were of bathrooms with no grab rails, the sink was too high, or the red emergency cord was in the wrong place. There was, however, a photo that even I was shocked at a disabled bathroom with five steps leading in. You must go up five steps in a wheelchair to access a disabled bathroom. How do they expect me to access the toilet in a manual wheelchair, let alone an electric wheelchair?

When I saw this, my jaw dropped, and I had to pinch myself to ensure I wasn't dreaming. I had no words; I laughed, not because I thought it was funny. I laughed because I was astonished that someone thought it was a good idea to put an accessible bathroom on a floor that could only be accessed by going up five steps. This is another classic example when the restaurant only did it to tick a box. Regulations are so vague that companies can get away with poor access because there are no clear instructions. A door has to be wide enough for a wheelchair, but it's no good if it's on a floor with no lift or ramp! It's all well and good having a venue with hearing loops, but if they are in a wheelchair and the venue has no elevator, they are screwed anyway.

People don't think that you can have more than one condition! It's completely beyond me!Let's talk about people parking in disabled bays when they don't have a blue badge. Let me paint the picture, you have just spent 15-20 minutes trying to get your wheelchair in the car, taking the wheels off, and it's also pissing down with rain. You arrive in town to do your weekly shopping. The sun has just appeared, and the rain has stopped. You think things are looking up! You get your blue badge out ready and look for the sign for disabled parking. You then find that every disabled bay is being used! Not to worry, seeing so many people with disabilities visiting the town is fantastic. As you pass each car parked in the disabled bay, you realise that only 2 of the seven cars have a blue badge.

You see a group walking, jumping, and laughing towards one of the parked cars in the disabled bays. You stop and ask them if they need to be parked there. "We were only going to get a KFC! We were only there for 5 minutes." The worst examples are when the person sees you are disabled, so start limping to pretend they are disabled. I bet some of you are laughing in embarrassment because you have done it yourself. To be honest, I would like to say I wouldn't if I was not disabled, but as I said at the beginning, I wouldn't hold the same values as I do today if I was not in a wheelchair. So the moral of the story is that if I ever see you parked in the disabled bay when you shouldn't, you will wish you were disabled. That is not a threat, that's a promise! Wheelie Bins, I promised a friend I would talk about wheelie bins. I kid you not; 95% of our conversations are about wheelie bins and how they are the enemy. I once asked them to talk to me about why they hated them. 2 hours later; I was still on the phone talking about wheelie bins, not even exaggerating! So why are they an issue? The law is that the wheelie bin must be placed on the pavement rather than the driveway. So yes, there was a debate in parliament, and MPs had to vote for wheelie bins to be on the pavement rather than the driveway. It must have been a quiet day in the office if that was all they could debate about! Anyway, She lives at the end of the street, and if she takes her daughter to school, She will need to do about 30 slaloms, even before leaving your road.

It's even worse if the pavement is only wide enough for the wheelie bin. You will need to hope and pray that there is a dropped curb; otherwise, you will end up wheeling backwards to the nearest drop curb because there is not enough pavement even to do a 180° turn! Now can you see why we hate Wheelie bin day? This is a good Segway to talk about Pavements and roads. Hold the front page. Pavements don't all have dropped curbs. I know! With 1.2 million people who use a wheelchair in the UK, you would think all pavements have a drop curb. Let me again set the scene. I'm in town trying to get to a shop. I enter a busy road and make sure I'm on the pavement. I realise I'm on the wrong side of the road! The obvious thing to do is cross to the other side. But, there is no dropped curb near you!

You don't want to carry on down just in case there isn't one for miles, so you turn back. You have probably done 3 miles just to get to that one shop! Another situation I have found myself in more than once is a drop curb on my side but no dropped curb to get onto the other pavement. I haven't finished; the lack of drop curbs isn't my only issue with pavements! People are parked in ligament places alongside the pavement, but they seem not to realise that the space is on the road rather than the pavement. I have lost count of the number of cars, mainly vans, parked halfway on the pavement, and it's always just before the next drop curb, public transport is my worst nightmare. The only thing that can cause my anxiety to go is in 0.2 seconds. Why? Cause if something goes wrong, I'm screwed and properly screwed! I know I am not the only person in a wheelchair who finds public transport a nightmare. I have friends who have never taken public transport unless with friends or family. That is entirely understandable! So let me share with you some of the horrific situations I have been in.

Let's start with buses...

So, It isn't necessarily the actual vehicle that causes me anxiety. There is much preparation that takes place even before I have left the flat! How long will it take to push to the bus stop? Will the bus stop be raised? Will the bus stop at the other end, be wheelchair accessible? Is it past 9 am? Will I need to get multiple buses to get to the destination? It is no secret that it takes a while for me to get ready! Not because of my disability, but because I get distracted by watching youtube on my phone! Seriously, my phone is like, "You have plenty of time! Just watch one more video." And every time I fool for it and watch the following video and then the next, and instead of having 2 hours, I have 20 minutes! So, In my head, I need to shower, shave, get dressed, put my back brace on and then wheel to the bus stop 5 minutes away. I also need to make sure I have enough catheters.

So as you can see a lot to remember and think about! No wonder I forget my keys sometimes! Always remember my phone but never my keys. Due to Covid-19, I need to make sure I have my mask! Anyway, I get to the bus stop on a steep incline, meaning when the driver puts the ramp down, it is at a 90° angle! Too steep for me to push without tipping back. Yet again, not the fault of the company but the council! The beautiful NHS! Let me start by saying the NHS is amazing! The number of hours the doctors and nurses spends to ensure we are healthy and kept safe. The only thanks they get is us spending 1 minute a week clapping, and even that routine ended as soon as we came out of lockdown. So why have I directed the question to them? I haven't directed the question to the doctors and nurses but the management. The guy in charge of the NHS, The Right Honourable Sajid Javid. The newly appointed Health Minister after Matt Hancock, his predecessor, was caught cheating on his wife by the CCTV Cameras in his office. I'm not even making it up! Why is my question directed to him if he has only been in his role for a month? Because he is in charge of making sure there is enough funding for the NHS.

The NHS is and has been underfunded for over a decade now! If the NHS were adequately funded and properly staffed with no cuts, there would be no waiting lists for new wheelchairs. Getting assessed for an adapted home would take weeks rather than months. People who need weekly physio would be able to rather than a select few. I get we are in a pandemic; however, these issues have been happening for a decade now; Covid has just highlighted the importance of a well-funded health system. People say we need to be grateful for a free health system, and I am. I am so thankful, but all I am saying is that it could be so much better. Doctors and nurses need a good pay rise. If it weren't for them, our vaccine rollout would fail. The government spends each day telling us what they have done to beat the virus, but they have yet to say what the hundreds of doctors, nurses and care staff have done to keep us safe.

Later in the book, I will discuss my experience through the lockdown. I, unfortunately, spent a week in the hospital. I was in during the week before the national lockdown. I will never forget one doctor coming in to tell me that visiting restrictions would be cut to one visit 20 min a day. She was both emotionally and physically drained. So I want to end this chapter by saying thank you to every doctor, nurse and healthcare assistant, paramedic and emergency call handler. To everyone who maintains the NHS, from cleaners to radiographers, it is because of you that I can live my life and will never take it for granted! May the clapping never stop!

CHAPTER 3
Education, Fit For Purpose?

"Ask me my three main priorities for Government, and I'll tell you: education, education, education."

Tony Blair 1st October 1996

Every government says that education is critical and that the education system fits its purpose. The question is, does it work for the 21st century? Is the education system inclusive? Is the current system partly to blame for dividing "Disabled" people and "Able-bodied" people? Over seven months, I met with different groups of people that helped shape and form the EHCP. I created surveys which were then sent out to parents and students. I also had meetings with SENCOs to get an understanding of the process and understand the process, what the school's involvement is with the EHCP and what the changes to the system mean. EHCP stands for Education, Health and Care Plan. The Education Health and Care Plans have replaced Statements of Special Educational Needs and Learning Difficulty Assessments.

Professionals in education put together the plan, health and social care to ensure children with SEND have a package of support to help them through to adulthood (until they are 25). In this chapter, I will be sharing the process that takes place for the EHCP. The main topics and some of the issues that need to be addressed have yet to be discussed. When was EHCP introduced in 2013? What was the experience of a physically disabled young person in mainstream school, and what could improve that experience?

Before 2013 any child with a physical or developmental disability was given a statement. This document would help the school, social worker, Occupational Therapist and any other professional involved in the student's life to understand how best to support them. In addition, this document would be reviewed at the annual review meeting, where any problems or plans were discussed. In 2013 the government decided that there needed to be a new system that made it more student-centred. So they scrapped the Statement and brought the EHCP (Educational Health Care Plan). This plan was welcomed by Special Educational Needs Coordinators (SENCO) in secondary schools and, more importantly, gave the students a more powerful voice.

In this chapter, I will examine how the Statement and the EHCP differ and how each process supports the child with special needs. I have spoken to SENCOs, Parents, Support workers and Students to get their perspectives on how the mainstream education system helps students with physical disabilities. I was on what's called the old Statement until Year 10. Every year leading up to my annual review, I had to fill out a two-page form that included questions about how I felt the year had gone so far. It was to clarify any problems I wanted them to discuss on my behalf. The form was used during the Annual Review and meant I did not have to be at the meeting. I did go into the meeting, but it was only for 5 minutes in the end. In the forum, several different professionals attended. I remember always hated going in as I never had a chance to speak, and the only way I could get my voice heard was through a two-page document.

In Year 10, I transferred over to the EHCP. The idea was to make the EHCP more student-centred, and one of the elements that allowed that was called a "One Page Profile." This was a Powerpoint Presentation that the student completed. I was then allowed to present the presentation in my Annual review giving me a more significant voice in my future. As a young disabled person who participated in the pre-2013 system, I have identified two crucial issues with this system. Firstly, the voice of the student was often barely heard. This led to the inevitable outcome that plans of support were made, which were not shaped by the student. I think it is essential that the meeting was about the student, and sometimes the student was there in the forum, but they'd only have 5 or 6 minutes to talk. So many plans were made for the student, yet the student did not have much voice.

So, why are Mainstream Schools important?

Most disabled children have been educated in special schools for over a century, excluded from their non-disabled peers. Only in the last 30 years has this started to change as more disabled children have been increasingly given the right to mainstream education. As a result, this form of apartheid is slowly exposed and removed. I strongly believe in mainstream education because of the right of non-disabled and disabled children to be educated together. Mainstream schools provide disabled children with the exact expectations to succeed as their peers. In addition, the social skills needed to compete in a non-disabled world which special schools fail to do. Mainstream schools prepare disabled children for the real world, not to say anyone deserves to be bullied.

My views on mainstream education do not mean I do not believe in special education. On the contrary, I firmly believe everyone should get the specific education they need. I think the criticisms against mainstream education by parents and others are because many children are integrated into their schools rather than included. Integration is when the child is required to fit in with the school simply, and no consideration of their needs is considered.

This is not proper inclusion, where the school reasonably adapts its policies, practices and teaching methods to accommodate the child's specific needs. There will always be some middle ground where the child must learn how to adapt to the school. In the same way, they will need to adapt to other situations throughout their life to succeed.

In a recent interview, Dame Tanni Grey Thompson said:

"Special schools are 'sold' to parents based on promises and exploiting the parents' fears of how their disabled child will cope in the real world. Like everything, special education has been ruled by fashion and trends over the years rather than anything else. The policy of free schools allows parents and others to set up their special schools on any ideology they choose. This is a further step into this consumerism 'fad' culture where the parents' wants come before the child's needs."

She went on to say:

"My concern with the government is that they have turned the issue into a matter of parental choice, where parents of disabled children should have the right to choose a special or mainstream school, arguing they wish to end the 'bias towards inclusion. This standpoint assumes in this instance, as opposed to any other, parents are suitably experienced to make decisions that would determine whether or not their child will have an opacity to be properly included into Society."

This scenario that Dame Tanni Grey Thompson shares is, unfortunately, something that happens frequently. I recently spoke to a Secondary school student who lived in London while at primary school. He explained his difficulties while finding a primary school that could support him with his physical disability. Tom, now 17, has Epilepsy and Spina Bifida and Hydrocephalus.

When I met with Tom, we started by talking about the process of getting the local authorities to issue him with the old Statement.

"It was difficult as the mainstream schools that we visited were not able to support me. The reasons behind this were not to do with the fact that I was in a wheelchair or that I needed to self-catheterise but with the epileptic fits that I occasionally have.

Most of the TAs were not trained by the local authority to deal with the fits, and the ones who were trained left while I was still at primary school."

This had a massive impact on Tom's education and resulted in him needing to be placed in a special needs school where the TAs were trained to deal with epileptic fits. This, however, meant that he could not do GCSEs like the rest of his friends and was not given the same opportunities to look for further education and work.

"The issue for people like me going to a special needs school is that I instantly feel isolated and not prepared for the real world. They like to wrap you up in cotton wool and pretend everything is fine where that is far from the truth."

First, I wanted to find out why Annual Reviews are so critical. When I was a student, Jane Ettle was the SENCO at St Martin's Garden Primary School. I met Jane in October 2018 to talk about the process she went through her process to complete the Statement ready for the Annual Review. She talked me through the process for the old Statement compared to the new approach with the EHCP. Throughout the conversation with Jane, it was evident that the system has changed for the better in secondary schools. Still, she does feel that the new EHCP does not support students in primary school. She argues that,

"Kids at that age don't care about the paperwork. All they care about is playing and having fun. So, the paperwork has decreased;

however, it concentrates on the person's mental health and is student centred for primary school students."

Jane explained that when I was a student at St Martin's Garden Primary School, the Teaching Assistants tried to help me be as independent as possible. She explained that the annual reviews were there for the relevant people to make the decisions and evaluate the student's progress. Examples of such decisions include. Jane then explained why they asked the student to fill in a form about their reflection on the year. The review looked at the student's achievements, the stuff they have enjoyed, things they have not enjoyed and any targets for their next academic year. Finally, I asked her about her views on introducing the EHCP to preschools and primary schools.

Before meeting with her, I thought the EHCP needed to be introduced at the early stages. I have seen families where the child relies too much on their parents to be their voice. The issues can be, and I stress I can be, that the student grows up relying on their parents to be their advocate and finds it difficult to make decisions on their own.

After meeting with her, my views changed slightly when I asked her views on introducing the EHCP into primary and making the Annual Reviews more student centred.

She said, "This is not a good idea as it is tough to get the child to think about what they would like and their targets."

"We found that all they wanted was to play with their friends, and they did not want to make the big decisions that needed to be made. They don't know what they want!"

I then wanted to find out exactly what support is there for parents. According to the Government website, parents are advised to talk to the teacher or the SEN co-ordinator (SENCO) if they think their child needs al long list of different areas of support. However,

I am not sure if this is the case? I met with several parents who expressed the challenges that parents have to face. In addition, many people see how the process affects the child's family. I met with Anne, a parent of a 17-year-old boy with Cerebral palsy. Over the 2 hours, she explained the process from a parent's point of view. Anne is a single parent and has two other sons. They recently moved to Bath but lived in Swindon for six years. Anne's son has CP, but no cognitive issues, so he went through mainstream, now in his first year at college. He had a statement in preschool for 15 hours per week for some support. This was transferred to an EHCP. When we were discussing the preparation for the Annual Review meeting, Anne talked to me about the documentation she needed to do.

"I would say it's important to give as much information as possible about your child's situation; you know the best."

She also explained that involving the professionals who help with your child is essential. They can help the school understand some practical measures that must be met. We then talked about how easy the process is from start to finish. She explained the process from the parent's side and how they needed to fight to ensure everything was included.

"We didn't have any major issues, but we did keep on top of things and kept asking if we were unsure of anything. The EHCP should involve the child and all their needs and be reviewed annually."

"We found the school was not wanting our son to be involved and would exclude him from the annual review. They made the excuse that he did not want to attend, but when we asked him, he seemed eager to attend."

It became clear that the issues are not just down to the local authority; schools can make positive changes that help benefit the student.

"We were lucky to have good staff during school but had to be assertive and stick to our guns on occasion. Of course, things can also change, so keeping track and writing things down as and when they happen dates also help to change. Keeping track and writing things down as when to happen with dates helps build up any evidence should you need it."

I then had a meeting with another parent called John. His son just finished his first year at college. He spoke to me about the final years of school.

"I feel many of the 'helpers' in the classroom are poorly trained and don't always assist as they should. It is not as though a child will tell them they aren't helping them as they should or agreed in the plan. There is a huge amount that could change, I believe the people involved want to help, but staffing and funding is an issue, postcode lottery. For example, I suggested more speech therapy today but was hit with the funding could be an issue. They only have to supply adequate, not 'good' support."

I wanted to find out how the challenges discussed over the past few months have affected the student's mental well-being. So I decided to send school questionnaires I designed to hand out to students using EHCP. For data protection, I have changed the names of the students. Sam left school two years ago and transitioned to college six months after receiving an EHCP. Sam has Cerebral Palsy, Which means he uses a manual wheelchair. Kat has Spinal muscular atrophy type 2 and is in year 9. She uses a manual wheelchair when she is feeling weak. Imogen is a year 12 student. When she was 9, she had a stroke that left her right side paralysed. She has gained some movement but still finds it difficult to walk. I firstly asked What is your experience of being a young disabled person?

Kat explained that she is missing so many days of school due to her health and the number of doctor appointments she needs to attend. So after every meeting, she has to catch up on her lunch break while all her peers are on the playing field.

"I'm in constant pain with fluctuating symptoms, and doctors seem to be doing guesswork as far as medicating me goes. They either don't listen or don't know what to do and say they can't give me anything stronger than what they are giving me."

When asking Sam the same question, he shared that the Heath side of the EHCP was missed. Unfortunately, this is not the only example I have heard of where catheterising is missed off the EHCP, so schools are not prepared. In addition, teaching Assistants have not been trained the support the student while catheterising.

"It was difficult to add things to the "Health" Section of the EHCP as the TAs in my new secondary school were not Medically trained in helping me self-catheterise."

Imogen shared about the challenges of feeling accepted within her friendship group but also trying to navigate all the buildings and, at times, uneven surfaces. This resonated with me due to my own experiences at school with bullying and the inability to access certain building facilities without a TA. If the lift was to break or a building had no access, I would be forced to work alone in Learning Support. It wasn't until I started my GCSEs that every building had a lift or GCSEs

"My experiences are very mixed as some aspects such as meeting many amazing friends are very positive, but some are much more negative."

"I find navigating the built environment very difficult as a mobility aid user, and I find the attitudes of people I do not know as well or of elderly people are often quite negative or stereotypical. For me, this can require much emotional Labour."

We then started to discuss What it is to experience a mainstream school. The students seem to have had many socially and physically active opportunities like sports days and school trips.

"Being involved in inclusion sports gave me more opportunities to make friends and being chosen to be a tutor group mentor to younger kids in an inclusion tutor group."

However, Kat shared that her school was not as inclusive regarding activities such as school trips and sports days.

"In my first high school, my teachers ignored my problems. I get called lazy by my teachers for not doing enough in PE and getting tired out easily or unable to write fast enough. Here at Hope (the school I moved to) is very different. My Teachers understand that I have limits and my condition won't get any better by pushing past them."

Sam shared about sports camps for students with physical disabilities to get sports.

"Getting to go to different sporting events and meeting Paralympians."

As I said at the beginning of the book, there are many opportunities and strengths of being a disabled young person. So I was fascinated to hear what the students' views were.

"I think being disabled has taught me how to fight for what I want and that disability doesn't mean I can't do something. It's more mind over matter."

This is a value that I now hold. As soon as you say we cannot do something, take a step back and watch us prove you wrong.

"You gain a new view of life. Coming to terms with the fact that you're different is the hard part, but finding people who understand what you're going through strengthens the voice disabled people have and helps spread awareness. I try to encourage people to ask questions since my main condition is relatively unknown but not as rare as people think, so it's nice to be aware of the signs and symptoms and hint parents or people of what to ask their doctor about if they show those signs."

Give the young disabled person a say in what they feel would help them during their time in mainstream school. Take into consideration that all young disabled people's needs are different. I think disabled people need to be much more active in educating non-disabled people about access and the issues that affect our community and us. What is your experience of being a young disabled person in mainstream school?

"Overall, my experiences in school were positive. Although there were some instances where I did not feel included in activities due to my impairment and teachers not knowing how to include me fully."

I was also bullied in school, but this was only partly due to my condition. However, it did have a massive impact on me as I did not have many friends at school. I did not see anybody outside of school. I was very lonely, especially in secondary school. Missing a lot of years 7, 8 and 9 due to health issues did not help with this.

When I asked Sam his thoughts on Special Needs Schools, he shared, "I have no problem with Special needs Schools, but for me, I can learn the same subjects as my peers. I wanted to feel normal and complete my GCSEs like everyone else."

At the end of our conversation, I wanted to know what the challenges young people face at the challenges young people face. After a few minutes of thinking, Imogen took a deep breath and said, "Society!" Then, looking around the table, each student smiled, nodding in agreement.

She said, "Society's perception of people with disabilities. I think we've come a long way with becoming more accepting. However, we still lack appropriate accommodation and fail to facilitate everybody's needs."

Many improvements still need to be made, whether accessed in and around hospitals, offices, shops, schools or any other social venues. I feel that so many non-disabled people overlook the luxury of being able to be completely self-sufficient. Unfortunately, these are some of the issues I face in Society. I feel like the government should be more aware of the needs of disabled people. They take away benches to stop homeless people from sleeping on them, but what are disabled people meant to do? Most of us struggle to get up off the floor, myself included. Angela works for an organisation called Shine. She helps and supports families who have disabled children that are not on EHCP. They have found that this process is inconsistent throughout the UK. For example, they have had parents move from one county to another and were accepted in one county, but once they moved, they were denied a Plan.

Angela explained that there is much confusion around parental rights and how much their child is entitled. In addition, there is a lack of info for parents. Shine has added a page on their website explaining to parents and cares what EHCP is, what the process is and how to start the process. Many parents do not realise that they can start the process themselves. In addition, councils are not recognising medical needs. For example, some students in wheelchairs need to be catheterised, and panels do not remember this as a health need and therefore do not follow the appropriate procedure. I asked her the main issue she comes across the most. She explained, "Difficult to help the council understand cognitive issues with Hydrocephalus." She then explained that it is not just the students that suffer. It is the support network around the child that also gets affected.

"Many parents are now fighting for their child's needs."

It was clear from talking to her that many parents find their children sitting in a classroom writing or reading while their peers are playing sports. This was down to the lack of funding for sports chairs and the lack of resources for coaching in disability sports. "The Paralympics in 2012 helped schools develop their PE Sessions to be more inclusive, but it has slowly gone backwards. Students are now segregated and excluded as the schools don't have the funding or expertise."

After all of my conversations, it got me thinking: does the government encourage Disabled children in mainstream schools? The only time "special needs" was mentioned in the 2010 Manifesto is on page 53, where it states:

"The most vulnerable children deserve the highest quality of care, so that we will call for a moratorium on the ideologically driven closure of special schools. In addition, we will end the bias towards including children with special needs in mainstream schools."

When questioned further, the Prime Minister, David Cameron, said, "Our manifesto says that we will 'end' the bias towards inclusion. It does not say we will 'reverse' it."

The implication being, they said, is that they will free up parental choices by ending the bias and not pushing children towards a particular form of education by reversing it. It's a "clear implication", they said.

Despite not outlining this part of the policy in their manifesto, they stressed: "Our approach to special educational needs is all about supporting parent choices." Bartley expressed that he felt, in practice, there was not even a good policy of inclusion at the moment. So he feared the Tory manifesto pledge meant even more hurdles for parents who wanted their disabled children to be taught in mainstream classes.

He said: "They do talk about ending the bias in their manifesto. And yes, many parents would want their children to be educated in special schools. But in my experience, if a local school can cope with a disabled pupil and is adequately resourced, they would love their child to go there. He added: "Labour is staying very silent on this issue, and I am not impressed by the Lib Dems either. So this issue has not been a feature of this campaign – despite Cameron talking about the Great Ignored."

NASEN, formerly known as the National Association for Special Educational Needs, is a leading organisation in the UK that promotes the education of those with special and additional support needs. It said the bias towards educating disabled children in mainstream schools had emerged in the past 20 years. Still, the difficulty of getting a special needs child into such schools very much depended on the local authority. So whereas some parents faced a fight, others found the process much easier. However, the Alliance for Inclusive Education campaigns on this issue were far more critical of Cameron. Its director Tara Flood told FactCheck;

"The moment your child is deemed to have special needs, you shift out of the system; you go into the special needs framework, and then the pressure turns on the parents. There is no bias. It is tough going."

While doing this research project, I came across 4 Themes that seemed to come up repeatedly in my conversations with students, teachers, parents and support networks.

1 Misunderstanding of the student's medical needs

This theme keeps coming up with both the parents and students I spoke with. There is a miscommunication about what medical needs students have and what raining the Teaching Assistants to have teaching assistants' training.

2 Mental health of the students

A lot of the mental health issues that students with Physical disabilities face are exclusion and segregation from their peers.

3 Pressure on schools

Secondary Schools, in particular, are now having to turn students with Physical Disabilities away because they do not have enough staff. Unfortunately, this means many students with physical disabilities are forced to attend special needs Schools.

4 Local Authority

Many parents I spoke to said it was challenging to help the council understand cognitive issues. Some students were academically able but found writing difficult. I feel there can sometimes be a lack of communication between schools, parents, and the local authority. The consequence is that the student gets stuck in the middle, and their voices get drowned out. The student needs to be able to communicate about their future and need opportunities to voice their concerns. There needs to be a more accessible pathway for schools to make changes easier. I think that mentoring is a vital part of improving the EHCP.

Mentoring, especially with someone with a disability, can help boost the student's confidence. Someone they can look up to and see that their disability should not stop them from achieving their goals is an integral part of their school life. It is unlikely that they will encounter any other teachers or students with disabilities, and therefore they can feel isolated. Disabled people are bullied more than any other child. This is due to their disability and therefore considered to be different. I feel this happens more when there is a lack of understanding about the student's disability. Why would they, as they probably do not have anyone in their life with a disability? If there were opportunities for guest speakers to come in and talk in Assemblies and PSHE

Lessons about their experiences, this would start a conversation. It can also give the young disabled person the confidence to talk about their disability to their peers. If the child cannot join in with the sport, they must be able to get an activity they can participate in. Unfortunately, there have been several scenarios where disabled students have had to sit in a classroom and write essays rather than play sports. This is bad for several reasons. Firstly, it segregates the student from their peers. Secondly, the chances are that the student is stuck in classrooms all day, and this is their one chance to play sports. Another critical issue that keeps being raised is that the student is on their own with the TA, either doing physio or playing sport.

The student must be able to play sports with peers as this is an excellent way of making friends and introducing people to disability sports. The education system has improved massively over the past decade. Mental health is talked about a lot more than it used to. However, a lot can still be done, which needs urgent attention. The issues that I have underlined in this chapter are only the beginning. This chapter only uncovers some of the problems that students with physical disabilities face faced by students with physical disabilities. The issues of exclusion need to be looked into in more detail. The students need to be consulted more on improving the education system to help them achieve their goals.

Their education needs to be tailored more to suit their needs. They need more support to get their voices heard. The student's voice is usually the last to be heard when many professionals are involved. As soon as children have people they can aspire to be like or who can be role models, it is amazing how much their confidence grows.

CHAPTER 4

How Can I Believe In God?

"Now faith is the assurance of what we hope for and the certainty of what we do not see."

Hebrews 11:1

Does this mean believing in a God of love and kindness is easy? Does it mean I go to church every Sunday religiously? Do I pray every night? The answer to all those questions is no. I have not been to church for at least five years, I don't find it easy to pray, and I have indeed not found it easy to believe in a God of love and kindness. Yet I believe that Jesus is the son of God, that he died on the cross to set us all free. I believe in what the Bible says. I listen to many talks from different churches around the UK and in America. I was born into a Christian home, and my parents have been involved in the church for over 40 years. Mum & Dad now give most of their time building and growing friendships between leaders in the city. As a kid, every Sunday, we would all go to church. The church met in the city centre of Bath. For me, the church was something I went to but didn't understand. As a six-year-old, I thought church was a building where people sang songs and heard church leaders preach.

It wasn't until I was in my teens that I realised what church meant. Most of my closest friends are not Christians or call themselves atheists. I already found school hard enough to feel accepted as a disabled person, let alone a disabled person who believes in God! Many of my issues at school were due to my faith rather than my disability. I remember the day that my school life changed forever. My PET Lesson! It no nothing to do with animals; it stood for Philosophy, Ethics, and Theology. We were asked if anybody believed in God.

I thought they would accept me as we were in the 21st Century. Ha ha, how I was wrong! Yeah, I was 100% false. Just because we are in the 21st Century most definitely doesn't mean we are accepted for who we are, and I would go further and say that even today, in 2021, it is still the case. It feels like we are all now figuring out what tribes we are in and if you're not in the same tribe, get prepared to be ostracised. You may laugh and think this is an over-the-top comment. Still, a staggering 260 million Christians in the top 50 countries on the World Watch List face high or extreme levels of persecution for their faith.

My teacher started by sharing that he was from a Jewish background But wasn't religious. I think that is why I have all the courage to share my experience, that I was brought up in a Christian family, that I went to church, and that my parents were church leaders. But, before I carry on, I must describe the classroom and explain why I was not the most comfortable afterwards. Because I had to use an adjustable table, my desk was at the front of the classroom. This meant that my back was turned to the rest of the class. I never saw my peers' facial reactions. I could never see them laughing at me.

Looking back at it, there were probably signs I missed that could have told me what I had just said, which caused me much trouble later down the line or even on that day. I left the classroom feeling pretty confident and thinking that people would respect me or sharing. Again, how wrong was I!

It's funny now that past experiences haunt you for the rest of your life. That was the only time I ever publicly shared my faith. To this day, I have never transferred anything about my relationship with God. You may ask, what about my parents? Don't you talk to them about your faith? I love my parents and am so grateful they brought me up in a Christian home. It should be easy for me to talk about my faith to them, but I have the same anxiety. It feels like faith is so personal to me that I don't dare to speak to anyone about it, including my own family. It goes back to what I was saying earlier about the label disability. Society sees my chair before they see me as a human. When people see the chair before they see the person, they tend not to take me seriously. They start talking to me like I'm a child as if I don't understand what is happening. It is like they think I'm just copying what everyone else is doing without understanding what is happening.

Why have we got to the point where some people in society see a wheelchair and instantly assume that we are idiots? I'm not saying my family or friends treat me like this; far from it! However, my anxiety tells me these things will happen because of past experiences. So Where was I really at school? I was lost! I was unsure, I was insecure with myself, I was hurt, and I was alone. I was unsure what to believe. Is there a god? Does he hear my prayers? At the time, it felt like he wasn't listening to me. But, then again, I didn't talk to him, so there was not much to listen to! They always say you will feel the Holy Spirit, and you will feel his presence and peace. I never felt anything. Nothing. I would go to church, and people would shout, talk in a particular language and shake, but I never felt anything!

I started to doubt everything. Are they all just pretending? Am I missing a trick? Is there a magic word I need to say to allow me to talk to and feel God? The short answer is no! There was no secret password or ritual that I needed to do. There was nothing I needed to do except talk to him. I'm saying all this now, but this was not clear back at school! I didn't understand what a Christian meant. I was so caught up in feeling left out at school and in society that I forgot that there was a loving God that never failed, never left me, and never forsake me. I was so caught up in my own problems that were all 100% down to me and the idiotic mistakes. I became increasingly distracted and distant from the one person I could trust who would never leave me, no matter how many mistakes I made. I felt hurt; why would a creator ever create something that was broken? You're going to start to see a running theme here! I felt hurt because I felt like society didn't accept me, and my hurt got in the way of my relationship with the one person who had never hurt me. How do I know this? Because I believe in what Genesis 1:27 says,

> "So God created mankind in his image, in the image of God he created them; male and female he created them."

I was hurt because of my mistakes, but I was blind and kept blaming God when It was down to my actions, not his. It's easy to pass on the blame rather than take responsibility! I want to say it gets easier as you get older, but it doesn't! I was hurt because I was being bullied for something I couldn't help. I was hurt because my friends left me once they knew I was a Christian, and I blamed God for basically being him! I was a hypocrite! I was angry and rejected God because I felt hurt and rejected and wanted someone else to feel the way I felt! He knew exactly how I was feeling. He always knows how we think and feels! If you have faith, you believe God can feel what you think. He's not like your friends or family who watch from the outside, and then it moves them because of their love for you. He can think in his own Spirit your suffering. Isaiah 53:4 says,

> "It was certainly our sickness that He carried, and our sufferings that He bore."

The Bible continues to say,

> "Jesus was moved with compassion and healed the sick. He knew the hearts of men."

By the way, I am not saying it's easy; far from it! Where am I now? I am a Christian. I pray, play worship music, and am at peace for the first time in my life. I attend church both online and in person. I sit at the back so nobody can see me. I believe God has a plan for me; I trust him and believe things happen for a reason. I am at peace for two reasons; first of all, I now know what it truly means to be a Christian. It's now about the building but about fellowshipping with others. I know that we were made in his image. I now truly understand what that means. Secondly, I don't have to be brave or put a mask on when talking to him. I have stopped blaming him for things that society has put me through.

I have also become more assertive in my values. This is where things start to get controversial, and party leaders have fallen because they were not clear on their beliefs and values. I believe in what the Bible says. I believe Jesus told stories to illustrate God's everlasting love for us. The Bible is full of illustrations of how we should live our lives. For a long time, I believed that if I didn't follow the ten commandments, I was not a Christian and would go to hell.

What commandments have I broken? I have said the name of the Lord in vain. I have worked on the Sabbath. I haven't always honoured my parents. I have lied multiple times. So anyone with an IQ higher than one will be able to tell you that I'll be sent to hell as I have broken several commandments. Wrong! I truly believe Jesus was here on this earth to teach us how to follow him. I believe he died on the cross, and because of that, my sins are automatically forgiven. All our sins are forgiven. That does not mean we can now do whatever we want because God will forgive us.

Before becoming a Christian, I was scared of death. I felt restless. Have I done enough on this earth? I felt like I wasn't contributing anything to society for a long time. Compared to people like Nick Vujicic, I was a lazy person. I wasn't travelling around the world sharing my story. I was sitting in my bedroom on Facebook and feeling sorry for myself. During this pandemic, I have been able to join different churches here in Bath and around the UK and the US! Isn't technology great when it works? Despite everything and my lack of faith, the one thing that I have always done is listen to worship music.

The only "gigs" I have attended have been worship events. At school, we were allowed to listen to music in lessons. So my iPod was just full of worship music. Songs like; In Christ Alone, 10,000 reasons by Matt Redman, Amazing Grace (My chains have gone) by Chris Tomlin. A very close school friend I grew up with introduced me to an artist called Lecrae. I recently bought his book "I AM RESTORED", honestly I can't seem to put the book down. He is honest and open about losing his faith after becoming a "Celeb".

I bought the book not because of his music but because of his story of becoming a Christian. There was one particular video titled "How I Lost My Religion". For a long time, I have been struggling with the idea that I needed to perform for God, to hide the fact that I have a disability. As long as I was the person I thought God wanted me to be, so be it, even if it is not me. It wasn't until I watched the video and then read his book that I realised I was still stuck in the religion and not the relationship I longed for.

As soon as I realised it was a relationship with my heavenly father, that anxiety of death vanished. That question of having done enough on this earth vanished. For the first time, I was not performing for anyone. I was not acting anymore. My Identity became less about my condition and more about how I live my life following Jesus. That whole that I have tried to fill got smaller and smaller. I will end with these two quotes that I now understand,

and I hope and pray I will live by them for the rest of my life. For too long, I have let my condition define me. I am tired of being angry with God. I no longer want to be determined by my condition but by my relationship with my Heavenly Father. I recently spoke to someone about my current situation and how I am not proud of who I am and how I am not happy with who I am. They said I should read 1 Corinthians 6:19-20.

"Apostle Paul asks, or do you not know that your body is a temple of the Holy Spirit within you, whom you have from God? You are not your own, for you were bought with a price. So glorify God in your body."

They then asked if I was taking care of myself or destroying God's creation. As I thought about my life, I started questioning it. The damage I was doing to my body was physical, emotional, and spiritual. I stopped eating good food, I wasn't catheterising when I needed to, and I didn't take care of my fitness. Since 2020, I've been getting pressure sores. Whenever they're healed, they'll return and I'm back on bedrest. By the way, this realisation happened 7 days ago. I could use my hydrocephalus as an excuse to not look after my body.

I could blame the pressure sores on my dislocated hips. Maybe I used the disability card unintentionally to avoid taking responsibility. I've neglected myself physically and spiritually for too long. While I've tried to change for a long time, there's been a piece of the puzzle missing. And if I don't realise there's a piece missing, I'll not only be stuck in the same old routine, damaging myself in the process, but I'll never fulfil God's plan for my life. I don't know if you believe in God or not. I don't know your circumstances but what I have learnt in the last year or so is that everything happens for a reason. I have heard over the years that we only pray when we are in need of a miracle.

We never take the time to thank God for everything he has provided for us. This has always been true for me. As I stated earlier I don't pray every night. I don't read my Bible as much as I should. I only pray when I have hit rock bottom. My prayers are always short, and they are always selfish prayers. My faith has to grow stronger for me to change my life. My relationship with my heavenly father needs to be rebuilt. It doesn't matter if I'm at rock bottom or not, I need to talk to him all the time. Rather than watching trash on YouTube and scrolling endlessly on Instagram, I should read more. It doesn't matter what I'm working through, I should be praising him. There's always something good in life, even when I can't see it. I recently wrote in my notes some random thoughts.

One evening when I was just sitting thinking about my conversations with my friends that day I realised that I am great at building routines. There is however a problem with my routines. The routines I have successfully built and maintained are harming me more than they are helping me. The routines that I have maintained not only exclude my medical routines but also exclude my relationship with God. This may sound awful and when I first spoke to a friend about it I felt ashamed of myself. After our long conversation, I transitioned from feeling depressed and ashamed to feeling proud and motivated. Why? Despite my condition, I have proven I'm capable of building routines, I'm capable of building a healthy lifestyle if I want to. I need to remember that I have seen miracles in my life. Where mountains tremble and walls come crashing to the ground. In Genesis chapter 3 8-9, it says

"Then the man and his wife heard the sound of the Lord God as he was walking in the garden in the cool of the day, and they hid from the Lord God among the trees of the garden. But the Lord God called to the man, "Where are you?"

For many years I took that verse as if God was asking Adam where he was physically as if they were playing a game of hide and seek. The thing you need to remember is that God knows where you are. He watches you every second of every minute of every hour of every day of every week...you get the picture. God asked that question because god wanted to know where Adam was emotionally and spiritually. Adam and Eve had just eaten an apple from the tree God had cursed. As Adam did, I have hidden from God as a result of my shame and guilt over my past mistakes.

There is a sense of shame I feel now about the life that I have led. The reason I have hidden so much is that I am afraid of finding out that my actions have angered God. Despite that, I also know I will always be loved by him no matter what I have done or how I have behaved. Later on, I will be talking about my past and the lessons I have learned from it. The biggest lesson that I have learned recently is that when I give my problems to him, not only do I feel a huge weight lifted off my shoulders, but I have also seen my life change for the better. Which brings me nicely to the subject of prayer. I am not very confident in my ability to pray, I normally do not say my prayers out loud when I am with others.

This is not because I don't know how to pray or don't have anything to pray about, but rather because I feel self-conscious and embarrassed about how I pray. I feel a lot of pressure in my mind, but I cannot explain why. The only person that puts pressure on me when I pray is myself. I am not under any pressure from anyone else. There is a great deal of controversy surrounding prayer in the disability community. Throughout the years, my view of prayer has changed as I have grown up. There was a time when I allowed my friends' opinions to override my own opinions. There was a time in my life when I was scared to speak up when I disagreed with someone about their stance on religion. Honestly, I am still a bit worried about speaking up at times, but I am learning as I go along. A lot of my friends and even people I follow on social media find it somewhat hurtful if they are asked in the street if they would like prayer.

Whenever a friend of mine is asked if he wants prayer, he would reply, "Why would I need prayer?". For a lot of people who have a disability, the question will come across as if you're saying, "Well there is obviously something wrong with you and you need healing.". Even though the intention is to talk about Jesus and his love and to share the gospel as soon as you begin with that question, you will have no chance of ever being able to have a meaningful conversation.

I was recently asked if I had the choice of keeping my disability or being able to walk what would I choose? This is a question I have been struggling to answer for some time. I am proud of who I am, I am not ashamed of my disability and I will never let my disability stop me from achieving what I want to do in my life. I believe I was put on this earth for a reason. I believe I was born with Spina Bifida for a reason. I was not given it as a punishment but as a way to share God's love. I may not have had the miracles that I have been praying for but I have seen miracles in my life. I have seen situations that could never have been resolved without God. For some people, this will be a load of nonsense and they will believe that the situations were resolved because of science and pure luck.

I will always be grateful to the doctors and nurses that have helped me over the last 20+ years. I am so grateful for the NHS and Local Authority services that have allowed me to gain independence. There have been situations that not even the top medical staff and social services could have resolved and yet the situations with in 24 hours were resolved. At a time when if you were looking for a council house you had to wait 18 months, but I waited 2 weeks. At the time I could not see God move. I could not see the walls come crashing to the ground. However, when I talk about it to family and friends there is no other explanation but God! The Lord's prayer is a prayer we would always recite at school. Looking back at it I have realised that I read the words without meaning them and so did 99% of the school. I have recently reread the prayer and now when I say it I will say it with meaning and I will concentrate on each sentence.

Our Father, who art in heaven, hallowed be thy name; thy kingdom come; thy will be done; on earth as it is in heaven. Give us this day our daily bread. And forgive us our trespasses, as we forgive those who trespass against us. And lead us not into temptation; but deliver us from evil. For thine is the kingdom, the power and the glory, for ever and ever. Amen.

CHAPTER 7

Disability Hate Crime

"Half of them aren't even disabled. It's a joke!" Let's spell it out TH IS IS H ATE.

I can't sleep. Maybe it's because I have had too much caffeine, or because I have a UTI, or perhaps because I can feel a storm brewing both literally and metaphorically. It's probably a mixture of all of them. I had a phone call this evening, which infuriated me to the point where I was scared of society for the first time in a while. A close friend of mine rang in tears as a family member got attacked because they are on the Autistic Spectrum by children his age. So what are we teaching our kids? Teaching them that it's okay to hurt people who are different? Teaching them that disabled people are worthless, that we are not human beings, because if that's the case, then I'm done.

Eight thousand four hundred sixty-nine people last year, eight thousand four hundred sixty-nine people were attacked due to their disabilities. Eight Thousand Four hundred and sixty-nine! However, The National Crime Survey estimates an accurate figure of 70,000. As you are reading this, that number is going up! Somewhere in the world, someone is being attacked.

After all, they are different because they use a wheelchair or see the world differently. Every year the government publishes the latest statistics on hate crime. There are five centrally monitored strands of hate crime:

Race or Ethnicity – 76,070 Cases in 2020

Religion or Beliefs – 6,822 Cases in 2020

Sexual orientation – 15,835 Cases in 2020

Disability – 8,469 Cases in 2020

Transgender identity – 2,540 Cases in 2020

For the past five years, the media have not reported on the issue well when the government releases new statistics. They seem to be obsessing more about Brexit than critical issues that most of us face daily. Instead, they would rather talk about an institution nobody knows, understands or cares about. If you're female, you are more likely to get attacked than if you are male. If you're black, you're more likely to get shot than if you're white. If you are gay, you are more likely to get attacked than heterosexual.

In this chapter, you will read three accounts of real hate crime incidents from the perspective of the victims, their families and friends. The following stories will include topics of violence, abusive language, and suicidal and self-harming thoughts. Names have been changed to protect their identity.

#WEAREHUMAN

River's Story

So, it all started on Christmas 2018, when I went shopping. Three car parks were near each other, every disabled space was being used, and probably out of the fifteen, three had blue badges. Then, a gang of youths came out, carrying cases of beer, jumping around, jumping into the car, and driving off. It annoyed me that I had struggled for the last 10 minutes to get my door open enough to get my prosthetic leg out to get to the shop. I was at the back of the car park because that was the only place I could park. So I dragged my leg in paipainn as these kids came out laughing and joking, jumped in the car, and drove off, which annoyed me so much. I just had my leg amputated not long before then, and, you know, I was dealing with anger issues of how now I was looked at and have to think before I act.

I can't be, 'Let's just jump in the car and go away for the weekend,' because I need a disabled room. So I need you to know before we'd go down and just jump on Airbnb. I need the wet room and my wheelchair; I need access. And when you ask places, 'Is it accessible?' and they say yes, nine times out of ten, they're like, 'Well, there's only three steps, you know, other than that, it's acceptable.' And so, I'm learning all this and getting a little bit of a temper. I say, 'Well, wait a minute, you said this was completely wheelchair accessible.' They say, 'There is a ramp. It's at the back, we've never had it out, but we've got one.' And then when you ask them to use it, nobody knows how. You've got two steps when they figure it out and get the ramp up. You've got to flip your wheelchair somehow to get in, but it's a kid's party, and you don't want your daughter to be the only one that didn't turn up because you can't get through the party's front door.

So yeah, things were building up tension-wise for me that day. On Facebook, there's a site called spotted in, and this one is spotted in Derby. And I had a bit of a rant saying people need to think about where they're parking before they park, because if they park in the disabled bay for only five minutes, then that means I can come and shop.' I could have been driving an hour to the specific shop, and I get to the disabled bay and guess what? Now I have to turn around and go home because I can't just park anywhere. I need to be able to get out. And so, I had my little mini-rant about, 'Please think before you do this.' And a few people agreed, apologised, and said they'd do this. A few people had said that maybe they forgot to pull their badge out. You can't judge a book. Many people had said yeah, but you know when you just need to, you just got to pop in quick, or you know, the disabled accessible toilets, they're right next to them, the non-disabled toilets.

Still, there's a massive queue, and you need to go to the bathroom quickly because I've got an appointment. I'll be busy, or whatever their excuse is, just to nip in. So, yeah, I don't get to go; okay, the disabled bay is being used. I'll just pop into the others. You can't; that's the only toilet I can use. So, it was annoying, basically, and I'd had my rant. And two days later, I had a Facebook inbox message from a gentleman asking if he could help, saying he understood because he too was disabled. And it was nice to talk to somebody else with a disability. As we talked online, it turned out he wasn't physically disabled. He said he had a mental disability. And again, I'm not to judge; he was just lovely. I was making friends in the community. And previously, I had just lost £3000 to a con man who said he would fix my garden so it was accessible for the wheelchair.

Which meant a lot because it's a massive, beautiful garden, I look out the window, and it's like, it's teasing me because it's there, it's in my reach. I can see it, and I can't touch it; I can't quite get there. The guy offered the moon and the stars, took the money, and destroyed the garden I have, leaving it unusable for my daughter right now, which was usable before and ran off. He was never to be seen again. There was nothing wrong with it; it was a beautiful garden with many rabbit holes and no ramp. This guy on Facebook said he would come, fix it, and make the park accessible for me. Part of me was grateful but also worried because I didn't know him. I was desperate, so I said yes. He assessed the garden, but something did not feel right. He was very strong-willed with what he wanted to do to the park. I felt uneasy then and like something was wrong, and I know I should have said no, there and then.

And then my mother had come to visit just as he was leaving, and even she said, No, don't use him, we'll find someone else, we'll pay somebody, something's not right. You know, when you have that gut feeling, but through desperation, I had pushed that feeling to the back. The next day, he came out of the blue with his wife and daughter. His daughter was the same age as mine, so the girls played, he cracked on with a garden, filling in the holes, and his wife made burgers for everybody. As the day went on, he got a lot of the rotten wood in the garden and built a huge bonfire. He carried the chair and me, and I got to the bonfire and hotdogs, and the kids loved it, and I loved it; it was a nice day. The next day, they turn up again, and he's taking the stuff to the tip, and she starts cleaning my house, just out of the blue. It was excellent, and I wanted to believe that this could work, and I'd get in the garden and have help. I was looking for a carer at the time, so I just mentioned it to her.

She had a full DBS and enhanced DBS check from working as a part-time teaching assistant at a school. So, I thought again, she could probably help Gia with her reading and writing, and I took her on. She was terrific, and I genuinely really let her come in. The house was spotless, the washing was done, I could rest, you know, we talked, we got on, and she was a very, very good carer. As time went on, though, I have to admit that looking back, and she knew what was happening. I had begged her for help a few times to stop Eddie from coming around and letting himself in. I was scared of him. My carer knew these things and let them carry on because I think, to be honest, she knew what he was capable of, and while he was harassing me, he wasn't harassing her. So, for her, it was a win, win. Either way, very quickly, his mood changed. He started talking about joint suicides, asking how I could carry on with the pain I was in. And how poorly I was and did not want just to end it. And, you know, he understood because he wanted to end it. And I didn't, I said, I've got my daughter, I've got my life, to think of that I owe her to try. And yes, I'm in pain, and yes, I'm not sleeping, but that will change, you know, I have faith, and I just have to carry on. But, again, he came out with some crazy things, and sometimes I didn't know whether he was joking. It became clear very quickly that he liked to drink, and there was never any alcohol in my house.

And he joked saying that there was the one problem with my house, it wasn't that it wasn't accessible or adapted, it was that there was no beer! So, he started fetching it and bringing some for himself, but he was always trying to get me to have a drink. I explained that I wasn't going to have a drink because of the medication I was on. I don't know what it would do to me, and I've not had a drink in many years due to the infections.

He was quite forceful at times, but I still said no. And he also tried to get me to take the medication that he had. So, his doctor had given him diazepam and Zovaflam to help him sleep, and he was always trying to get me to take them. He'd take them out of the packet, put them in my hand, and say, just take it, take it, just take that, and you'll be out of pain. Once or twice, I pretended to take it to shut him up, just to calm him because he was being quite aggressive in front of my daughter. Finally, I got to a point where I kept inviting my friend to come around because I didn't want to be on my own with him. He had said that he was money-crazed, had a love child, and nobody knew about it.

He was a proper Cockney and was a gangster, nobody knows why, but he was a gangster. He'd asked me how much money a wheelchair would be, like, a proper nice one that would keep me more comfortable than what I was in. Long story, but the hospital had messed up with wheelchairs, and I ended up buying one on eBay for a while, but I'm not going to go into that. It's a different story. Anyway, I had said that a blade is about £10,000, and the wheelchairs are about £5,000. I just don't have any money left even to fix my garden since, like, and I had the three-grand taken, you know, being disabled, I've spent much money adapting my house because of red tape.

Anyway, he had come up with an idea of a place he wanted to go over, and he wanted me to be the getaway driver! To me, that was the stupidest idea in my life! Why? I've never committed a crime, but who would ask somebody with one leg to be the getaway driver? Like, you know I do drive, I use an adaptive car, but it's an adaptive car. And he was talking about me driving his Jaguar because it's a swift shift and a manual car. So I'm thinking, I don't know how you presume I'm going to change gear and all that stuff with one leg, like, it just was funny to me, and I thought he was joking. I make many jokes about myself and very light-h stuff; I just presumed he was the same. Now and again, as I say, he would go into this deep conversation of suicide and joint suicide, and then he'd joke, but you knew he was honest.

And he was seeing this girl who wanted to do it, and he would do it with her, and I don't know, it was crazy. So, he came to the house, and as I said, the mood had changed entirely. His wife had said, 'Just kind of agree with him, and eventually, he'll come out of this, and he'll go back to a normal, nice guy fixing your garden. So just be nice, play along.' So, I thought maybe that would help; he wanted to take my daughter to the shops to buy a toy for her and a toy for his daughter. They were going to pick it up on Friday, so then on Saturday, they could play together when we were all going to go to the park. Now we'd all planned to go to the park, as in my carer, his wife, his daughter, my daughter, and me, we hadn't planned him coming, that wasn't the point. But he decided he would come, and she said to play along again. It's easier. Once her car was fixed, she would have nothing to do with him.

So, she asked me to please play all so she could get her car. So, I did, and we all went to the park that day. He then decided to take the girls for this toy. I had said no because there were no car seats and all kinds of different things, but unfortunately, I had an accident which meant I needed to go and get changed. So, while I was in the toilet, he took Gia in the car, in my car to the shop, and then he dropped her off at his wife's house and said she was going for a sleepover. I had not agreed to this, and I phoned his wife and said, what the hell?

No way is she sleeping over. No way is he staying at my house. This is all crazy; please bring Gia back. She agreed; the girls had a play, they were happy, there was no reason to upset them, let's let them play, and then she would bring them back and take him out of my house. This time, he wrote down the plan and the idea of stealing these things. He'd gotten a bottle of champagne, which he was toasting to new things, and planning what he was doing with these thousands and thousands of pounds when we did this job. You know, moving to Tahiti, and God knows what. I was petrified of this man but wanted my daughter, but I knew she was safe with his wife. I knew she was, but I still wanted her here. But out of all of it, it was me that didn't feel safe in this scenario. I was scared of what he was going to do. Why was he so adamant that he wanted to stay over and give me drugs first? He was about getting weed that helps with pain, the diazepam, some champagne, and I'll have a good night's sleep.

But why did he want to stay as well? So anyway, Gia came home that night, and I then asked him not to go again the next day. I had said he had scared Gia; he'd scared me. It wasn't appropriate, it wasn't right, and I didn't want anything to do with him. His wife and daughter were still welcome, and she would still work for me, but I did not want him here. And that was it. He had gotten a bit pissed off but then was okay. And said okay, I understand, but he wanted his tools back, which was fair, you know, he had his tools and some things I put in my house for storage. I said his wife would pick them up and give them to him, and he said he didn't trust her. He wanted to come himself. I wasn't happy with that, so he asked me, could I put them in the front garden at least? And I said yeah, that's fine, and I would put his helmet and leather jacket that he had bought me on the front as well. He immediately said, no, you can keep the helmet; you might need it. And I said, why would I need a motorbike helmet? Do you know? And he said, no, keep it. You might; you're going to need it. It felt like a threat, so I ensured the helmet was on the front, and he didn't take it. The next few days, I didn't hear anything from him, and I didn't hear anything from his wife, which worried me a little, but I was also happy that I was left alone. She wasn't due to work anyway, so my daughter and I had a weekend to ourselves. Finally, on Monday, she came and explained he had fixed her car but then decided to take it for a ride with her as the passenger. He was doing 140 down the country lanes and scaring her unbelievably.

She said she'd never been so scared for her life, and again, it scared me even more. Tuesday, there was nothing, and then Wednesday, it happened. I had been hiding in the house, curtains shut, doors locked, just in case he ever turned up. Because he used just to turn up, my daughter and I had been hiding in the back bedroom, my room, for two or three days, with a friend. My friend I'd kept calling to help me get rid of him rang to check If it was okay. He said yes, I'm fine; I'm hiding in the back room. And she said, I can't, you cannot live like that, he is not coming back, you're okay, you're safe. Get a shower, pull yourself together, and I will pick you up in an hour and take you for coffee. And I thought, yeah, she's right, you know, what am I doing? It was stupid.

So, I showered, put my makeup on, and got ready. There was a knock at the door, I answered a knock at the door, expecting it to be her, and it wasn't, it was him. He grabbed the level balls of the wheelchair by the footplate and tipped me, but not out, just tipped tilted slightly. I held on to the doorframe while he punched, and he hit my leg, anything to try and get me to let go. I don't know whether he was trying to tip me out of the wheelchair or take the wheelchair with me, but he was trying to pull me out the door.

The dog was trying to stop him, and he was kicking the dog as well. The dog bit him once or twice, but he always had thick overalls and all that motorbike stuff. And the dog wasn't biting; it was a nip. I have a small pug. But he tried his best, and he was getting kicked and beaten, and what was probably three minutes felt like an hour. I realised how vulnerable I was at that moment. Before losing my leg, I did kickboxing, which made me feel safer because I was trained. I was never trained and taught how to use a wheelchair. I don't know how to defend myself now. I put my arm up to protect myself when he started punching my face. Suddenly it was this warm feeling in my tummy like somebody had poured hot water over me. Then the wheelchair went down; he had let go. I didn't even see where he ran off to because he let go, and I looked down to see what the warmth was, and there was blood everywhere.

He'd cut through my arm; I don't know what to do with it because I did not see it. The dog was black and blue. It was black and blue, but I've got this gash now on my arm. We phoned the police, and we explained what happened, we explained what had happened, and told them the whole story about him, and my friend was there at the time, and she had arrived just two minutes after he'd gone. The police weren't that quick getting here, but it gave us time to clean up. I wrapped up my arm as best I could and cleaned the blood from around the front door, as my daughter was due to arrive from school at any moment. I gave my statement, and my friend tried to give her a statement idea, and they wouldn't take it; they said they'd contact her later. As far as I'm aware, they never actually got her. Still, she did write a statement and emailed it to them with the whole story of how she had to escort him out of the house about half a million times.

She talked about how crazy he was and obsessed with me, but they didn't listen. I'd explained that he'd been sectioned a few times. My wife knew that at the moment, he was going through some hell of a manic moment. But, yet again, the police didn't take it seriously. None of it was taken seriously, if you ask me. It took them three days to find him, and when they saw him, he said it was all a lie. He said that I and his wife's wife and I had made it up so that she would get custody of his daughter. Their doctors checked him to ensure he was mentally capable and said there was nothing wrong with him; he was bailed. Two days later, I had a phone call from his wife, explaining that I didn't need to be scared anymore because he'd had a motorbike accident. He'd gone out in the storm and into the back of a breakneck speed.

He used to say that his motorbike would do a 180 to 200. I don't know what speed he was doing that night, but I'm sure it was speeding fast. He was around motorbikes since he was a child, you know, he'd take them apart, and put them back together, he was a very good man excellent mechanic. He was and put them back together; he was a very good man, an excellent mechanic and a good rider. I don't believe it was an accident, 100%; I know it wasn't an accident. The day he was bailed, I got a phone call saying he'd been told not to contact me. Anyway, I was to know them if I had any contact with him.

The day after, I had a lady in a wheelchair and a man dressed as a lady. This was her husband, and I knew this because they had the same glasses, the same scar on their face and the same watch on their wrist. Anybody could see a picture of him and this lady and know that was him. So I phoned my best friend to come round. She came, and we looked at the profile, every one of the friends was a female in a wheelchair, not one male, and not one able-bodied-disabled. I asked who he was through messenger, and there was no reply. And then the day after, say, I have a phone call from his wife. We phoned the police station and asked if it was true. I stupidly was going crazy myself with fear and was scared that he had taken her phone maybe and texted me that, and he's kidnapped her.

Thinking he's letting me get my guard down, and then he's coming for me. Either way, I was scared. I didn't know if that was true. It was a text, sorry, not a phone call; the phone call came later. And I texted all day and did not have a reply, and that's what I thought that, and then she did phone. It took the police after I had phoned them three times three times after I had phoned them to find out if this was true. I was told that the officer dealing with my case was on leave, and they could not tell me anything about another issue. So, nothing was said to me for 14 days. Then, at seven o'clock at night, I knocked on the door by the gentleman dealing with my case. He came into the house and said, we're sorry to tell you this.

Still, he had an accident, possible thinking of suicide on his motorbike, so your case is done, said, we're sorry to tell you this. Still, he had an accident, possibly considering suicide on his motorbike, so your case is closed, and that was it; that was all I got. I felt guilty that this had happened. I then learnt about the 'devotee community,' people obsessed with women in wheelchairs, and the dangers of these devotees. How much he had stalked me all came out later after he died. The fear is still there. It's horrible; I have an awful scar, but more than anything, mentally, I go to the hospital, and I stay at home. The public's fear and reactions to somebody in a wheelchair are pretty horrific.

No one has ever shouted shit to me before; no one has seen me walk past and yell something at me. Like, okay, I've heard a bird or wolf whistle, but, never like, come along blade runner, or it's a pirate, or look, it's Jack Sparrow. And yet, now I do, and it's as if it's acceptable because no one says anything. No one sticks up for you, and no one says what the heck? Like, why are you doing that? Do you know that woman? No, you don't. So, at the minute, I'm still adapting, learning, and trying to move forward.

Tom's Story

I have dyslexia, so I will keep things brief. I also had a stroke five years ago, so effects from that include memory issues. This is something people like to prey on. The first one was when I was doing athletics, but due to MS, I can't do crouch starts but rules in that league said you have to. I got told off on the line, which put me off, and I was told I should be grateful. Eventually, I did get through to England athletics, but this was after an s a coach said I broke the rules. When I pointed out that including practices was illegal, I came to a positive conclusion working with EA for inclusion schemes. However, the coach invented an incident about me. The incident turned out to be accurate but not about me. Another individual has done similar incidents (abusive to officials).

I now do masters athletics which is all standards so long over 35. Amount of people who tried me to get para-classification. I want to take part but not compete.. o why the humiliation of taking part? In triathlon, I can't ride a bike; even in para classification, you can't ride trikes. However, I got an exemption. Onto the "mate crime", A guy moved in next door in March. I am very community spirited and help people. I am involved with a local food bank and work for a charity, and I have two cats; one is a long-term foster.

I have no family and live in a house with a vast garden. He quickly got me to help him obtain stuff. He said it was money but his reiki business, which he is not qualified for. I liked growing veg; he wanted to exploit my skills. He wanted to do things in my garden, build into my garden, and take the fence down. He demanded money for work even though he never approved it. He took gravel from my driveway and removed footpaths so the bins in the front block communal pathways. He told me to put a roof on the communal garden and grow plants on shelves attached to my wall. He moved bins and took stuff from the garden either by severe hinting or taking it and borrowing it but never bringing it back. He has moved fruit trees as they are not where he wanted them to be, as he had plans for a greenhouse in the set area. He tried to put a fence around my garden and called it "the garden". He put the CCTV camera over the communal area. He put gates up, which I was okay with, but as it damaged my wall, he threatened me when I challenged it. He wanted me to let him control my bank accounts and sign the house over to him.

Telling me my friends hate me. A friend who helped me with money said he was abusing me; he told the police the story was made up by this friend wanting to buy my house. He liked using keywords like "my friend". When I got stuff for the place thought it was for him. He took some plants in his greenhouse, denied me entry, and refused payment. He sat shouting at me, 'You are mentally ill, and no point asking you anything as you forget it!' He stopped friends coming to the house to do work like lay the patio or do pallet stuff. I quickly noticed nothing was going by my side. He demanded £300 for stuff and called me ungrateful.

I had a few panic attacks, one so severe that it was a suspected stroke. Of course, he feels not to blame but blames my friend who supported me with the police. He demanded keys to my house, car and shed. He even took the shed keys. A house key went missing, and stuff was moved when I came home. So, I thought it was my memory as my anxiety worsened. The moving of stuff stopped when the locks were changed. He said I was the only person working, so I had to pay for work to be done in his garden.

Jane's Story

My daughter has Cerebral palsy. She started college when she was 17. She was befriended by a group of people from college. She had her bank account, which she managed very well and thrifty. After a while, we noticed that her money was being spent on mobile phones. She had at least four contracts out. She told us she had got them for her friends so they could keep in touch with her. They had the money but no bank account, so they would pay it back monthly to her. But, of course, they never did. They were selling the phones for drugs. She was left with £4,000 in debt.

The so-called friends kept her out overnight against her will, and we had the police out on several occasions. By now, she was 18, and the police said she was old enough to make her own decisions even if they were terrible. She wouldn't speak up against them; she considered them her friends, so she put up with them whatever they did. I got in touch with social workers, police, the police and crime commissioner, and the Head of social services. I got the same answer. She was 18 and could do what she wanted. However, she wasn't doing what she wanted; she was doing what her so-called friends wanted her to do. Over the next three years, the friendship with these people continued. Physical and emotional abuse towards my daughter got worse.

I had massive concerns for her well-being and safety. I continued to contact the police and social workers during this time with my concerns, and no action was taken. Eventually, the so-called friends backed away as my daughter had no more to give them. Social services and the police finally agreed that my daughter had been a victim of a hate crime. Two people were charged with harassment and got a few hours of community service. Seemingly the court did not deem it a hate crime! Unfortunately, there is not enough information or training for social workers and police to recognise and stop this hate crime.

I recently read a statistic that has been playing on my mind. Online abuse towards disabled people went up by 50% last year. I have recently had multiple conversations with friends about what we need to do to educate society. Still, there has been one factor until now that has been missing from our discussions. The question isn't what we need to do; it's why these members of society commit these crimes. What myths and lies have they been told that have made them conclude that disabled people are damaged goods? I don't want to sound like a broken record, but it all comes down to the mindset of society. Instead of treating people with different conditions as equal, we first need to see them and discuss Community law. Society needs to see us as human beings before our disabilities.

The community needs to cater for each need. This does not validate using the term 'Special Needs' as everyone needs market is essential. It should not be singled out to make the individual feel a burden on society. Until we see everyone as a human being, we will not see hate crime statistics decrease. But, once we have changed our mindset, we will see the other pieces of the jigsaw come into place. Bus stops and train platforms will be raised. Taxi firms will increase the number of accessible vehicles. Retail shops, cafes, places of worship and any other public building will have ramps, lifts, accessible toilets and hearing loops. We will see pavements with more drop curbs and triple the amount of disabled bays in car parks.

Our World
By Kate Green

Words cannot describe what you have called me this time
In our world, we call it a disability hate crime
You think it's a great big deal
My question to you is, do you know how we feel?

That feeling of hatred that you are giving
My question to you is, what do you do for a living?
We disabled fight for our rights and
anything that's within our sights.

We may suffer with cuts be we don't need plasters
We budget for things so money can last us
Our budget is small, just like your mind
So stand up and start to be kind

You may one day have our needs
Don't look down on us like we're weeds
For we are strong
I would like you to know
The question is, now where are you going to go?

There are more disabled people than you think.
The pain of hate crime that you have caused stinks
So quit now while you think you're ahead
Or you, the attacker may one day be dead

Do you want to spend your life doing hate crimes?
Or the rest of your time doing hate crimes?
So just remember the scarring you have done
We disabled want to see you permanently gone

CHAPTER 6

Redefined Politically

"Today, for the first time in history, the largest group of Americans living in poverty are children."

— Jed Bartlet, The West Wing

If only Jed Bartlet, portrayed by the legendary Martin Sheen, was president today. I have no problem with the current president, Joe Biden, but he isn't Jed Bartlet. No Prime Minister or President has ever made a speech that is so poignant that people remember them. Slogans are so important in political campaigns; the campaigns that seem to win have short slogans and are to the point. For example, "Take Back Control" was used by The Vote Leave Campaign in the 2016 EU Referendum. The campaign led to Britain voting to leave the European Union or, as my friend calls it, "the European Experiment"! They say never talk about religion or politics…well as I have already spoken about my faith, then let's talk about politics. I will not tell you who to vote for or not vote for. I am not here to promote one political party and talk rubbish about the others. Instead, I will talk about my journey and what I look for within a party when I put the "X" on the ballot paper. I joined the Green Party in 2017.

Before joining, I never joined a political party because I felt rejected, excluded and forgotten about in politics. In October, the Home Office published a report about Hate crime in England and Wales between the financial year 2019 -2020. Over the past few years, we have been seeing a gradual rise in the statistics relating to disability hate crime. Hate crime, in general, has been on the rise and has increased over the past few years. Some blame Brexit for this; in some cases, they're right. Between 2019-2020 8,256 cases of disability Hate crime were reported.

However, The National Crime Survey estimates an accurate figure of 70,000. So what is happening? We are meant to be in the 21st century, where everyone is treated equally. UK Prime Minister David Cameron 2016, introduced equal marriage. He said, "Everyone should be treated; equally. People should be able to be themselves and not worry about what people think of them or how they should act around others." For too long, government after government has ignored and neglected disabled people. As a result, we are cutting public services that people like myself rely on. People say we are better now that we have left the EU. However, leaving the EU has meant we have lost the European Social Fund. The loss of the European Social Fund has been disastrous for disadvantaged groups, including people with disabilities.

The fund gave £500m a year to organisations in the UK that provide employment and training support for people whom mainstream providers often neglect. The government has yet to create a funding stream for these organisations. These organisations and charities have lost so much funding since Brexit and now the pandemic. We are at a point where we have a government that can do whatever they want and an opposition that doesn't call them out. We have just been dealing with the worst pandemic in our lifetime, with 129k deaths! That is 129k, too many deaths. Our government needed to have been stricter with the lockdown instead of dithering and delaying. Instead, we have a government that will set rules for us while breaking the laws themselves.

We need a strong opposition, keeping the government to account. Make sure the government sticks to their agreement for a net-zero carbon roadmap. This might make me sound like I am just talking rubbish about the Conservatives. However, if Labour were in and I felt like they weren't helping disabled people, I would say the same about them. I'm neither Left nor Right. I vote for a party that I feel will help disabled people and hold the same values as me. If I believed a Tory Leader had good policies and the same values as me, I would vote for them. But, unfortunately, there is no Tory that I would feel comfortable voting for at this moment. I can't vote for a party that sets out rules and guidelines to keep society safe yet doesn't follow the laws themselves.

A government that seems to have an answer or excuse for every mistake they make. Politics have become a three-word slogan. "Take back control" or "Strong and Stable". These slogans, up to now, have made campaigns work. Currently, the government's motto is "Levelling up Britain". But what does that mean? When members of the party were asked at the conference what Levelling up meant, 99% were unsurprisingly unable to answer. Does levelling up look like the society we live in now? Because if it does, I'm not sure I want to be a part of this! Homeless people still do not get the support they need, with unemployment rising yearly and an education system that is failing pupils across the UK.

We have now got to a place where it is up to the teachers to teach, write, and grade the exam. By the way, students take the exam three times, and the teacher just has to take the highest grade and not average the scores. This means that more students attend top universities; however, how many of them deserve to attend those universities? Furthermore, how many of those students will drop out after the first year? Is it levelling up when we see over 8000 disabled people being attacked just because they are deemed "Damaged goods"? As I write this, fresh allegations of rule-breaking in Downing Street have emerged. It's been reported that Boris Johnson is looking to reboot his leadership after a bruising week.

So how have we got to a place where the prime minister's future is now the subject of playground teasing? The only sector that is not struggling at the moment is the comedy sector. Every day has become a new comedy routine. Every statement the government makes has now become a meme. And yet this is why he will still be prime minister for the foreseeable future. These memes, Comedy routines have made the crises less severe. "Oh, Well, it's just Johnson being Johnson." I'm all for political satire, some of my favourite comedians and political impressionists. However, we can't allow them to get away with breaking the laws they set. No wonder people think it's one rule for us and another for them. Russel Brand is known for not voting in general elections. Arguing that the current political system is not fit for the 21st century.

All the Political leaders have been well educated, silver spoon fed and never had to live off of Universal credit. They had it easy! "There's no point in voting when the main political parties are basically indistinguishable, and the relationship between government, big business and factions of the media make it impossible for the democratic will of the people to be realised, which is a more nuanced point and plainly true."

In 2013 Brand wrote an article for The Guardian titled "Russell Brand: my life without drugs". In the article, he shared his relationship with alcohol and drugs and his journey to recovery. It's funny how we tell ourselves not to judge a book by its cover, yet when we hear someone is a drug addict, we suddenly feel the need to look down on them as if they have the plague. This is where true tribalism is shown.It doesn't matter what they have been through, the hurt they feel because they use drugs and alcohol as a mechanism to deal with life. We cannot have anything to do with them. They are peasants amongst us. Yet, I bet if you had been through everything they had been through, you would also use some kind of addiction to ease the pain.

"There are some things you should know. We're seventh in literacy, twenty-seventh in maths, twenty-second in science, forty-ninth in life expectancy, 178th in infant mortality, third in median household income, four in the labour force, and fourth in exports. We lead the world in only three categories: number of incarcerated citizens per capita, number of adults who believe angels are real, and defence spending, where we spend more than the following twenty-six countries combined, twenty-five of whom are allies.

We sure used to be. We stood up for what was right! We fought for moral reasons; we passed and struck down laws for ethical reasons. We waged wars on poverty, not poor people. We sacrificed, cared about our neighbours, put our money where our mouths were, and never beat our chest. We built great big things, made ungodly technological advances, explored the universe, cured diseases, and cultivated the world's greatest artists and the world's greatest economy.

We reached for the stars, and we acted like men. We aspired to intelligence; we didn't belittle it; it didn't make us feel inferior. We didn't identify ourselves by whom we voted for in the last election, and we didn't get scared so easily. And we were able to be all these things and do all these things because we were informed. By great men, men who were revered. The first step in solving any problem is recognising there is one America is not the greatest country in the world anymore."

Will McAvoy - The NewsRoom

Okay, I need to stop using quotes written by Aaron Sorkin. Sorkin Wrote the first three series of The West Wing and all three series of The Newsroom. I have watched all seven series of The West Wing twice, and I'm on the 3rd series of The Newsroom. It's become a weekly Friday night routine with my friend, who hooked my parents and me on The West Wing! Every Friday evening, we have a beer, usually an IPA, and watch an episode of The Newsroom.

I'm getting distracted! Why are we the most incredible country? Without sounding like Will McAvoy, We are not the greatest country in the world. I would say no country is at the top and is more significant than all the others. London has the highest Knife crime than any other part of the UK; we have a health system that hasn't been adequately funded for over a decade. We have politicians that have never had to live off of PIP or Universal Credit. Yet, they govern us without considering how it will affect millions of people. Instead, politicians use Taxpayers' money to employ university friends in their departments. Politicians use Taxpayers' money to hire a staff member they're having an affair with.

No wonder people are sceptical about COVID-19. Why would you believe a government that has blatantly lied multiple times? Just a side note, If I were an MP today and accused the government of not being truthful, I would be thrown out of the commons for the rest of the sitting. Yet we seem not to give a...! We have an opposition leader, a former lawyer whom Her Majesty knighted for his work as a lawyer, who appears to be unable to hold this government to account. As a lawyer, he should be good with evidence and ensure the government is telling the truth and holding them accountable for their actions. See, I said something negative about the left! Are you happy now? Here is another one despite everything wrong with the conservatives, the labour party don't seem to mention the issues disabled people face. For those who are not in the UK or do not follow politics as much as me (and if you do follow it more than me, that's just sad!)

Every Wednesday at midday, the Prime Minister is put in front of MP's for 40+ minutes. It is meant to be a time where MP's can make sure the Prime Minister and, more importantly, the Government as a whole is accountable. I say they meant to be because nine times out of 10, the opposition leader doesn't seem to follow up on anything the Prime Minister says. Also, other MP's are only allowed to ask one question, whereas party leaders are entitled to ask six questions. If you haven't seen "Prime Minister's Questions", you would be forgiven for thinking it's a quiet, civilised debate. A debate where the questions and answers are heard without any shouting. Ha, think again!

It looks and sounds like a classroom with all the noisy, misbehaving kids put into one classroom with a supply teacher. It's the most uncivilised thing I have ever watched. But, again, no wonder people are switched off and fed up with politics. If you're looking for a grownup, the civilised debate looks no further than the US Congress, allowing people to speak without drowning them with constant shouting. Can we not just once have a debate where people don't need to call names, *Cough* *Cough* Dennis Skinner? Can we not allow others with other opinions to share their thoughts on society? It is healthy to disagree with others as long as we do it respectfully. I became political and not in a good way. I got too engrossed in all the drama and became tribal. It wasn't until the past few months that I realised I was as bad as them!

I became the politician that I despised. I have a significant problem with certain people on the far left. They are against anybody on the right, anybody with centralist views in their party; they're always looking out for any mistakes they can write articles about or create a video for their youtube channel. However, this is not journalism, as they will not have anyone to balance the argument. The left reminds me of a tribe. When the Tribe leader is kicked out of office, their predecessor becomes the enemy. They are criticised for doing an awful job and are just as bad as the Tories!

Yes, I'm talking about Momentum and the people associated with them. Momentum rose when Jeremy Corbyn was elected Labour Leader. In their words:

> "Momentum is a people-powered, vibrant movement. We aim to transform the Labour Party, our communities and Britain in the interests of the many, not the few. Our proposition is simple: if more of us come together, we can use our skills and energy to tackle every challenge head-on. Using our collective power, campaigning, networks and tech, we can transform society for the better."

What's not to love about it? If that is all they want, then sign me up! But it doesn't seem to be the whole picture, only one pixel from a larger photo. The Momentum project is not a movement; it's a tribe full of far-left people. A tribe that is not welcome for debate. The issue with the left is that we are weak; we always have been. We have allowed the media to rip us to shreds. But, unfortunately, momentum was just the start of the now never ending far right slur against the fight against injustice. Fighting injustice, wanting everyone to have security at work, and giving everyone a safe place to call home are not something I am ashamed of. It's being human and caring for others. Socialism isn't all about taxing the rich and sharing the wealth equally. It's a lot more than that, yet we have allowed society to stereotype us and label us as soft hippies who can't be trusted with the financial crisis we have found ourselves in! If the current system works, why do we see the NHS at the breaking point?

If the current system works, why are we not seeing homelessness declining? We need to shake up the system, start from fresh, and bring in proportional representation. Proportional representation works; we have seen it work for decades in our system when electing our local councillors. Yet, Westminster is scared to use this concept because it will destroy the tribalism, and they will have to work together as a team to run the country. Egos will collapse and have to take their roles seriously rather than organising parties with "bring your own booze!" Egos are not just on the right, and there are many egos on the left that need to be taken down a peg or two. Left-wing journalists say they highlight the issues society faces and yet never mention disability issues. MP's say they want to support people struggling to cope and yet get caught up in political campaigns in other countries.

I genuinely believe that Momentum was set up in good faith, and its mission was sincere. However, I think they grew more extensive than they could ever imagine and got caught up like me in the "Westminster Politics." I will end by saying this: Politicians become Politicians because they want to make the world a better place. I know it doesn't feel like it at the moment, especially with the UK Government breaking the laws they set to keep us safe. Yes, I'm angry and annoyed, and yes, I would like to see the Prime Minister step down, BUT I don't think It would change anything. The reason for that remark is because the next Prime Minister will be an Eton-educated, silver spoon-fed, white, middle age man with no Disability. Nothing will change until we get away from Westminster politics. So how do we move forward? We need to stop being cynical and tribal, and let's share ideas, and maybe just maybe, our voices will be heard.

"I HAVE A DISABILITY, BUT ALL THAT ACTUALLY MEANS IS I NEED TO TAKE A SLIGHTLY DIFFERENT PATH TO YOU."

CHAPTER 7

Am I A Stereotypical Disabled Person?

"A stereotype may be negative or positive, but even positive stereotypes present two problems. They are cliches, and they present a human being as far more simple and uniform than any human being is." - Nancy Kress.

"Sim, are you a stereotypical disabled person?" Not in a million years, and neither is anyone else for that matter! What does a stereotypical disabled person look like? What does a stereotypical disabled person do? For the past six years, I have been going to schools talking in PSHE lessons about what it's like using a wheelchair to get around in today's society. At the beginning of each session, I ask them to discuss in groups what they think of when they hear the word disability. It's strange seeing their reaction when asking their opinion. A few are probably thinking, "Is this a trick question? What should I say without offending him?" I then reassure them that I genuinely want to know their beliefs and that I won't get offended.

After a few more minutes of awkward silence, each of them says what they think:

"People with disabilities can't do anything."

"People with disabilities use a wheelchair."

"People with disabilities need 24-hour care."

"People with disabilities can't communicate."

"People with disabilities are not able to work."

Okay, so let's break each of these down and determine whether these are accurate!

"People with disabilities can't do anything."

Tell that to Baroness Tanni Grey-Thompson. Over the course of her career, she has won 13 gold medals. As she prepared to retire from racing, she expanded her television broadcasting career on BBC Wales, S4C, and BBC One. In addition to serving on UK Sport's Mission 2012 panel and the National Disability Council, she sat on the Sports Council for Wales Board, the English Lottery Awards Panel and British Lottery Awards Panel for three years. Besides her current position on the London Legacy Development Corporation, Grey-Thompson served on the board of the London Marathon in 2007 and the London Legacy Development Corporation in 2008 and 2018. Currently, she is the chair of the UK Active board. Among the charities, Grey-Thompson supports are the Duke of Edinburgh Awards scheme, the Wembley Stadium Legacy Trust, Sports Leaders UK, the leadership of UNICEF, and the Winston Churchill Memorial Trust.

Grey-Thompson is also the Patron of the Tees Wheelyboat Club, a group that gives disabled people access to the River Tees. In July 2011, Grey-Thompson was announced as President of the Leadership 20:20 Commission. On 14 December 2011, she launched the Commission's recommendations. Her previous roles include Trustee of V, the Tony Blair Sports Foundation, Sports Aid Foundation (which she received as a young athlete), International Inspiration Ambassador, and Chair of the Women's Sports and Fitness Foundation Commission.

Since July 2015, Grey-Thompson has also been Chancellor of Northumbria University. The House of Lords Appointments Commission (HOLAC) appointed Grey-Thompson a Life Peer on 23 March 2010. As a result, she was given the title of Baroness Grey-Thompson, of Eaglescliffe in Stockton-On-Tees, despite her previous interest in a Welsh title. On 29 March, Grey-Thompson swore the oath of allegiance in English and Welsh, sitting as a cross bencher. During the run-up to September's Scottish independence referendum, Grey-Thompson was one of the prominent public figures to sign a letter opposing Scottish independence. Oh, and she's got Spina Bifida!

Tell Ade Adepitan, the bronze medalist at the 2004 Paralympics. In addition to acting and presenting, he also appeared in series for the BBC and Channel 4. In his campaigns against racism and disability discrimination, he often uses television as a platform. In 2002 BBC One did an ident Hip-Hop, where he was one of three wheelchair basketball players. He was one of the main hosts of the children's program Xchange for CBBC and appeared in EastEnders. In addition, he starred in the TV series Desperados as a wheelchair basketball coach, "Baggy Awolowo". Adepitan participated in Beyond Boundaries, a four-part documentary in which he trekked through Nicaragua's rainforests, deserts, rivers, and mountains. As part of the Documentary, Ade made a video diary filmed between London and Spain, talking about his sporting aspirations and how he coped with living in Zaragoza without speaking Spanish.

He presented the London 2012 Paralympic Games on Channel 4 and co-presented That Paralympic Show with Rick Edwards. In addition, he has become increasingly involved in creating documentaries for Channel 4. In 2013, he did a Channel 4 Dispatches show called Britain on Benefits and an Unreported World documentary on Cuban basketball players. Along with Clare Balding, he presented the Channel 4 2014 Winter Paralympic Games and Rio 2016 Paralympics. In addition to presenting the Invictus Games, Adepitan has also guest-hosted The One Show with Alex Jones. In addition, Adepitan co-hosted New York: America's Busiest City with Anita Rani and Ant Anstead in 2016 on BBC 2. He has co-presented the BBC's Children in Need appeal since 2016.

He co-presented "World's Busiest Cities" with Anita Rani and Dan Snow. In 2019, he presented a four-part series for BBC Two Africa travelling across Africa, from Lagos in Nigeria - to the deep south of the continent. Earlier in life, Ade was diagnosed with Polio. Where do I begin when it comes to the late great Stephen Hawking? Hawking extended the singularity theorem concepts first explored in his doctoral thesis with Penrose. He hypothesised that the universe might have started as a singularity. The 1968 Gravity Research Foundation competition placed their joint essay runner-up. Using Alexander Friedmann's models of physical cosmology, the scientists proved that the universe should have begun as a singularity; if it obeys the general theory of relativity.

As a result, Hawking was awarded a Specially Created Fellowship for Distinction in Science in 1969 to remain at Caius for several years. He proposed a second law of black hole dynamics in 1970, stating that black holes can never shrink. In an analogy with thermodynamics, he proposed the four rules of black hole mechanics with James M. Bardeen and Brandon Carter. The graduate student Jacob Bekenstein, a student of John Wheeler, went further and applied thermodynamic concepts literally, to Hawking's dismay.

It was in the early 1970s that Hawking's work with Carter, Werner Israel, and David C. Robinson supported Wheeler's no-hair theorem. The theorem states that no matter what the original material was or how it was created, it can be entirely described by its mass, electrical charge, and rotation properties. He won the Gravity Research Foundation Award in January 1971 for his essay "Black Holes". In 1973, George Ellis published Hawking's first book on the topic. He began to study quantum gravity, as well as quantum mechanics, during the 1970s. A discussion with Yakov Borisovich Zel'dovich and Alexei Starobinsky led him to this study. They showed that rotational black holes emit particles based on uncertainty.

Hawking's much-checked calculations contradict Hawking's second law, which states that black holes cannot get smaller due to their entropy. In 1974, Hawking presented results showing that black holes emit radiation, known today as Hawking radiation, that may continue until they exhaust their energy. Hawking radiation was controversial at first. However, after further research was published in the late 1970s, the discovery was widely acknowledged as a significant breakthrough in theoretical physics. A few weeks after Hawking's radiation was announced, Hawking was elected a Fellow of the Royal Society (FRS). At the time, he was one of the youngest Fellows. Amarone was appointed to Caltech's Sherman Fairchild Distinguished Visiting Professorship in 1974. He is a distinguished academician. A colleague on the faculty, Kip Thorne, got involved in a scientific wager about whether Cygnus X-1 was a black hole.

The wager was an "insurance policy" against the proposition that black holes did not exist. Hawking conceded that he lost the bet in 1990, the first of several he made with Thorne and others. As a result of this first visit to Caltech, Hawking spent almost every year after his first visit. Hawking was promoted to the Cambridge University faculty in 1975 to become a reader in gravitational physics. In the mid-times and late 1970s, physicists were interested in black holes. Hawking was interviewed extensively for print and television. As a result of his work, he also gained increasing academic recognition. In 1975, he received both the Eddington Medal and the Pius XI Gold Medal; in 1976, the Dannie Heinemann Prize, the Maxwell Medal, and the Hughes Medal. However, it was in 1977 that he was appointed a professor with a chair in gravitational physics. The following year, he received the Albert Einstein Medal and an honorary doctorate at the University of Oxford. Hawking was appointed Lucian Professor of Mathematics at Cambridge University in 1979. "Is the End in Sight for Theoretical Physics?" was the title of his inaugural lecture, and he proposed N=8 Supergravity as a solution to many outstanding problems in theoretical physics.

Though reluctantly, he was experiencing a health crisis during his promotional period, which allowed him to accept some nursing care at home. His approach to physics was also changing, becoming more intuitive and speculative rather than insisting on mathematical proofs. He told Kip Thorne, "I would rather be right than rigorous.". He proposed in 1981 that information is irretrievably lost when a black hole evaporates. During the Black Hole War between Leonard Susskind and Gerard Hooft, the information paradox violated the fundamental tenet of quantum mechanics. You're right; people with disabilities can't do anything!

"Disabled people use a wheelchair."

While this is true for some people, it's not the case for all! There are currently 1.2 million people who use a wheelchair in the UK, which sounds like a lot. Still, when you compare it to the number of people recognised as disabled in the UK, it's not even 50%. It's only 8.5%! So, why is the wheelchair the first thing people think of when it comes to disability? The wheelchair symbol is used on everything from accessible toilets to disabled parking to disabled access. It has been a symbol for decades and is recognised around the world. So what can be used instead? To be honest, nothing!

There are so many disabilities that they can't all be identified in one symbol. It's practically impossible. Suppose we want to get away from the wheelchair as the symbol. In that case, we need to develop a colour or shape that can be used that still indicates those facilities are for disabled people only. Many disabilities are hidden, so people wear lanyards to help society understand. Unfortunately, there is still a long way to go for the community to understand the different signs.

"People with disabilities need 24-hour care."

Before discussing this, I must stress that **NOBODY** is entirely independent. We all need some kind of support, whether it depends on your employer to pay your wage on time. You rely on the mechanic to fix your car. You depend on the shop to have enough food on the shelf. We all need help, and it is okay to ask. I need help and support! Now, at the moment, I am depending on my mum to allow me to borrow her laptop to write this chapter while mine gets fixed. We need to stop worrying about how much help we need and concentrate on what we can achieve with the service we get. I have a fantastic support worker! He does not get enough credit for the amount he supports other people and me.

We laugh, but we also get a lot done. Without his support, I would be living in a pigsty. I'm not saying I am a messy person. However, I am physically unable to take the trash out, and I am unable to clean the bathroom thoroughly. I can change my bedding, but it's a marathon. I could probably manage with enough practice, but it's easier if he does it. I do the clothes washing as it only takes 30 seconds. So, some people with disabilities need support 24/7, but who cares? Does it affect your life? No, so just concentrate on your life rather than going on social media and telling us we are "worthless" and that our parents should have aborted us. Instead, let's use the support we have to empower us, give us a voice, and give us the ability to participate in life. Rant over!

"People with disabilities can't communicate."

Okay, so tell that to Stephen Hawkins, Every deaf person who uses sign language. Tell that to Lee Ridley (lost voice guy), who has created a whole comedy routine because he cannot talk the "Normal way" and needs to use a computer to speak. We all communicate; there is no conventional way of communicating anymore. The way we communicate is unique. Languages and spellings are different worldwide, and nobody seems to bat an eyelid. Yet, people are so hung up on how people with disabilities communicate.

Again, Does it affect your life? No, so just concentrate on your life rather than going on social media and telling us we are worthless. If it affects you that much, then learn their way of communicating. A few years ago, the UK Parliament debated if BSL should be compulsory in schools like Maths, English and Science. I was over the moon to hear that it was finally discussing this subject. It was the first time a debate at this level included a BSL interpreter, so it was as inclusive as possible. The arguments for the motion were solid and compelling. We had MP's who went above and beyond to learn their speech in BSL. At the end of the debate, the government minister had time to respond. But unfortunately, despite the millions of people who had signed the petition and the compelling arguments from all members across all the major parties who were for the motion, the government decided that BSL should not be a compulsory subject.

After this shocking event, I was preparing for a talk at a local school. I was so enraged that this government had the nerve to disempower many people. It was quite frankly the craziest thing I have seen and watched. With the help of youtube, I decided to learn my full introduction to my talk in BSL. After weeks of learning, I could sign my whole introduction confidently. Our ability counts; our voice matters. As I am writing this, I'm smiling like the Cheshire Cat! The UK Government have now finally recognised BSL as a language. Thank you, Wayne Barrow and

Rose Ayling-Ellis, for campaigning for a more equal society.

"People with disabilities cannot work."

I don't want this to be a chapter full of rants but for crying out loud, have you asked why people with disabilities cannot work? No, then you should. Society is inaccessible. Culture is partly to blame for millions of disabled people who can't work. The disability employment gap, the difference between the proportion of disabled and non-disabled people in employment, stands at nearly 30%. Since 2013, the gap has closed by five percentage points, and the number of disabled people in employment has risen by 1.3 million. But disabled people still face unacceptable barriers to finding, staying in and progressing in work. The UK Government has targeted getting 1,000,000 more disabled people into work by 2027.

They will say they are on target, but is it right to force people with disabilities to work? While I believe that everyone who can work should work and pay their taxes, I also think that people who cannot work because of their condition should not be forced to work. I will also argue that employers should be encouraged to employ more people with disabilities and should have government support. To answer the original question, there is no such thing as a stereotypical disabled person; we are only human. We all participate in today's society.

CHAPTER 8

A Minority Within A Minority

"We are a minority within a minority."

Simeon Wakely

What do I mean by that? As stated earlier, there are four minority groups; LGBTQ+ Community, The Black Asian and Minority Ethnic Community, The Disabled Community and the Faith Communities. No community is greater than the rest, and each person has the right to have a voice in today's society. The term "minority" is often used to refer to groups lacking social or political power and, combined, having the loudest voice. When I say Gender and Sexuality Minorities, you will probably think of the LGBTQ+ Community. Still, it is a much wider Community consisting of those who have transitioned and those who identify as non-binary. Those who identify as part of the Gender and Sexuality minority community have previously been refused equal rights and protection under the law.

I should also state that although Western Society has become more progressive regarding LGBTQ+ rights, in Eastern countries such as Saudi Arabia and Afghanistan still illegal to be in a same-sex marriage and is punishable with the death penalty. This is, of course, wrong on so many levels. People belonging to religious minorities have a faith distinct from the rest of society. Most countries, if not all, have religious minorities. It has now become widely accepted in the Western world that people should be free to follow and believe in their own religion. You may think I am just stating the obvious; however, this freedom is constricted in many countries.

For example, in Egypt, a new system has been put in place to force all citizens to state their religion on their identity cards, but the only choices for them are Islam, Christianity, or Judaism. "Black Lives Matter" is a phrase and notably a hashtag used to highlight racism, discrimination and inequality experienced by black people."race" and "ethnicity" refers to two different social identities. The term "race" defines people using physical characteristics such as skin colour and facial structure. The term "ethnicity" is used when talking about someone's shared heritage, language and culture. Ethnic and racial minorities exist in nation-states across the world.

However, they are not always gauged by apparent differences. As I said at the beginning of this chapter, the term "minority" is often used to refer to groups lacking social or political power. An excellent example is that during the apartheid in 1948, black people in South Africa owned the majority in the nation-state; however, this did not prevent institutionalised racism by the white minority. This was mainly because the National Party gained power with its all-white government and immediately began enforcing existing policies of racial segregation.So here's to educating so many ignorant minds. I suggest they are disabled, rejecting our place as part of humanity. We have so much to impart, unbound amounts to give, but lots of them have the relief; we have no point in living. We embrace them as they are. So, why not welcome us? For being just how we are, they need the blinkers off. Despite the intelligence man prides upon himself, disability issues remain low on the shelf. Awareness is something a lot of them need.

If only we could eradicate their ignorance and greed. If they took just a moment to think it through, they too might end up disabled; how would they cope? What would they do.? In a world just like us with disability issues to bear, I'll bet they'd all start crying, finding so much so unfair. So in desire of spreading knowledge of the discrimination we all have to face, I try to write words with the wish that we're treated as we should be and take our rightful place. Too many people are entirely ignorant of disability issues and do not accept us as normal human beings with so much to offer to society.

They need to get the blinkers off, smell the coffee, stop stereotyping us and get a grip on how much we have to give. It might take time, it will not happen overnight, and it might not happen in our lifetime, but it will for your kids and their kids. Isn't it remarkable that the former leader of the labour party, the one who said he was "For the Many, Not the Few", and yet we felt last in the queue? The last to be mentioned like a student in detention. It's as if our life is worthless than Joe's Blogs, on the surface, has more purpose. Yet, what gives Joe Blogs the right to have a voice when he himself is disabled?

Not physically or mentally disabled yet blind to the injustice in today's society. In the midst of society's chaos, you will find 6 million voices drowned out by the "remainers" and "brexiteers". Six million voices are drowned out by people who think they can talk louder because they are not damaged goods. They believe that because we are damaged goods, we are somehow the only ones broken and yet we are all broken; society is broken, and yet we just forget each day that it could be a hell of a lot better. So let's put down the megaphone and talk to your neighbour. Let's share ideas rather than see who can shout the loudest cause; in the end, we will fail miserably. We can all agree that society is broken, that much we can agree on, right? So the next question is, how do we fix it? What needs to change to make society a more equal society that doesn't rely on violence and name-calling? I think we need to see more disability sports showcased in the media.

We have an opportunity to build on a sector that, let's face it, is changing every few months. The media as we know it is changing all the time. Mainstream TV is dying, and media outlets like Netflix, Amazon and Youtube are thriving. People don't have time to sit on the sofa and watch TV. They want to be able to watch football on their phones on the train or listen to podcasts. They want to be able to learn a new skill or would like to be able to have a variety of films instead of what is scheduled on TV.

We have an opportunity to have an equal playing field with disability sports. A sector that has yet to thrive. We all have smartphones, tablets or laptops. We have the capability to showcase disability sports in a way that no other media outlet will— showcasing heartfelt stories of the athletes and shaping and shaping Disability Media. Secondly, we, as the disabled community, need to grow up! If someone stops us in the streets and asks us a question about our disability, we need to stop taking it personally and start a conversation.

Yes, they might not say it correctly, but who cares! We will not change society if we don't change our own and will not change the culture if we don't change our mindset. I am always open with people about my disability. I try to explain that it's not the condition that has disabled me but society. I am fed up with hearing that people are scared to talk or socialise with disabled people just in case they offend them. We have a voice; we need to use it. We have a platform; we need to use it. We have our stories; we just need to use them. Stop passing on the responsibility and help make society a more equal society. Last of all, we are a minority within a minority. My condition is different to yours. We have all got a disability of some kind. I am, at this moment, fuming with certain members of the disability community. Words can't describe how angry I am.

WHY ARE WE FIGHTING WITH EACH OTHER?

I have officially left every single Facebook group that supports people with disabilities. Why? Because for some stupid reason, people think it is acceptable to write that they are more disabled than everyone else and accuse others of not being disabled enough to be a part of the group! We all have the same condition, for goodness sake! It doesn't matter if you were born with the disease or if it developed as an adult. The state is still the same! Just because I get back pain and Joe Blogs, who also has Spina Bifida, doesn't mean he is not as disabled as me. Each person is unique and gets different symptoms unless you're in their position, which you're not; then, you can't judge them and discriminate.

"Handicap people are nice, Leonard; Everyone knows that!" - Penny, The Big Bang Theory

THIS IS TOTAL RUBBISH! We are just as judgemental, Tribal and obnoxious as the rest of society! Until we change, I won't be involved in any social media groups. I'm going to lose friends with what I am about to say. I am against the LGBTQ+ Community, I'm against the religious communities, and I am against the black and ethnic race community. Does that mean I'm racist or homophobic? Does that mean I'm anti-Semitic or Islamophobic? Not in a million years! I'm against how tribal each community has become.

They don't want to hear about it if it doesn't affect them! By the way, I am not for one moment saying the Disability Community is high and mighty amongst the rest; as I said, we are just as judgemental, Tribal and obnoxious as the rest of society! I am all for communities; I feel we are at our best when we act as a Community. We need to start sharing ideas, helping those in need and cheering each other on. My anxiety is that we have made our communities into tribes, which is getting out of hand. Those voices that could not be heard before will not be heard amongst the shouting and name-calling. The Disability community is still seen as a Community of those in society who are damaged goods.

A Community that is judged on their appearance before anything else. You wouldn't go to someone and say, "You don't look like a Christian" Or "You don't look gay", so why on earth do we accept comments like "You don't look disabled" or "are you in it for the money?". What money are you talking about? Oh, the £600 a month we get from the government? Let me ask you, can you live off £600 a month, paying all your bills plus what I like to call the disability tax?

So instead of saying yeah, but I have it worse because I'm gay or the Jewish Community gets it the worst, let's say we all get judged and get our fair share of discrimination. We get judged for our looks, beliefs, and how we talk or walk. We get judged the moment we step or push out of the door. We get judged on how we socialise; we get judged on how we learn and study. Instead of building walls, we need to build bridges. Instead of hard borders, we need to create paths and different paths to reach the same goal of making society more equal.

Owen Jones, author and journalist, is someone who, in the past, I have disagreed with strongly. I would say he is further left than me, but I admire, or should I say admired, him for his campaigning and standing up for injustice. I do, however, have a significant issue with him. It's not because he is gay or he is surrounded by people who are antisemitic. Owen has done over a hundred interviews, talking to those on the left and the right. However, he does seem to have one key issue that he stands for, which is fine, and these issues are close to his heart, but then he says he wants to create content highlighting different social issues.

After looking at this YouTube channel, Owen Jones has done 220 videos; 25% of his videos are on labour leadership, 65% on LGBTQ+ rights and the other 10% are interviews with politicians on both sides. Only two videos are on disability; even then, you must scroll through to the very first batch of videos to find anything on Disability.

In his review last year, he said:

> "We gave a voice to otherwise marginalised working-class people and minorities. We fought racism and bigotry. We gave a platform to promising alternatives."

And yet, no mention of Disability issues. No mention of the lack of adapted housing, no mention of the lack of accessible work, and no mention of the 8000 victims of Disability hate crime. It is all for one and none for all. I now don't call it minority communities; I call it minority tribes. Please, let's stop this and give everyone an equal voice. Don't shut down as soon as you hear the word disability because we are all in this together. I don't want this book just about my views; I want to create a book that will inspire you to become passionate about your hopes and dreams for the future, so I have given you space to write down your thoughts. I want you to physically write in this book so that five years down the line, when you pick this book back up, you will see that you, too, played a part in creating an equal society. Let us start a conversation; take a photo of what you have written and post it on social media.

Tell your dreams to your family and friends. Why? So that together, we can make it happen and keep us all accountable to each other. It's all well and good having a dream, but unless we are accountable to someone, we won't have the motivation to carry out our ambitions and our goals.

What are the top 3 things that need changing?

1 ....

2 ....

3 ....

What can you do to change point 1?

....
....
....

What can you do to change point 2?

....
....
....

What can you do to change point 3?

....
....
....

CHAPTER 9

The Housing Crisis

"The UK has a housing crisis."
Every Headline in the UK

Is it a shock that we are in a housing crisis? In 2008 we had the most significant financial crash ever recorded, and governments have yet to pay off the deficit. House prices tumbled all over the country as a result of the financial crisis. The average UK property's value fell by 20% over 16 months, while transaction levels slumped from 1.65 million in the decade up to the crisis to 730,000 in June 2009. Recovery was slow! It took around six years for prices to reach pre-crash prices. Arguably, in some areas of Britain, they had still not recovered. However, the housing crisis, in my opinion, started way before the financial crisis! Disagree? I dare you to go to every homeless person and tell them there is no Housing crisis. I dare you to say that to every person on the housing list waiting for a property that is either already adapted or is able to be adapted.

These crises were there long before 2008; unfortunately, they will be there until we stop this injustice! We will always have a housing crisis until we explore the reasons for our housing crises.

In this chapter, I am going to share first-hand why there is a housing crisis and my experiences and share some thoughts on how to improve the process of finding a property that needs to be adapted. For us to get to where we are today, we began in April 2019; I was having an annual review with my social worker. I say, my social worker, what I mean by that is a social worker, as since becoming 18, I no longer have a social worker assigned to me. So this Social worker turns up, and we talk about what I am doing and discuss my future. What do I want to be doing for work? Where would I like to be living?

These are all things I have been struggling with over the past few years. It's strange that once you're out of the situation, you can look back and review it with a different view. There are so many pivotal moments to this story, Different sides to the story, and many barriers to overcome. Renting a flat is not as easy as you think when you have a disability! The process is long, exhausting, stressful, emotional and scary! Firstly, there are so many people that I need to mention that have been there for me during this whole process and who, without their support, I wouldn't be living where I am now! Without my support network, I wouldn't be here today. So to those who have been there for me over the past 25 years, thank you! Nobody, especially me, would have ever thought we would be in this situation!

Let me set the scene. It's 2018, and I have just started my annual review with my social worker…no, sorry, I mean a social worker. I'm sitting there explaining my life story for the millionth time. I have it down to a tee, Explaining how college was not the best and my work is non-existent. We then go on to my living arrangements. At the time, I was living with my parents in a semi-detached house. We had been living there for 14 years and loved the community. Social events were difficult to organise due to the lack of public transport, and taxis were expensive. I explained that I wanted to be on the housing list and asked for their help and advice. As always, there are many forms to fill out. I swear my life is just filling out forms.

After explaining all the documents and the numbers that I needed to call, she left me to get on. By 5 pm that same day, I had gotten my name on the housing list, sent forms to the local authority and signed up for support from one of the housing associations, which is now my landlord! I was determined! Anyway, the system is different in each local authority. In Bath and North East Somerset, you have your own username and password to log in to their website. Once you have logged in, you can see all your details, which is scary how much info they have! You're given a "band", depending on how urgent your case is.

Now, because my parents' house had been adapted for me, and my parents could cook for me, I was, unfortunately, a low priority. Anyway, every Friday, I would stay awake until Midnight to see what houses, flats, and bungalows were available to "bid" for. The bidding process was simple. Click on the property, read through the info and click bid! It was that easy. Anyone could do it, even BDUs. Once you have checked your details, i.e. Your Age, Gender, Marital status, Do you have any dependents under 18, then I can see the properties that are available for me. Not all "Social Housing" is available for me as each property has specific criteria. For the first few weeks, there were no properties suitable for me. Most of the flats were on the first floor with no lift, or the bungalow was up on a steep hill with pavements with no dropped curb!

After a few depressing weeks of not bidding, I found a flat that was ground floor, 15min push into the city centre and had a beautiful community garden. The block was only five years old, with underground parking and a local cafe 30 seconds away! As soon as the property was up, I pressed Bid! Weeks passed, and I had not heard anything until one morning; I woke up and saw that I had been moved up to Band B. They must have realised how desperate I was to get my own place! Still, no news if I had got the place, I went back on to the bidding site. There was another flat that was on the same block as the previous flat. Of course, I instantly pressed "Bid".

My Dad had booked to go away for two weeks to visit friends. A week into his time away, I had a phone call from an 01225 number. Now, I have a lot of calls from the hospital that start with "01225". I was in the Kitchen at the time and, for whatever reason, had put my phone on silent. After seeing a missed call and then hearing the voicemail, I immediately dropped everything and rang straight back! A guy called Tim Oldrini Answered. He explained that the second flat I had put my name down for was available for me to go and visit. Before I go on with the story, I do need to say how grateful I am that he took the time to explain the process and answered all of my queries without hesitation. I did feel like a BDU asking all of these random questions! Some were probably obvious, but I was new to this, so give me a break...

So, we agreed to meet the following Monday with my mum. After putting the phone down, I shouted to my mum upstairs in her study. We decided what time we would be leaving, how long it would take to get there and where to park! Meanwhile, my dad was in another country without any idea what was happening. I think I called one of my brothers first, who was at work at the time, but he had been involved with many discussions about me moving out. I sent Dad a WhatsApp message! How amazing is it that we can send instant messages to anyone in the world with just one tap?

Yes, After asking my Dad to call me, I did miss his call! Excitement? No, I just forgot to take my phone off silent...sorry dad! After calling him back, we had a conversation. To be honest, the only information I had for my dad was the address and a map, and that's about it. It was more the idea that I was looking at a flat that I was able to call home. My home. Over the coming days, the idea of having my own place started to sink in! Excited and Scared, all mixed into one. Fast forward to the day of the viewing. As agreed, I met my mum in the city centre after meeting with a friend. We drove up to the local Homebase, which, now looking back at it, we could have easily walked up, but the parking is awful. We arrive outside the block with 15 minutes to spare. We started wandering around the area, getting familiar. I instantly fell in love with the area. It reminded me of some places in Europe. Tim arrived with the key and started to show us around. If you have ever been to University or a Premier Inn, The corridors looked exactly like that. A blue carpet with white walls looked like it needed a brand new lick of paint. We entered the flat; I had no idea what to expect. I went in with no expectations. I was overwhelmed by how much room I had. The kitchen was non-existent.

The living room had so much light! One wall had a multi-coloured wallpaper that turned out later was hiding a very dark purple wall. The bedroom looked small; however, after looking at the measurements, I had enough room for my wheelchair to manoeuvre. He then went on to show us the garden...You can play a full-size football match! Raised beds and the most stunning plants and trees. He then said he would contact me within the next few days to find out what I think. When I spoke to my Dad, he asked if it felt correct to say yes.

I spoke to my mum and agreed there and then that I would have the flat and that there wouldn't be anywhere better. My dad was due to fly back later that week, so he would help me sign the documentation. All good so far, right? Now, this is where the housing crisis starts. Social care! We informed social care that I have a property that needs adapting. We asked them what the process was. They explained that an Occupational Therapist was required to visit to do an assessment. He quoted eight months before I got assessed, Then another two months to find companies to do the assessment. All this while I pay rent, council tax, gas, electricity and water for a property I cannot live in.

After several months of writing to various people, I was at my flat as a family friend was decorating my bedroom. I suddenly received a phone call from a withheld number. It turned out to be an occupational therapist assigned to my case. After discussing the following steps, she asked when would be a good time for her to come and do the assessment. Being cocky, I mentioned I was at the flat now.

She was free, so she agreed to come down within the next 15 minutes. Still shocked at the idea of having the assessment done earlier than planned, I rang my mum to see if she could pop by to help me explain everything I needed. When the Occupational Therapist arrived, we started discussing the adaptations. I was worried about what to ask for as I wasn't sure what they could provide. Again I was overwhelmed by the options. I would have to buy the appliances, but the rest would be funded by the Disabled Facilities Grant run by the council.

After a couple of months of writing up the report, we had two companies to quote for the bathroom and two companies to quote for the kitchen. All in all, this is now six months from when I got the keys. Six months of paying bills. The council then received all the quotes and decided on the two companies to complete the work. After back and forth ironing out the details, we could start building work! Perfect, end of story! Haha, if only that were the case. It's only just begun. My next task was to get hold of social services again to organise an assessment for support when I was in my flat. Again the waiting list was massive. My thought process was that we could get the support organised by the time the adaptations had been put in. That would make sense, right?

How I was wrong! The assessment I had only completed the year before took place in February as the kitchen was just finishing. I have so much respect for social services and understand how much pressure they are under and are poorly funded. However, with that all being said, none of what I am about to tell you is down to just funding. Don't get me wrong, budget plays a big part but so does lack of communication. After the assessment, the social worker informed me that I would have a report within two weeks. Five weeks later, and still no report. After emailing him multiple times and no reply and phoning his office and still no reply, I managed to get hold of him on his mobile.

Either he had a day off, annual leave or was dealing with an emergency case. I then had to go to the hospital for a week; I'll explain more later. After I was discharged, I got back into contact with him to see his progress. He promised the assessment by the end of the week. Again three weeks later and still no report. This continued for months until the assessment finally went to the panel in December, 24th December to be exact. Finally, I will find out how much support I will get. Haha, if only that were the case! What a fantastic Christmas present that would be. The panel decided that they could not decide on the support! They needed the Reablement Team to assess my needs once I moved into my flat.

That assessment will be sent to social services, who will present it to the panel for the third time. They say the third time's a charm! Yet, in this situation, the third time was not a charm. It's as if they stab you in the back and then promise to take the sword out but then push it in further and further to increase the wound. Now, The news was not given to me by my social worker, his manager, or anyone else on that team. The information was given to me by the manager of the Reablement Team Manager. I have so much respect for that team! Their reason for not supporting me is that I can cook, wash, and order groceries myself. I can't, however, clean the flat, empty the bins, change my bedding on my own, but who cares if I live in a dirty, smelly flat...Oh, wait, I do!

For me to get the support, I needed to do a financial form explaining what income I have and what benefits I have. So, they know I can't afford to pay for my own support and yet that is the only option. Fuck sake! Fortunately for me, a family friend who used to babysit me when I was a kid lives only 15min walk from me. The agreement is 15 hours a week to help me with the tasks I can't do myself. He comes every Wednesday morning at 8 am with pastries. We put the kettle on and ended up doing Morecambe and Wise sketches.

We also tidy the flat, which is a good arrangement even if 'The boy's a fool'! I had finished this chapter, but then a close friend, a social worker, informed me that I had the right to see my assessment. I have never seen the assessment that the social worker did. I have not had any paperwork from him at all. I have no idea what was on that report If it was highlighting what the challenges were for me. I brought this up with my Occupational Therapist; she also had never seen the report and was shocked that I had never seen the report. So there may have been a report, but there might never have been a report. All I know is that the system has failed me.

CHAPTER 10

What Is Normal?

"We all have something living in our lives that is stealing from us. That thing that is stealing from me and you is comparison. It's the way we compare ourselves to other people."

Andy Croft.

What is normal? Nothing...end of the chapter! What is normal for me will not be normal for you, and what is normal for you will not be normal for your neighbour. Today I asked a close friend what is normal. Their answer "There is no such thing as normal". We look and follow people on social media, in magazines, and in the news. At the beginning of this book, I said The label disability had become a negative label that then diminishes our abilities. This is 100 per cent correct; the second thing that diminishes our ability is the expectation of having the perfect figure, two legs, or no deformations on our body. That is not normal; that is living in a dreamland. I feel that Social Media plays a massive part in this horrendous scandal.

It is a scam, showing you that it is possible to have a perfect life. That there is a formula that these "Influencers" follow. I went to two mainstream schools where I was the only person in a wheelchair my year. I grew up surrounded by people who could walk. I felt like the odd one out. This scam we fall for every day was happening before social media. I call it the British Culture Scam. It's been going on for decades and, unfortunately, is being redeveloped by people and organisations such as GB News, Piers Morgan and Jacob Rees-Mogg. The scam is simple and easy to do at home, but I don't recommend it! All you need to do is get all your emotions, push them as far as possible to the back of your brain and pretend all is perfect in the world.

Piers Morgan calls it "Manning Up!". The issue with "Manning Up" is that we bottle up our emotions until we can't cope, and then we lash out at the people whom we love most. We bottle up until we can't manage, so we self-harm or even commit suicide. I have been a part of the scam. I was on the inside seeing how the scam works. Like every scam, there needs to be a "Mark" or "Victim". They need to be weak and easy to manipulate, and the reward needs to be significant. The "Mark" is someone who is deemed to be different, Who in the eyes of society is "Damaged goods." The story to rope you in is, "You are worthless and useless. You cannot participate in society." The Reward is that society feels superior, as if everyone's life is perfect and yours isn't. Society gets something (You feeling shite about yourself) for absolutely nothing. I have stopped all social media.

I don't want to wake up every morning seeing what I don't have. It hurts. I'm glad you're doing well in your life but please, for once in your life, share something shit just to make me feel human. No filters, no photos, and a post on how you feel. Let me turn the question around, What isn't normal? It isn't normal to be emotionless. It isn't normal to tell strangers on social media that their parents should have aborted them. It isn't normal to physically attack someone because their hobbies differ from yours. And yet, unfortunately, all these things have become routine, and the worst thing is that society is blind and unaware of all of this. Is it normal to say to someone, "At least It gives them something to do", as if to say they are useless and don't participate enough already in society? Hell no, and yet we have allowed it to become normal. I'm sorry, but another rant is coming! My family means everything to me. I'm not just talking about my immediate family but my friends. Those who have been there for me and supported me through everything. Those who have mentored me over the past decade. I am blessed and will never take you guys for granted. So when someone maligns a member of my family, I'm sorry but not just going to sit by and do nothing.

So let me explain what we do; We study, work, socialise, watch sports, cheer on our friends, and support each other. So no, we were not all born for the Paralympics; we don't all have the same passion for sports. So stop telling us that we are only suitable for the Paralympics because that's just a load of...um, rubbish! You wouldn't say that about any of the athletes who compete at the Olympics, would you? So why say it about the Paralympic Athletes? Because society still sees the imperfection before they see the person. Can you see a running theme throughout this book?

Let me introduce you to James MacSorley. Despite not liking the sport initially, James stuck at it, and The Knights provided the platform for the Belfast-born athlete to develop his wheelchair basketball skills and progress. His progression was rewarded with attendance at his first GB Junior Camp in 2010, and in 2012 he was one of eight flag bearers at the London 2012 Paralympic Games Opening Ceremony. James is no stranger to podium finishes at the international level, having twice been part of historic GB performances, including on his GB senior debut at the 2018 World Championships, where the GB Men claimed the World title and brought home the gold. But that's not all; whilst achieving all of this, he also graduated from Queen's University in Belfast with a degree in Law. Feeling worthless sucks, trust me! I have battled with this demon many times, and I guarantee I will battle with this feeling again at some point.

90% of the time, I don't allow it to take charge of my life. The other 10%, I will admit that, has become too strong for me to ignore. Later, I will talk in-depth about my mental health, but for the past few months, my mental health has been down. There have been no reasons or significant situations.

How do I know my mental health has been wrong? Loss of appetite, not being motivated to get up in the morning, not being motivated to do anything! It is okay not to be okay. It is normal to feel like this sometimes or even every day. It would be abnormal to feel anything different, especially in this climate! I'm not saying it's all doom and gloom, far from it; there is a lot to smile about, but what I am saying is that we are all human, we all feel things, we all participate, and we all contribute. Let's not diminish someone's abilities and feelings just because they have to use a wheelchair or take a longer time to understand their tasks.

Covid-19 has brought two new expressions "Stay safe!" and "When things get back to some sort of normality". Now, I'm not sure about you, but I don't want it to go back to normal. I'm not saying for one moment that I want to repeat the past year. However, I don't want to go back to how I was before Covid-19. My Life was full of uncertainty. What do I want to do for work? Am I going to be having operations or not? Do I have enough money to last me until the end of the month? Don't get me wrong; Covid-19 has brought uncertainty and anxiety about the future. However, It has also meant that for the first time, we have seen key issues brought to the forefront of the debate. Voices that have been silenced for decades now have an equal opportunity to be heard, or so I thought.

During the pandemic, we saw the climate emergency taken seriously for the first time; we saw the world unite against racism. We saw America elect their first female Vice President. Teachers finally got the public recognition they deserved. Careers were reassessed, and horizons were broadened as many companies collectively realised the viability of remote working. And yet, this should already be the norm. It should already be the norm that people with disabilities who want and can work should find it easy to get employment; it should already be the norm that disabled people who want to live independently can without any dither or delay. It most definitely should be the norm that disabled people can have a social life and have the ability to go out without anxiety due to the lack of accessible pubs, restaurants, and nightclubs. It should be the norm that you can order a wheelchair-friendly taxi whenever you want. And yet this is not the norm.

If you turn on the Tv, I guarantee that either the football or Rugby Or Formula 1 will be on and yet no disability sports. I believe that to inspire the next generation of athletes, there needs to be an equal opportunity to be able to view disability sports. As we know, disability sports happen every four years for the Paralympics, but every week of every year, other events and competitions are going on. We need to change the game.

Changing the Game isn't just about creating more sporting opportunities but about ensuring the wider world has a better understanding of disability sport and generally a more forward-thinking approach to persons with disabilities. A recent survey that was carried out by The Great British Wheelchair Basketball Association showed that 78% of members said that wheelchair basketball had had a positive impact on their mental health. Giving them a platform to express themselves and their sport will provide all disabled people with an opportunity to see what is out there and available to them.

Sports governing bodies need to come together to discuss a plan on how we can better populate, make disability sports and make events inclusive. I want to talk about what my everyday life looks like. In some of it, you will be able to find similarities within your own life, and there will be some parts of my regular daily routine that will be different. However, that is the same for your regular daily routine and your partner's normal daily routine. What is normal for you will be abnormal to somebody else.

I am 25 and live on my own in a one-bedroom flat. I have brothers and sisters, nephews and nieces, uncles and aunties and cousins. I play sports every week. I go out for coffee with family and friends. I go to the pub with friends. I have volunteered for charities. I have worked as a Youth worker. I have had driving lessons and have owned a car. I read books, watch TV and play video games. I pay my own bills and buy my own shopping. I attend my own doctor's appointment. I use public transport on my own. What is not typical about any of that? There is no such thing as normal. What is normal for me will be abnormal for you. There is no normal way to enter a building. There is no normal way of eating; there is no normal way of communicating; there is no normal way of working.

Everyone on this earth has a different way of participating in today's society, yet certain parts of society have a problem with disabled people living their lives. I remember that at school, I never really wanted to socialise with other people who had a disability. I know how strange that sounds. Let me explain; I have never felt normal. There was nothing in my life that was normal compared to my friends. I was attending too many doctor appointments, missing too much school, and using a wheelchair. I needed something in my life that could make me feel normal, and unfortunately, hanging around with other people that were deemed to be anything but normal doesn't make me look normal. And I know there's a bad thing to say and I 100% Do you not have the view now. It's because certain parts of society have created this stigma around people who are, in their eyes, not normal. I didn't want to be a part of that stigma.

I had to ask a Teaching Assistant to help me access the toilet. I had to complete my exams in an office with a reader and scribe while everyone else completed their GCSEs in a hall independently. Every second I was reminded that I was not normal. I would turn on the TV and see people I could not relate to. Comedians that I could not relate to. Every children's program highlighted that I was different from everyone else. Game shows were impossible to participate in due to the nature of the activities and the studio not being designed to include people with all abilities. As I got older, I did start seeing programs that included people with disabilities. I have already mentioned one of my childhood programs, Desperados. I want to share with you another pivotal moment where I saw disability being normalised on TV. I have to be careful what I say as I have become close friends with this person in the past decade, and the last thing we need is for his ego to get bigger than it already is!

I came home from school and turned on the TV to watch one of the nation's favourite prime-time shows, Blue Peter. Now, if you have never heard of or watched Blue Peter, I'm sorry but have you been living under a rock? Blue Peter is a British children's television entertainment programme. It is the world's longest-running children's TV show, having been broadcast since October 1958. This particular episode stood out for me and is the only show I can still remember. One of the main presenters, Helen Skelton, went to Essex to meet a 16-year-old boy with Spina Bifida. As soon as I heard that sentence, I screamed to my mum to come into my bedroom. Thinking I had fallen out of my wheelchair or injured myself in some way, she dropped everything and rushed to my bedroom to find out there was someone on TV with Spina Bifida, Sorry Mum!

James Ireland, born with Spina Bifida and Hydrocephalus, is a professional wheelchair dancer. Helen was challenged to compete in a competition as a Combi duo. Combi is when an able-bodied dancer dances with a wheelchair dancer. The episode tracked their progress leading up to the competition. This was unusual to see the topic of disability positively portrayed in the media. I hate to admit this because I know his ego will increase, but that program, seeing James inspired me to carry one and that there is no such thing as normal. Over the past decade, I have become very close friends with James. He has become family. He has become a grandfather figure for me. His memory is shocking, and he keeps falling out of his wheelchair when doing house jobs around his bungalow.

I have lost count of the number of times I have had a phone call from him saying, "I have fallen out of my wheelchair." Being a caring and compassionate person, I make sure he is okay by asking him if he had a nice trip and if he enjoyed going down under. I'm such a caring person, aren't I? We are always teasing each other; his problem is that he keeps giving me ammunition. The story that makes me laugh just by thinking about it was when he phoned me one Sunday morning. One thing you need to know about James is that he is never a morning person, so when he called at 9 am, I knew it was serious. So I pick up the phone thinking something is wrong. James is known to be rushed into hospital for various reasons. I, therefore, instantly thought this was him telling me he was in the hospital with another infection. This is how I remember the conversation went;

"Hey mate, everything okay?"

"No, I'm stuck, and I am not home."

"Stuck where?

"In a disabled bathroom in a pub."

"Isn't it too early to be in a pub drinking?"

"I have been in here all night!"

"What? Why? How?

"I fell asleep in the bathroom, and the staff locked up the place and went home."

"You Idiot! Why did you not call anyone?"

"My phone ran out of battery."

As a result of all of these situations he has found himself in, he has told me I will never be his best man as he doesn't want the world to know these stories. Sorry James, the world now knows these stories. There is a serious point to these stories, and it goes back to my original point. What is normal? We are all programmed to seek friendship and relationships and to have a purpose. As a society, we have become too concerned about how we contribute to today's wealth, and those with a higher wage contribute more to society than those on a lower salary. Those who are deemed not to be damaged goods are contributing more than those who are considered to be damaged goods. This is false and is undermining the many talents each and every one of us has. My other thought is, why do we care about how other people live their lives? Why am I saying this?

I have lost count of the times I have been in town, and people have stopped and stared at me. I'm not talking about kids; I'm talking about adults. Recently, I went into town to meet with a close friend from church. After we said goodbye, I started to head back to my flat. I stopped to answer a call. I wheeled to a bench to take the call. While on the phone, the most strange and quite awkward thing happened. This lady in her late 40's early 50's stopped in front of me about a meter away and stared at me. She looked at me up and down for a good few minutes. I was, to be honest, speechless and in shock. I stopped my conversation on the phone and asked her if I could help. As soon as I spoke, she walked off. It was like she had never seen someone in a wheelchair. As if I was an alien, and was scared off as soon as she realised this alien could speak her language. This is obviously not the worst thing to have ever happened, but it does make you think about what particular parts of society think of us.

Do they see us as unimportant? Hopeless? Ignorant? Lonely? Weak? Disgusting? Limited? Useless? Helpless? Worthless? Burden? Abnormal? Because I can promise you nobody on this earth is any of these things, and if you feel like you are, I am sorry you feel like that. This is just untrue, and you should never be made to feel like that. I hope that one day you will be able to find your true identity again and that anxiety of feeling abnormal leaves. Once we can eliminate that anxiety of feeling alone and abnormal, we can thrive on the fact that we are all unique, and none of us is normal.

In the book of Psalms, David writes in chapter 139, verses 13 and 14:

"For it was You who created my inward parts; you knit me together in my mother's womb. I will praise You because I have been fearfully and wonderfully made".

Fearfully when translated from Hebrew, means with great reverence, heart-felt interest, and with respect. "Wonderfully", when translated from Hebrew, means unique and set apart. Fearful in this context does not mean to be literally scared or afraid. It means quite the opposite - that you were created with great reverence, heart-felt interest, and respect to be unique and set apart! As a Christian, I believe you would desire an ongoing relationship with Him. We were made with a hole in the centre of our souls that only one thing fits. Until we find that definite something, you will never be fulfilled. And that very specific something is God Himself. We were designed with an intense need for our Creator, God. Without a relationship with Him, you will always search for something to fill that void. Drugs, alcohol, food, money, material goods, occupations, hobbies, travel, success, and fame are how we try to fill that void and feel normal.

But none of those things will ever be enough. They are like round pegs in square holes. The vacant areas at the edges will still leave you wanting more. Whatever you attempt to put in there will evaporate because it never fills the void. Those things were never meant to fill the space; they never can. Sadly, many continue to shove mismatched pegs into that hole. A little of this, a little of that… hoping they will one day feel complete. They surmise this thing over here didn't work, but maybe this other thing will do. They just haven't found the right thing yet, but they hope they will one day. One day I'll have enough money to feel safe and secure.

CHAPTER 11

The Disability Card

"No, I have never used the disability card."
Every Disabled person

Where do I begin when talking about this using the disability card? If you went into a room with 20 people with different disabilities and asked them if they have ever used the disability card in their life, they will all probably nervously laugh, look up and not give you any eye contact when replying, "No, I have never used the disability card." We all have used the disability card. And unfortunately, it is this society that has forced us to use the disability card. It is the system that is forcing us to show the negatives about living with a disability.

Of course, some people use the disability card to their advantage to get discounts, benefits, and money from the government. But most of us who are ashamed of using the disability card use it because it's the only way to get care. The only way we can get adapted housing is the only way we can get an adapted vehicle. It's the only way we can live. So using the disability card isn't about how much money I can get from the government? Or can I use the disabled space? Using the disability card is the only way. To get anywhere with the system, the system that for generations of failed disabled people. So what does it say about a society that disabled people must use the disability card to get Any support? What is the say about a society where the last resort is to play up the disability? What does it say about a community that we can't create an accessible society that treats everybody equally, that sees the person for who they are instead of that wheelchair, instead of the hearing aid, instead of their walking thing, instead of the kind of thing they can't talk before they see the person as a, as a human being.

I was struggling, to be honest, to work out what to say in this chapter. I don't understand how we've got into this mess, And the media doesn't help. The media Sees us playing the disability card and can create headlines that put a negative mark against our names, "Disabled people are benefit thieving scums." Says the Sun Newspaper. "They were only in it for the money from the government" by the way, what money? Trust me; I'm not claiming to have a disability for the money. The government does not provide sufficient support. And I'm Not ashamed about using the disability card, which, to be honest, if you'd asked me a week ago, am I ashamed to use the disability card? I would have said Yeah, I am ashamed of using the disability card.

And I would probably deny using the disability card, but while planning for this chapter, I realised that I'm not ashamed because I wouldn't be able to live independently. I wouldn't be able to play wheelchair basketball. I wouldn't be able to travel without using the disability card. The system is corrupt; the system we find ourselves in is corrupt. It's damaging us; it's damaging society. I'm embarrassed to use this card is because, for our whole lives, we've been trying to get away from the negativity that comes with the label disability; concentrate on the positives, what we can do, not what we can't do. The disability card immediately highlights what we can't do. It goes against everything that many people with disabilities and I stand for. The idea that we have to hang in on the negativities is not Easy to handle mentally. It's giving people who comment on social media that "people's disability should be aborted." It gives them ammunition.

It provides the haters, the trolls ammunition. And it's because the system is corrupt. So yes, I will be the first to admit that I use the disability card. I am not ashamed of using disability because the system is corrupt. And until the system changes until society changes, I will still use the disability card. Do I hate using the disability card? Yes, I wish I didn't have to o use the disability card, but I have to because otherwise, I would not be able to live an independent life the way I want to.

I wouldn't be able to achieve what I have been able to achieve without using the disability card because society would not let me; the system would not let me because the system and society see us as damaged goods. They see us as little kids who need 24-hour care, can't participate in life, and sit on their sofa all day watching TV, waiting for the government to pay us so we can go shopping. The vast majority of us who have the privilege of being part of the disabled community are not like the stereotypical disabled person that society has created.

Society has created a stereotypical disabled person that does not represent anybody within the disability community. I am proud to be part of such a fantastic community, a community that needs to be heard but isn't being listened to. The disability card using disability card gives us a voice in a system that doesn't listen to society. The government and Private companies see damaged goods.

The media sees us as damaged goods and that we are Dumb and stupid. We are just Human beings who have no voice. It's depressing and shameful. I am proud to be part of the disability community. I am not proud to be part of the society we live in today. I am proud of who I am. I'm not proud to be part of the system. And yet I am; everybody is, whether we like it or not. And until somebody stands up And fights the system, nothing will change. Nothing will change. And like Martin Luther King, like Nelson Mandela, like Rosa Parks, we need leadership that can change the course of Society. Many hoped that Jeremy Corbyn would be that leader; however, I feared the system was too strong for a new way of politics. I was reading an article on minority groups by Pragati Kalive. In the article, it talks about social, Political and economic issues each minority group has to face across the world;

> "People with disabilities are not only disadvantaged by their impairments but also by society. They are at a higher risk of being subjected to violence and poverty."

There are three ways of using a disability card. I have explained the first way, but the second is even worse and inhumane. It's happening all over the UK, and 90% of people it affects don't even know it's happening. Let's take the first sentence of the quote you have just read;

> "People with disabilities are not only disadvantaged by their impairments but also by society."

Certain members of today's society think they can use people's conditions to get away with lousy care practices. Now, I need to be clear that this does not mean that everybody in the care sector is taking advantage of people with physical and developmental disabilities. It is, unfortunately, a small minority of people, usually in high levels of care, that give the care sector a bad reputation. This small minority take advantage of people mainly with developmental disabilities. If by any chance a family member or friend finds out they are taking advantage and makes a complaint to either the company or the local authority; it would be their word against the care company's word.

I recently had this scenario happen to a very close friend who may be a BDU. Still, they understand what is going on and are capable of not only looking after and caring for their eight-year-old daughter but also organising and managing her own care package. As wheelchair users, there are specific house jobs that we need support with. In the UK, you can have two different types of care packages. You can either hire a care agency to support you, or you can recruit somebody of your choice to become your support worker or carer. In the past, they have gone for the latter option. There are several reasons why they have gone for this option; the main reason is due to the fact that they want to be able to build a friendship with their support worker. I feel that is so for a lot of people.

To be fair to the care agency, many of the patients they support, if not all the patients they support, have learning difficulties or developmental disabilities rather than just physical disabilities. This means that if they don't turn up or don't complete the tasks they set, either the person won't have the communication skills to complain or if they do, then they will lie and say the patient has forgotten due to the medication they are on. This is using the Disability card to get away with bad practice.

Uber has been found to also use the disability card for profit. Uber discriminates against people with disabilities by charging them a "wait time" fee. At the same time, the passenger enters the vehicle, according to a new lawsuit filed by the US Justice Department against the company. Uber instituted a wait time fee in several cities starting in April 2016, eventually expanding the policy nationwide. Passengers would incur the fee two minutes after their Uber car arrived at their pickup location and were charged until the vehicle began its trip. Passengers with disabilities, such as those who use a wheelchair or a walker, often need more time to get into the car than passengers without disabilities. As we all know, People with disabilities deserve equal access to all areas of community life and heavily rely on private transportation services like Uber for hospital appointments, work and social gatherings.

When challenged on this, Matt Kallman, a spokesperson for Uber, called the lawsuit "surprising and confusing" in light of Uber's desire to work with the Justice Department to address confusion around its wait time fees. My experience with Uber has not always been easy, and I have had multiple instances where the taxi driver refuses to take me due to my being in a wheelchair. This, unfortunately, isn't the first time Uber has done this, and it won't be the last. Uber's failure to include wheelchair-accessible cars in its fleet of private vehicles has drawn a federal complaint alleging disability discrimination.

In a complaint filed with a federal judge in Washington, the nonprofit Equal Rights Center says Uber violates the Americans with Disabilities Act because none of its 30,000 cars in the nation's capital can fit wheelchairs that do not fold up and stored in the boot. I have had friends who have been charged extra at the end of the journey because the driver has back pain lifting the wheelchair in and out of the boot, or worse, they refuse to get the wheelchair out of the car until the passenger pays the extra charge without a valid reason. The third way to use the Disability card is nowhere near as harmless, but if used too many times, it will turn into the boy who cried wolf. We hear people saying, "I can't do that." Or maybe we have spoken to ourselves, "I can't do that because of x, y, or z." I have said, "I can't meet today as I am in pain", Or, "I don't have the ability to attend this meeting now due to my anxiety and depression issues." While this is true, and It's good to have healthy boundaries, it can quickly turn into a daily excuse, and the next thing you know, it's Friday, and you're still in bed, bored and alone.

Our attitudes and mindsets set so much of what we can and cannot do, yet often, we are limitless if we let ourselves be so. When I think about the people I admire, the people I see out there who are happy and enjoying life, They aren't making excuses. They are doing everything. These people live their lives to their fullest despite their disabilities or life issues. They are no one special; they don't have a unique title; they are just human beings trying to earn a living and a safe environment for their families. These people see their abilities and not their disabilities.

These people have challenged me and pushed me to be the best I can be. They are not inspirational because they are disabled but have inspired me due to what they do at work and their vision for a more equal society. They don't care about labels, they don't care about people judging them, and why should they? I want to introduce you to four people in my life that have inspired me, encouraged me and made me a better person. This has nothing to do with them needing to use a wheelchair or prosthetic leg. They have inspired me because of their skills and attitude to life. I Promise they are not all athletes!

Jen Browning

I first met Jen and her husband, Mike, in 2008. Jen, alongside her husband Mike, started a wheelchair basketball team called Southwest Scorpions. Now, I have to thank my teaching assistant Jan Smith for introducing me to Jen because if it weren't for Jan handing me a leaflet for this new basketball team that was starting, I wouldn't be where I am today. I definitely wouldn't have met Jen and wouldn't have made the friendships that I have made through leagues and matches. The sessions started off being fortnightly on a Sunday afternoon.

My dad had agreed that we would try the sessions after church. I have had extraordinary and sometimes depressing experiences with multi-sports clubs. When found, they run flawlessly for many years until leadership either gets greedy or handles a situation that then snowballs into a disaster that then leads to the club closing. Unfortunately, I have seen that happen many times, especially within the disability sports world. So I, of course, went to the first session with quite a lot of anticipation and quite a lot of anxiety. However, I knew that this was something that I'd dreamed about doing for ages, being part of a basketball team. It was about 45 minutes journey from Bath to Filton College in Bristol.

As we got there, I saw a very close friend of mine called Dave, whom we had met with in previous sports clubs, and we'd kept in touch and kept very close. When we wheeled into the sports hall, we were greeted by Mike and Jen. Jen is originally from The US. I quickly realised that she competed at the 2004 Paralympics for our women's wheelchair basketball team and was assistant coach of the women's GB wheelchair basketball team. So to say that I wasn't in safe hands and that I had the best coach is probably a bit of an understatement.

The first session, I remember, had around four athletes attending. Jack Davey, whom I'm still really good friends with to this day, Jordan Bright, again, somebody who I'm in regular contact with, Ben Fox, who is now representing GB on the men's basketball team and Dave Watts, whom I have met through different sports clubs and events. These sessions, which started fortnightly on a Sunday afternoon, suddenly grew under both Mike and Jen's leadership into a club that was every Sunday morning with two different teams under fifteens team and an under nineteens team.

Both teams were put in junior leagues and the national leagues. As a 12-year-old, this was something that I'd always dreamt of being part of. I had numerous conversations with my dad saying I always wanted to be part of a basketball team. Now I've got to explain that most of that ambition was watching People like Ade Adepitan On TV at the Paralympic games or the children's drama Desperados. For me, sport is one of the only sectors that are fully inclusive. Under mike and Jen's leadership with the club, we started to see two powerful teams develop. We saw new players come in every week; Players were returning every week dedicated. We were seeing funding coming in like no other sports team. We were a team where people took us seriously, And It was an honour and a privilege to be part of the team. I didn't just become a better athlete, but I also became a better person because what makes a good coach Isn't just about how they make you a better athlete; it's How they help you to become a better person.

A good coach can help you and develop you to be the best you can be in every circumstance. And that was Jen, somebody who Mentored me and still someone I can go to for help and guidance. When they decided to step down from the club, it was a shock. As I said, the team was taken seriously. Fast forward a few years after they've left. And I had become an assistant coach as I was too old to play in the junior league, and there was no adult team yet.

I was then allowed to take over the club as head coach from the previous coaches. I knew I wanted Southwest scorpions to have the same atmosphere, drive, and ethos as when the club started. The only way that happened was to get back in touch with Mike and Jen. I asked questions; I wanted to make sure that I was doing as much as I could to develop the team. Now it's no secret, especially with my family and friends, that the club was nowhere near where I wanted it to be. It was going to be a massive task for that to happen. However, I knew that I wanted the club to carry on, and I knew the potential club. I knew my vision was to get the club back to how Mike and Jen ran it.

I wanted to be a coach that didn't just coach in basketball but became a mentor to the kids coming through the door to show that it doesn't matter what disability they have. I wanted to create an environment that allowed them to achieve exactly what they wanted, like when I first wheeled through those doors back in 2008, dreaming of being in a basketball team. I wanted to give these kids the same opportunities. I can't put into words how much it has meant to me to have that mentorship, that friendship, and that coaching has made me who I am today. If I had never met them or had never had coaching from them, I would not be in the position I'm in today.

And I think it's straightforward to take friendships and those who have mentored us for granted. I think it's so easy to get caught up in everything, life, dramas and the news that we forget how we got to where we are today and those who played a part. Mike and Jen paid a massive part in who I am today. I wouldn't have started The Disability Sports Channel if it weren't for them. If it weren't for them, I wouldn't have made the friendships I've made today. If it weren't for them, I wouldn't have learned how to deal with life as a wheelchair user. I owe a lot to them, more than they will ever realise. So if you're reading this, Mike and Jen, thank you.

James Ducat

Brother of three sisters and a brother, Uncle James, grew up in Bath. He lived a "normal" life, teaching at a local catholic Secondary school and supporting the local rugby team with his mate maz. Life changed in the 90s when he had a stroke which left him paralysed and needing to use an electric wheelchair. My earliest memory of Uncle James was visiting him with my mum; I had only just got my first wheelchair, it was bright yellow, and my legs stuck out to allow me to wear splints. We were in his living room; there was just about enough room to have a race from the sofa to the wall. Due to my legs sticking out, I remember getting caught between the sofa. James was the first person I saw in a wheelchair. He taught me so much, even if our relationship was cut way too short.

His can-do attitude inspired me. He showed me that despite the label and all the issues that come with the label, I could do anything. It is a value I still hold today. A few years ago, I met a close friend of James's; we shared memories of James. He shared how James would campaign for disability rights, and if he saw a car parked on the pavement or disabled bay without a blue badge, then he would stick a poster on the windscreen that he had created. I am not for one moment saying I have the confidence to do that, but it is because of James that I am writing this book; it's because of James that I fight for equality. I remember visiting him in the hospital; it was just before he passed away. He was not on the ward but sat in front of a tv watching rugby.

There were two things that I remember from that visit, firstly his passion for the sport. Despite everything he was going through, he never let it get in the way of what he loved. The second reason that visit meant so much to me was that I discovered how close we were. We sat next to each other watching the rugby, and it was halfway through that I suddenly felt this hand grab hold of mine and rest it on his armrest, his hand on top of mine. I will never ever forget that moment, and even thinking about it now puts a smile on my face and a tear in my eye. Wherever you are, James, I hope I'm doing you proud. I miss you and wish you were still here.

Nicole Perera

When asking Nicole how we met, she reminded me it was at the mental institution, otherwise known as Basketball training! Her passion for the sport was shown by her willingness to wake up every Sunday at 7 am until she gave up after three sessions. Our paths didn't cross again until a few years later; I had started college, and Nicole was just starting her GCSEs. My role within the club had changed; I became too old to play for the team, so I became an assistant coach under the mentorship of the head coach at the time. We wanted to grow the team and decided to set up a satellite club at a local school in North East Somerset, where I was living at the time. It was around the same time that Nicole was doing her GCSEs. When I first saw Nicole, I could see that she was under a lot of stress and anxiety.

You could tell that she had been through a lot even at an early age, but it wasn't until a couple of years later that I found out what exactly she had been through. Raised without a dad from an early age and saw things that no child at six should ever see. Nicole was born with Spina Bifida and Hydrocephalus. I could see many similarities to me. We studied the same subjects, went to the same college and had the same tutors two years apart. Some would say we are in a relationship; we are that close, but we are just really good friends. We get each other; we know what each other is going through.

We support each other and have the same drive to see an equal society. Nicole doesn't see her disability and has never classed herself as disabled. Nicole likes to prove everyone wrong, especially me. She might be younger than me, but she is someone who has inspired me and who has and still spurs me on to carry on whatever challenges are against me. We might not see each other a lot or talk on the phone as regularly as we would like, but when we do, we are able to have a laugh, challenge each other and resolve challenges we have faced. Nicole, never ever change regardless of whatever hurdle society puts in front of you because I can guarantee that you can knock it down in 0.2 seconds.

Peter Harding

I have never met Peter face to face, but I was introduced to him through a mutual friend in 2019. We worked together for The Disability Sports Channel and remain close friends. From the moment we first had that zoom call, I could see his passion for showcasing disability sports, showcasing the heartfelt stories of the Paralympic athletes and breaking down the barriers that Society and the mainstream media have put in the way of Paralympic athletes. Ten years ago, Peter was diagnosed with a brain injury that affects mostly his left side but all four limbs. He also has learning difficulties and a slight speech impediment.

This has never stopped him from doing what he loves. Peter has worked for the past few years for the BBC in London and Manchester. His role within the BBC has allowed him to promote disability sports via the BBC Website through articles and research. Peter is also apart of panels that decide what content is shown. This leads me to how he has challenged me; we have had multiple debates on the lack of media coverage of disability sports on the BBC. For me, it feels like the BBC showcases Disability sports as a goodwill gesture, not because they want to. If you ever go on the BBC Sports website, it is a minefield to find the dedicated page for Disability Sports. The Page is rarely updated, and yet there is always a Disability sports event going on. We share the same ethos to inspire the next generation of disabled athletes. We agree that this view can only be done if there is better representation in the media. However, we have taken different paths to get to the same destination. I believe the mainstream media won't change because if they wanted to, they would have already. Peter's view is that the system can change, and working for the organisation means he can help bring change from within the organisation. I have lost count of the number of times we have been on a call, and he patiently hears me rant and then calmly explains why my approach is less effective, and nine times out of 10, he is pretty much on point.

He reminds me that there has been a dramatic increase in Disability sports compared to before 2012; we are seeing more Paralympic athletes on game shows and chat shows. We have seen more people on soap operas and an increase in presenters with a wide range of disabilities. Because of TV Personalities such as Rose Ayling-Ellis, BSL is now a recognised language! Peter, I know we will have many debates in the future. Without your wisdom, I would never see the bigger picture. Never stop challenging me and proving me wrong!

CHAPTER 12

COVID-19: The least of my worries

This pandemic has made us realise the amount of things we take for granted in life, not to mention, life itself.

To get to where we are today, we must go back to November 2019. As a wheelchair user, most people who use a wheelchair daily will be able to tell you that it is very common to develop a pressure sore. A pressure sore is when you apply pressure to a part of your body for an extended period of time. And the skin starts to break. Now, I've been fortunate in the sense that I've only had three pressure sores in my life. They've all been on my left hip because both my hips are dislocated, and my pelvis is not in the correct position. Now in November 2019, a pressure sore was developing. I had just got a new wheelchair with a new seat, and I was in my wheelchair from the moment I woke up to the moment I went to bed. One evening I noticed some blood on my bed and I was living with my parents back then. So I called my mum and asked her to check, which was broken.

Fortunately, at that point, the pressure sore was a Grade one, meaning it was just a graze. The skin is slightly broken, but it is superficial. By the end of November, it had gone from a grade one to a grade three, and the pressure sore was very deep and was increasing in depth and size. So over the 2019 Christmas, I was visiting the nurse or having district nurses come and visit me a few times per week. This was all happening while I was trying to navigate the flat being adapted. I was trying to get prepared for moving because COVID hadn't been talked about at this point. So my plans for moving in 2020 were still going ahead. In 2019, the UK Prime minister, Boris Johnson, announced a snap Election.

This was the first time that we had a snap election in the winter for a very long time. I didn't think we'd had a snap election in the winter during my lifetime. Now, at this point, I was very much campaigning for one of my local candidates, and I was invited to watch the count in my area, and as a political geek, I couldn't refuse. However, it would mean being in my wheelchair from around 10 pm till 5-6 am the next day. However, being naive and not taking my health seriously at the time, I decided to ignore advice and to go.

Fast forward to the end of February, early March of 2020, a handful of cases in the UK of COVID-19. My pressure sore was now the same size as the Palm of my hand and deep enough almost to see my hip bone. The Tissue Viability Nurse asked if I was able to go and visit the hospital for a couple of weeks for them to try a type of dressing that is connected to what I can only describe as a vacuum cleaner. And the idea of this vacuum dressing would be to suck all the bad tissue to help the new, healthy tissue development.

I had just had confirmation that my flat had been adapted and was ready for me to move in. So, the idea for me not to move in when I wanted was quite a big shock. I had to put my health first, so I agreed to go to the hospital for a couple of weeks. At this point, the wound was also infected. I was given my own room on the ward;

the first room I was given, the walls were painted bright yellow, and there was no TV. The room was just about big enough to fit a hospital bed. Plus, my wheelchair and the only window were on the ceiling and were probably the same size as an A3 piece of paper. I only spent less than 24 hours in that room before I was transferred to the room opposite. As you can imagine, I was already having cabin fever. I was not able to leave the room because of the infection. I was unable to sit in my wheelchair because of the dressing.

The next day I was moved to a different room, which was slightly bigger. I had an adorable frosted window which, after a few days, made my cabin fever go through the roof. I had a TV but never a remote, so my phone and laptop were the only entertainment I had. Before I go on, I have to say thank you to those who were there for me and kept me entertained by video calling, texting and sending me video messages! One person, in particular, has to be mentioned! A good friend of mine introduced me to a game on the app store called "Plague inc". The game aims to wipe out humanity with a virus. The more the virus spreads, the more points you gain. Probably not the best game to play in a hospital while the whole world is fighting a virus in real life! Visiting hours were early in the afternoon.

This was, of course, down to COVID restrictions, where care homes and hospitals visit were limited and were only between a particular time of day as the week progressed. The nurses and doctors were very friendly and very helpful. I could not have asked for better care. I will never forget one doctor coming in to tell me that visiting restrictions would be cut to one visit 20 min a day. She was both emotionally and physically drained. When asked how stretched the hospital was, she broke down in tears and shared how scared she was as they were not adequately staffed. Many staff are working overtime, not seeing their kids and wondering what will happen. The NHS has been underfunded for over a decade now, and Covid-19 just proved how our beautiful health service needs better funding.

Fast forward to 23rd March 2020, Boris Johnson announced we were all going into lockdown for three weeks. As we all know, this didn't quite go to plan! I was waiting for the go-ahead to leave for home, where I would finish my recovery. I was still connected to the Vac Machine Dressing; however, they were confident enough for me to finish the treatment at home. This was mixed emotions; I was grateful for the support I had from the hospital, physically exhausted from the lack of sleep and nervous about what the next few months would bring.

It's funny what we take for granted until it's taken away from us. We suddenly miss those situations that we used to hate, those work meetings we used to dread, the school reunions that we would try to get out of because we don't want to sit next to the school bully. The idea that we were not allowed out unless we were going out for exercise was alien to us! I was not only following the rules like everyone else but also in an even bigger lockdown as I was on bed rest. Now I could do a day-by-day journal talking about each day in lockdown, recovering from this pressure sore. But as somebody said on social media, the days of the week, all combined into one, there was no Monday, Tuesday, Wednesday, but this day, that day, another day, someday, yesterday, today, and next day, this was say true for me. I was talking to a friend on the phone recently, trying to reflect on that challenging period of my life.

We joked, saying that at the beginning, it was terrific. Being able to have breakfast in bed every morning and being able to have food served to me without having to leave my bed. For any parents, anybody who's working night shifts, that sounds like a dream. And at first, it was, but after a few days, and I mean, just a few days, the feeling turned into complete and utter misery. I was bored. I wanted to be ready to go out. I wanted to be able to get in my wheelchair. I wanted to be able to do things that I wouldn't usually do in normal circumstances. I wanted it to be able to go out. I want to be able to play sports. I wanted to do anything apart from being stuck in bed. I wanted the be able to have a shower.

I missed all the mundane chores we had to do, moan about, and take for granted. I want to do them because anything is better than being stuck in bed. I want to highlight five significant milestones during that year, Some thoughts I've had since and what needs to happen now, moving forward. I think it's essential that we learn from our mistakes, and I'm not talking about government mistakes. I'm talking about us as a society, as individuals making mistakes that led us all to be in lockdown. It's so easy to point the finger at the scientists in China, saying that it's their fault that we were in a pandemic, But is it? Isn't it all of our responsibilities? It doesn't matter where the pandemic started. It doesn't matter how it began. What matters is how it produced the biggest global pandemic we've ever seen in our lifetime. It's interesting as a society; we always like to blame other people and not take responsibility for ourselves.

Taking responsibility for our actions is the grown-up thing to do. We're always taught that the grown-up thing is to take responsibility. Some might argue why we should take responsibility when the government doesn't take responsibility for their actions. And yeah, that is a fair point, but that doesn't excuse your actions, my actions. We can't keep saying, "oh, the government doesn't follow the guidelines, so why should we?" Our actions have consequences; It is our actions that led us to be on lockdown. People criticise the government, saying they should have banned flights. People complained, saying that the government should have done a better job with test and trace.

Yeah, we should have, but name me one country except for New Zealand, which had a better system. Can't? Neither can I! Except South Korea, Germany, Singapore, France and America. At least Johnson didn't suggest that we injected ourselves with bleach! But he did ask his staff to bring their own booze to work. I could join the crowd criticising the government, yes, they made mistakes, and yes, they broke the law, but I then have to ask myself whether I would want to be Prime Minister during these unprecedented times. Would I cope? Not in a million years! I can't look after myself, let alone the country, which leads me to my mistakes in

2020. I need to take full responsibility for my actions. I must take responsibility because if I don't, I will end up back on bed rest which I cannot afford! At the beginning of the chapter, I said that the pressure sore went from a graze to a grade three pressure sore that was the same size as the Palm of my hand. So how did it go from a graze to grade three in 24 hours? The answer is complicated. Probably up to this point, only three people know the true story; who knows exactly what happened and how it developed? They say that there are three sides to the truth.

Each person has their own perspective of the truth, and that perspective depends on how much information they have because they can only come up with that side of the story with the knowledge that they have. And the truth is that those around me didn't have the complete information. Those around me didn't have enough information to know the truth. They had some of the facts, but not all. They knew it went from a grade one to four in less than 24 hours. But that was it. Was there anyone that knew the truth, that knew all facts?

What I'm about to share with you is me being completely honest, Because I know that there will be people in the same situation as me struggling with the exact same issues that I have to struggle with. I'm not for one moment saying it's easy, trust me. I'm 25, and I still find certain medical routines challenging, but I don't want people in my situation to have to go on bed rest. So I'm going to be blunt. I'm not going to sugarcoat it. It will be many things that not many people know. This book is different to every other book. I'm talking about topics that aren't discussed in today's society. I'm keeping it personal because somebody has. After all, we need to talk about these things as a wheelchair users.
I have to be very careful with what cushions I have for my chair. For many years the wheelchair service had provided me with a Roho Cushion. A cushion with air pockets that distributes my weight evenly. When I was born, both my hips were dislocated, and my pelvis was out of line.

This, therefore, means all my weight goes on to my left hip hence why I am prone to getting pressure sores on my left hip. When purchased, the cushion that came with my chair was not a Roho seat but just a standard foam cushion. This comes to my first mistake; I never went to the wheelchair service to ask for a Roho seat. Why? I was embarrassed to tell them I had got a private wheelchair. I felt like I owed them because of the care they had provided me for just under two decades. The embarrassment got the better of me; I didn't want to let them down. The truth is the day I went into the hospital for the Vac Dressing; the wheelchair service rang me as they had a referral from the Tissue Viability Nurse. The person who rang me knew me well and was very understanding as to why I got a private wheelchair. They took down the measurements and ordered me a Roho Seat as well as a temporary seat while mine was being made.

By the middle of the first week of being in the hospital, I had received not only the temporary seat but also my made-to-measure seat. It's strange and agonising that all this could have been prevented if I had called them as soon as I got my chair. People have told me I couldn't help but that I had a pressure sore; as I said earlier, there are always three sides to the story. I could have prevented the pressure sore if I hadn't been so reluctant to call the wheelchair service. I am one of those people who can't be forced to decide and have to come to a conclusion in my own time.

This was my outlook until recently; I have learnt that it is okay to ask for advice, it is okay to ask for help, and it is okay to need different medical equipment to allow you to live as independently as possible. This explains how the wound appeared but not how it went from a grade one to a grade four in 24 hours. If I thought phoning the wheelchair service was embarrassing, this is beyond embarrassing. I have been going back and forth to know if I should include this. Still, I feel like I have to for those of you who are also struggling because you are not alone, and if anything has taught me over the past few years, there are a lot more people than I realise who have to go through the same challenges.

As I stated earlier, I am paralysed from the waist down; this means I have no feeling below my waist. If I injure myself, I won't know. This has, over the years, caused multiple burns and other injuries if I'm not careful. The other challenge that I have to overcome is incontinence issues. I am meant to catheterise every three hours. I say "meant" because that is what the consultants have told me my whole life. I have always struggled with routines. I have always struggled with organisation.

Over the years, I have never known which category Hydrocephalus is in; It's not a physical disability nor a learning disability. A few years ago, I was talking to someone who works for a charity that supports people with Spina Bifida and Hydrocephalus. I asked them if Hydrocephalus is a learning disability, She paused, and in that short moment, I thought I had just asked a ridiculous question. It isn't a learning disability but an Executive Dysfunction Disorder. What does that mean?!

> Executive dysfunction is a term used to describe the range of cognitive, behavioural, and emotional difficulties which often occur as a result of another disorder or a traumatic brain injury. Individuals with executive dysfunction struggle with planning, problem-solving, organisation, and time management.

At school, I could not process information as fast as my peers; It took me longer to understand information. I knew in my head what I wanted to say, but when asked to put it on paper, I froze. In Primary school, we were asked to do mental maths. As soon as the stopwatch started, my brain went into overload. Imagine having 20 elastic bands around your head, getting tighter and tighter every second. As I have gotten older, I have tried to learn techniques to remember information. I have been attempting to learn techniques to remember routines. I have set alarms, tried to use mathematical tools, and written lists down. I have tried pretty much everything. I am working with a consultant to determine if there is more to it than just hydrocephalus. I promise you I'm not trying to sound like a broken record, but it's partly down to my mindset. We live in a world where Technology and Social Media rule our lives. Later in the book, I will discuss social media and how it is destroying society, especially with the Metaverse.

I want to talk about my addiction to social media, Youtube and other streaming services. I hate silence; I need background noise. I love music, and I love listening to podcasts. However, despite loving music and podcasts, I don't tend to listen to music and podcasts. When I wake up, the first thing I do is check my phone, messages, and the news and all of a sudden, I find myself tapping on the YouTube app. I look at the time and convince myself I have time for one video, and that one video turns into a whole day.

You can start to realise why routines for me are complex. I have yet to find a strategy to keep me focused without distractions. On a great day, I am awake by 5.30 and dressed, eat breakfast, and have done my Medical Routine by 9 am. Those "Great Days" hardly happened; I can't remember the last time it happened. On the "Great Day", I barely look at my phone, and if I do, It's only to check the news and WhatsApp messages. I have recently deleted Facebook from my phone and have found that I hardly ever check Facebook. Sorry to those who have messaged me or tagged me in posts, and I haven't messaged or commented. What does this all have to do with my pressure sore? Instead of looking after myself and phoning the wheelchair service, and working on my routine, I was stuck watching YouTube videos or video calling my friends whilst watching YouTube videos. My routine was non-existent; it is pretty much still nonexistent.

Instead of finding work or studying at college, I procrastinated. College was not the best experience for me for different reasons. I was not confident, I didn't enjoy the lectures, and I only made one true friend with whom I'm still in touch today. I applied for many Apprenticeships and had multiple interviews but was always turned down. I became depressed, and instead of fighting back, I held myself to a pity Party. Self Pity is a choice. I chose to feel sorry for myself and looked for sympathy. Everyone I knew had a life that was meaningful and impacted Society. I wanted to be like them but didn't have the motivation to find work. I didn't want to have any more rejections. I couldn't cope with another rejection. That pity party was dangerous, and until now, I haven't realised how perilous throwing that pity party was. That pity party led to me getting into a routine I am still in that I can't seem to change.

I said earlier that I couldn't stick to routines, but that was a lie; I can, but not the routines I should be doing. My daily routine consists of watching Netflix, creating amazon lists and talking to friends on video calls. I'm not throwing myself a pity party anymore, but I can't seem to motivate myself to stick to a routine that gives me a purpose. Up to now, I have chosen the easy path. The routine I'm in at the moment means I don't look after my health, especially my personal care. I said earlier that I could have prevented myself from making the pressure sore worse. I didn't look after myself; I didn't look after my personal care; it's because of that reason, and that reason alone, that my pressure sore went from a grade one to a grade four in 24 hours.

I am now working on building a new routine; I have been honest with myself for the first time, which is the first step to finding a new routine. I am now putting my health before anything else. As a friend of mine once said, "Health comes before work." As with every negative situation, you can always rely on British humour to make things a little easier. So, here are a few of my favourite quotes I saw on social media that summed up 2020 well, Enjoy!

"Pretty wild how we used to eat cake after someone had blown on it."

"Until further notice, the days of the week are now called This day, That day, Other day, Someday, Yesterday, Today and Next day!"

"**Friend 1:** Coronavirus pandemic could be over within two years

Friend 2: who said?

Friend 1: Yes, W.H.O said"

"In Germany, they are preparing for the crisis by stocking up with sausage and cheese. That's the Wurst Käse scenario."

"I got my COVID test today; it says 50. What does that mean? Also, my IQ test came back positive."

"Never in my whole life would I imagine my hands would consume more alcohol that my mouth"

"Strange times for cats. First, the dogs were kept inside, and now the humans. Must feel like they've won."

"Best believe I'm clapping on the plane the first place I go after lockdown."

"I find it so mature that every guy I was talking to are socially distancing themselves from me during this time. I really know how to pick a man."

CHAPTER 13

Mental Health

"The bravest thing I ever did was continuing my life when I wanted to die."

— Juliette Lewis

They say that if you have mental health issues, you just need to man up and grow up and take it on the chin. They say that you need to look on the bright side of life, That you don't need to take things too seriously, and that life isn't all gloom and doom. Life isn't all Mr positive; life can be rubbish. Life can be going good, and life can be tough. If several challenges come all at once, then no wonder somebody's mental health goes downhill. You lose a job, your house or your marriage breaks up. Your best friend dies; suddenly, a relative dies.

Suddenly You don't have the network, the support network around you, or if you do, it's too late. The waiting list to get support to get help is so long that You have to process it on your own for at least three years before being able to talk about it with a professional.

Mental health, especially amongst men, is essential. I say especially amongst men, not because I think men are more important than women but because men are useless at sharing their feelings. The stereotypical male is somebody who provides financial support for their family, Working class that goes down to the pub every Friday night to watch the football with his mates and who doesn't have any emotions, doesn't get anxious, and can man up. He doesn't talk about his feelings because why would he? He's not a snowflake; sharing your feelings means you're a snowflake, and who wants to be a snowflake?

Let me tell you, showing your emotions, talking about your feelings, and talking about what is getting you down is not a sign of weakness. It's a sign of strength For a long time. I didn't really know how to talk about my mental health. I didn't know how to express how I was feeling, how alone I was feeling. For a long time, I was suicidal. I was self-harming, and I was lost. I was alone because I was getting bullied at school. I had made terrible mistakes that led to consequences that I couldn't deal with. I'm not talking physically deal with; I mean mentally deal with. I had lied to people at school. I lost friends, and I couldn't trust anybody. All of a sudden, in 0.2 seconds, I stopped being able to trust everybody. It got so bad that I couldn't even trust my family, my brothers, my sisters, and my parents Early on in the book.

I discussed the stereotypical disabled person, The mentality of certain members of society who sees the wheelchair before they see the person. They see the guide dog before they see the person. They see the hearing aid before they see the person, and They see the learning disability before they see the person. We've got into a situation where some parts of society, not all, but some, still see us as a child who has to treat us like the child. Because as children, we didn't understand what was happening in the world.

We copy our parents, family, and friends, But we don't understand what we're doing. I'm here to tell you that we know what we're doing. My views are my views. My actions on my actions, nobody else's. I don't copy anybody. I do what I do because I want to do it. I'm not forced. I'm never forced to do anything I don't want to do. I believe in what I believe in, not because I am copying other people but because I genuinely believe in my values and my beliefs in my faith. I have seen things that have helped me build my beliefs, my faith and my values. However, growing up with a disability means that not everybody understands or gets it.

They still think I'm the little boy just doing these projects, doing this book, going to church, doing the sport because I can't do anything else. "Well, he has to do something. " or "Well, at least he keeps him busy." No, I do what I do because I enjoy it. After all, it gives me a purpose in life. And that's all we do; that's what anybody does. People work; they socialise because it gives them purpose. My mental health has been up and down. I have good days; I've had bad days. On a good day, my routine is awful. On a bad day, I didn't have the energy to cook, no energy to go out, no energy to do medical routines, to socialise. Over the last couple of years, I've had more bad days than good.

This year, So far, I've had more good days and I've had bad days. I'm not saying my days are perfect. I'm not saying that there haven't been things that have gotten me down. Trust me. There have been. In the chapter, I'm going to talk about some of the significant challenges that I've had a face, which has led to my mental health being shaken. As I've already mentioned, I was part of a wheelchair Basketball team. Southwest Scorpions was my life, whether training, going to leagues, playing friendlies or coaching. I loved going every Sunday, watching the kids develop as a coach. There is no better feeling than watching kids, enjoying playing the sport, developing, building friendships, And having the biggest smile on their faces. So when it all came to a close in 2019 because of me, I couldn't handle it. Now, back in 2018, I was handed over to the club, and I became head coach. This was a big honour and a privilege. I didn't take for granted the amount of Pride in being the head coach.

I was proud to be able to run and lead such a fantastic team, But I made mistakes that led to the club closing led to me letting down athletes of all ages and all abilities. And I let my mental health go downhill. I lost a very dear friend in the process, And I hate myself. And to this day, I still have the same guilt. When I took over from him, the finances were not in great shape. When running any sports club sports team, you need to be to pay for equipment, venues, insurance, and hiring a minibus to be able to go to matches and games. However, I didn't know how to fundraise for the team. And I was too young to take over the club as I had no experience. I was way too young. I didn't have an assistant coach.

The committee were terrific. I built a committee that knew me and that I could trust, But there were challenges with the club that led to me having to call it a day, closing the club. I let many athletes and many kids down that day, Which resulted in my mental health going downhill. The biggest reason wasn't that I had to call it a day; the most significant reason was that I let kids down. I had to tell them they could not come to basketball training anymore. That the 11-year club was coming to a close, that I let the founders down. Mike and Jen, I let them down. I hadn't carried on that legacy. I can't go back, but I can move forward. I can build bridges. After closing the club, my mental health went downhill considerably. I didn't even want to watch basketball on TV. I didn't want anything to do with the word basketball.

I didn't want anything to do with sport. I didn't want to talk to anybody from the world of basketball. Any of my friends who were playing basketball, I couldn't. It was the most depressing time. The number of nights that I couldn't sleep. The number of times that I couldn't focus. I couldn't even go on Facebook and see what the team was doing. I lost my motivation, but now I'm proud to be able to say that I have joined the basketball team in Bath. I am not a coach. I'm an athlete. I'm never going to say I'm never going to get back into coaching. I'm never going to say I'm never going to be running a basketball team in the future, but for now, I don't want any responsibilities within the club except to play, to compete.

And I feel a lot better because I don't have the pressure of letting anybody down. In 2021, I moved into my flat after a year and a half of waiting to pay, to move in the delays due to the system, failing to the pandemic and my own physical health. It was meant to be a day. That was amazing. That finally crossed the finishing line. And for the first few months, it was, it was terrific. I was excited. I was, my routine was perfect, but in the summer of 2021, things turned quite quickly.

My motivation again, to cook, to eat adequately, changed. My motivation to be able to go out, to socialise changed considerably. I moved into the city centre so I could go out in the evenings and socialise, say that I could cook for myself. There was no defining moment or reason for my mental health to go downhill. There were no events had caused my mental health to go down, but I became very depressed very quickly. I lost all motivation. I didn't care if my flat was clean. I didn't care if I ate. I didn't care about going out. This year I have been able to turn things around. I've had to slap myself and say, "wake up, smell the coffee. We need to get a grip." That's different from Manning up, by the way. Getting a grip and having a wake-up call is different from Manning up. Manning up is saying just ignore your feelings, don't talk about your feelings. Getting a grip and taking control of the situation means you recognise the need to talk.

It would help if you found somebody you could talk to. I've got the most fantastic counsellor I see every month, whom I've seen regularly for the last five years. Over the years, I have had counselling sessions through CAHMS and college. I honestly couldn't ask for better support from my counsellor. Without the help and guidance and that encouragement and wisdom, I wouldn't be here where I am today. They've challenged me on several occasions. They've supported me. They've shown me that I'm capable of achieving what I want to achieve.

They have helped me articulate my feelings, and they have helped me and supported me so that I don't get angry in no 0.2 seconds that I don't go from nought to ten in a split second. I think rationally about the situation and how it would affect those around me. They say that you set the atmosphere in the house, whether it's a friendly atmosphere or an angry atmosphere, and those who enter the house know in a split second what the atmosphere is like. For a long time, I set the atmosphere in my parent's house, and it wasn't good for a long time. I was angry.

I lashed out at my mum. I lashed out that my dad would come home early. I would have abused my mum because I didn't know how to talk and share my feelings. I didn't know how to express how I was feeling. All I knew was how to make a scene. And these are the consequences. People lash out at those whom they love the most. If you don't talk about your mental health, if you don't get the proper support, those around you, those who love you the most, will get hurt. The most those who bought you up will get hurt the most. Now I can't change the past.

I can't change the actions that I've already made, but what I can do is make sure that those actions do not happen ever again. I can ensure I'm talking about my feelings rather than lashing out. I talk to my family about how I'm feeling. I share with them what's going on, but I would also say state that it is okay to be not okay. It is okay not to be okay. And I'll go further and say, if you didn't feel okay, that is normal, especially at this unprecedented time with the pandemic. For the last five years, I have been on antidepressant medication. I take one tablet every night, which helps me with my sleep and helps me with my anxiety. I don't understand why we have to have an issue with it. What if somebody is on antidepressant medication because that doesn't make them weak? It doesn't make them worse and makes them strong.

I know when my mental health goes downhill, it's when I haven't spoken to my Support network. I want to talk about my family and my counsellor or my GP. I'm talking about my friends, my true friends, my best friends. Those who've supported me. Those who have been with me through everything. And I owe them a lot more than they will ever realise. They are my second family. It's not a massive group of people. It's a very, very small leap. And they know who they are. They have inspired me to be the best person I can possibly be.

Those who have challenged me. Those who have made me laugh in no 0.2 seconds. Those who have, in some cases, saved my life because I've wanted to end my life. I have three things that I need to clarify before I go any further. Firstly, it's okay to talk. It is important to talk. Do not shut yourself away in your bedroom and not talk about your mental health and how you're feeling. Secondly, if you are worried about your friend or family member, check up on how they're doing, but don't ask how your day has been. How are you doing? Honestly, ask how they are doing and allow them to talk. I think it's very easy to bypass the question, life has become fast pace, and the world is spinning out of control. We have become so absorbed in our own lives that we don't think we have time to check in on the people we love the most. This is a load of rubbish; if they are really important to us, we will find the time.

What I'm about to say is directed at specific people in the public eye. To those who have said that crying, sharing your feelings, and showing your emotions is weak, let me tell you, yeah, I am weak, but we all are. If you believe you are strong, not only are you lying to those around you, but you're lying to yourself. I have seen many friends bottling up their emotions, and then they break. They bottle up their feelings because they don't want the world to see them as weak. Recently we have seen those mainly on the right indirectly and sometimes directly shred those with mental health illnesses to shreds.

Telling them to snap out of it and that they need to quit being so negative will result in the highest rate of suicide for over a decade. I was suicidal while doing my GCSEs; I felt alone, angry and confused. I am no longer suicidal, but I must be careful about my mental health because I can slip anytime. I am weak, but three things have kept me going; my faith in god, my family and my friends. Earlier I talked about my faith, and I am now starting to talk more openly about my faith with friends and family. I'm tired of how I am feeling; I don't want to feel depressed anymore, and I don't want to feel anxious anymore.

I want to be confident and have the ability to go into a room with my friends and family without feeling like the walls are closing in. When I get anxious, I feel trapped. As a kid, I used to have a complete meltdown in front of everyone and make a scene. As soon as that has happened, I create an atmosphere where everyone is then treading on eggshells. You could hear a pin drop. This situation has resulted in me not wanting to be involved in family get-togethers and pretty much every social gathering. I choose not to be involved because I don't want to create an atmosphere where everyone is treading on eggshells. I have created a routine where I'm not always in my comfort zone. Where I will not get triggered, people won't have to tread on eggshells.

I hate that people are still cautious about what they say, just in case I lash out. I still have nightmares about how I used to treat my family. I don't want to be in that situation ever again. I am now a lot better; I am slowly becoming more confident in social gatherings. I have learnt techniques, breathing exercises and code words that allow me to express to those around me that I need to get out of the situation.

It is not easy to sit around a table with my whole family. However, I am going to social gatherings on my own that I wouldn't have gone to a few years ago. This may sound like a small step, but for me, the fact that I am getting myself to these places on my own and contributing is a massive milestone. I couldn't have achieved what I have achieved without my family, friends, counsellor and those who have supported me over the years. This leads me to my last point. Thank you to my family, friends, counsellor, GP, consultants, and teammates for putting up with me through everything. I know I can be a mess sometimes. I know I can be an idiot.

I've made mistakes, but your friendship and support have meant a lot to me. I am stronger because of you. So thank you. This evening pick up the phone, text someone you know and ask them how they are. Instead of watching that film, you have seen three thousand times talk to a friend or loved one. We are all human, we all have feelings, and we all participate in today's society. Let's not allow our one disability to get in the way of our many abilities. We will not break down barriers or cancel the stigma around mental health unless we talk. I know it's easier said than done.

It took me years before I had the courage to talk to my parents about my mental health. I showed a teacher a letter from my councillor. It had references in there that I was suicidal. I didn't know how to share it with my dad. The teacher picked up the phone and called my mum. She explained that I had a letter with information that was upsetting. We agreed I would show my mum the letter when I returned from school. I had to go through the rest of the day with the anxiety that I had to show my mum the letter. Once I got home, I sat around the kitchen table and gave mum the letter.

I left the room while she read the letter. She then came a hugged me, and we started talking about how I was feeling. The next day my dad took me out to a cafe, and I showed him the letter. We then discussed it and came up with ways that would allow me to be able to share how I'm feeling without anxiety. The truth is, even though those words were sincere, I still had doubts because I still was struggling to trust people. My parents and family didn't do anything to give me evidence that proved my hypothesis.

As I said, when you feel guilt, your emotions overpower all rational thoughts. I allowed those feelings to get the better of me; those thoughts destroyed my friendships. Those thoughts destroyed my education because I couldn't concentrate at school. When you are depressed, all your hobbies and everything you enjoy goes out the window. I didn't care about going to basketball or seeing friends. I did not want to do anything but curl up in a ball and cry, and sometimes I did, and that's okay. My biggest mistake was bottling up my feelings for too long and not talking about them. If a female cries, it's okay, but if a bloke cries, then they are seen as weak. I cried, I still cry, and it's okay and good to cry. For me to move on and get better, I needed to cry to let out all my emotions.

We are not in victorian times; we are allowed to be seen and heard. The issue is that even though my trust has gotten stronger and I can share more with my family, there are still situations where I have a little voice at the back of my mind saying nobody will believe me.

There will always be a voice at the back of my mind saying I'm worthless; nobody cares, I'm a waste of space. Society has made me years feel like this, and it has destroyed my mental well-being. I don't want to be scrutinising every conversation working out if they genuinely respect me and see me as equal. A close friend of mine called Chris Young has walked around the edges of the UK. Chris is a former senior social worker who left social work. He walked around the edge of the UK to highlight people who feel on the edge of society. We have only met a couple of times, but we have had countless conversations on the phone. We discuss many things, from politics and disability benefits to the mental health crisis.

There is one story that he told me about his time in social work that has been playing on my mind recently. He was asked to take a quiz; he was shown ten different people and was asked if he trusted each person. Out of the ten people, he only trusted one person, and that was only, so he didn't look so cynical. He realised that if he decided someone was a bad person, he would only see the negatives in that person, that he would be waiting for them to mess up, proving his hypothesis. When he started his walk around the UK, he wanted to put what he had learnt into practice. He was determined to make sure he saw everyone in a positive way. Everyone he met, he made sure he said hello with a smile. He was astonished by the number of people he had conversations with and the hospitality he received. I'm now thinking about how I can put this into practice in my own life.

Instead of expecting sarcasm and patronising comments, I will concentrate more on the time together. I'm not for one moment saying it's easy; it's going to take time before I can completely ignore the voice at the back of my mind. What has helped me recently is being honest with people, not keeping secrets, to be open to discussions. What has helped me is being confident in what I am saying, to talk with confidence and to talk from the heart. People respect and admire others who say precisely what they think without hesitation. I would be giving society a win if I gave up and stayed at home all day, every day. I want to show the world that there is nothing that can stop me. This is why I do what I do; this is why I enjoy what I do. I see people on social media getting attacked because they have a disability. This is what drives me to carry on, to fight for those who feel they don't have a voice.

Something that I have learnt over the years is that it is easier to give advice than to receive advice. My brother once asked me, if my friends were in the same situation as me, what advice I would give them. Without hesitation, I gave him my advice; he turned round and asked why I was not taking my own advice. The reason I didn't want to take that advice was that I didn't feel I deserved to take that advice. I felt at the time that I deserved everything that was happening to me. The truth is nobody deserves to feel the way I felt. We all should feel valued and respected. Our lives Matter. My Advice to anyone who feels alone and their life doesn't matter is to talk to your friends and family, talk to your neighbour, and talk to your GP. Do not allow society to win this battle.

CHAPTER 14
Postcode Lottery

Postcode lottery is dangerous because where you live determines whether you live.

In the United Kingdom, the postcode lottery is the unequal provision of healthcare, education and disability benefits on the geographic area or postcode. Postcodes can directly affect the services an area can obtain. Despite having many non-postal uses, postcodes are only determined based on Royal Mail operations and bear little relation to local government boundaries. More broadly, there is an unequal provision of services around the country, especially in public services, such as access to cancer drugs in the healthcare system or quality education. These are more likely to result from local budgets and decision-making than postcodes.

Postcodes were devised solely to sort and direct mail and rarely coincide with political boundaries. However, over time they have become a geographical reference in their own right, with postcodes and postcode groups becoming synonymous with certain towns and districts. Furthermore, the postcode has been used by organisations for other applications, including government statistics, marketing, calculation of car and household insurance premiums and credit referencing. In practice, there are geographical variations in almost all aspects of care. Recent examples include variations in charges for disabled people's home care; NHS availability of the multiple sclerosis drug, beta interferon; availability of NHS in vitro fertilisation services; waiting times for NHS treatment; assessment of children on social service "at risk" registers, access to NHS cancer screening programmes, and availability of drugs for Alzheimer's disease. Devolution has also brought the postcode lottery to the fore: Scotland plans to provide free personal care for people in residential and care homes, meaning that the cost of long-term care for elderly people will be significantly cheaper north of the border.

In Wales, fee exemption rules on prescriptions are more liberal, leading to the "drug runs" phenomenon whereby people on the English side of the border drive across to stock up on cheaper medicines. How did the postcode lottery come about? Since its inception in 1948, the government argues that there have been no national standards of care in the NHS. For five decades, services grew haphazardly: decisions on which treatments and drugs should be made available were made locally and on an ad-hoc basis by individual health authorities and influential medical consultants. For many, the epitome of the postcode lottery was GP fundholding, introduced during the internal market of the 1990s.

Patients of budget-holding family doctor practices (now replaced with primary care groups and primary care trusts) had faster access to hospital treatment than patients of non-fundholding practices, leading to a two-tier postcode lottery. The concept of a postcode lottery is also a by-product of patients and consumers becoming more aware: patient groups have become more adept at lobbying for their consumer "rights" to drugs and services, and the well-targeted survey with its shock findings of a "postcode lottery" is a crucial weapon in their campaigning armoury. The Postcode lottery still determines whether young people are likely to get a university degree or not.

So how does the postcode lottery affect me? How bad is it in reality? To answer both questions, we need to look at four areas of society that, to Joe Blogs, would presumably be the same in all regions of the United Kingdom; however, if not, you dig into the situation and realise each area is so different. You would be excused for thinking you have entered a foreign country with a different government. The truth is the government has let some local authorities make their own legislation and others not. This has meant that each local authority has a different housing scheme, a different wheelchair service scheme and different NHS Providers. So not many differences!

Let's discuss each one and how it has affected me, starting with the housing scheme. Earlier I spoke about how I moved out of my parent's house and the challenges that came with moving. I never spoke about how I managed to pay rent. The process to claim housing benefits in BANES is through Universal credit. You would be forgiven if you thought this was the same process in every area. Each Council has their own method and protocols for claiming Housing benefits. One of the best things about the disability community is that we support each other through social media pages and support groups. The major hurdle we have to battle is how we can help and support each other when the process is different.

A few months ago, a close friend and former teammate sent me a message asking for my help and guidance with getting a council house. As someone who has recently been through the process, I thought, how difficult would it be? As soon as I started talking to him, I realised I was out of my depth. I knew the process inside out for the Bath area, but this was for the Bristol area, which has a different housing benefit system and a different way to apply for a property. As stated earlier in Bath, I had to use a website to bid for other properties. The problem I realised was that Bristol's "Bidding" system was not the same process.

Two years ago, a dear friend of mine was made homeless. He has Spina Bifida like myself and uses a manual wheelchair. He was born in Essex and has lived there his whole life. When becoming homeless, he was taken to a hostel with his stepdad. I remember video calling him every night and seeing how emotionally and physically challenging it was for him. Months passed, and the process for him to find his own place was unknown. The questions about rent, council tax, and paying bills were still unclear. I remember him asking me about my situation, and I'm sitting there, unable to answer. It has got me thinking, why is Universal credit determined not by your circumstance but by where you live? The government has wanted to streamline benefits for a very long time.

However, the government spends millions on welfare due to the horrific postcode lottery. In a recent campaign organised by the charity Scope, in the southwest alone, 78% of people got their benefits after being forced to fight at a tribunal. The overall cost in the South West Region of these tribunals was £4,114,488. The government spent £4,114,488 that could have been saved if there had been no postcode lottery. In the Greater London Region, 50,509 people went to tribunal, the second appeal stage. 78% of people got their benefits after being forced to fight at a tribunal. The overall cost in the Greater London Region of these tribunals was £9,519,168.

In the past, the media, governments and some parts of society have branded people with disabilities as lazy and only in it of the money. As a disabled person, I can 100% tell you this is false. The debate on welfare is never going to be over until we get away from the postcode lottery. Let's talk about the wheelchair service; why is it in such a state? Postcode Lottery! Each wheelchair service is run and funded differently. Some, like the wheelchair services in Bristol, are run and funded by the NHS others are run and funded by private companies. NHS Wheelchair Services assess people with a wide range of physical disabilities that affect mobility to help them decide what wheelchair or other mobility equipment the patient should be provided with.

It is common for your GP, consultant or occupational therapist to make the referral. Even though it is a national service, it is regulated locally. This often means contracting out to private companies. Therefore, there are noticeable differences from district to district on what criteria the health authority applies and what equipment they will fund. So, in one area, only people in a chair 24/7 will get support, while in another, there might be a more generous approach to mobility needs.

I have no idea where to start with this, except to say I dread to think about how much the NHS has to spend on fixing issues if the chair isn't fit for purpose. I have had multiple wheelchairs from the wheelchair service. I remember my very first wheelchair was when I was four years old. When I was four, I had braces to keep my legs straight. This meant that my wheelchair had to accommodate those leg braces. I remember the wheelchair services measured me and put me in this giant bean bag, Which then sucked all the air out to create a foam seat mould. The choices for me were at that age unbelievable. I was able to choose the colour of the frame, the colour of the Cushion seat, and the colour of the backrest.

However, It's not until you go down the route that I have recently gone down with a private wheelchair that you realise that the choices you have within the wheelchair service are limited. I was allowed specific makes of wheelchairs, And I was only allowed certain cushions. In contrast, friends of mine who live in other areas of the United Kingdom were allowed wheelchairs and cushions that were not available for me. I'm not talking about not being available for me, but they weren't available at the wheelchair service in my area. We've reached a point where The wheelchair service has gone so far away from its original ethos and priorities that we see multiple times where patients have gained pressure sores, scoliosis and other health issues because the wheelchair they were given from the NHS was not fit for purpose.

The wheelchair services are not fit to provide the wheelchairs that the patients need. I must stress that this is of no fault of their own;

the wheelchair service is not to blame for this. I am always saddened that because they are the main point of call, they are always getting blamed for this mess. It has become clear that It is because of the postcode lottery that many people are ending up in hospitals because the wheelchairs they were provided were not made to measure and therefore caused them health issues that have, that have meant more operations. I have scoliosis; I'm not saying that, for one moment, it could have been prevented If I had the correct wheelchair in the first place; however, if I had the proper wheelchair from the start, it could have prevented my scoliosis from getting worse.

It's not just the wheelchair service that is affected by the postcode lottery. Medication prescriptions are now becoming a thing of the past, and GPs have been known to give patients Amazon links for catheters, dressings and other medical equipment. How have we gotten to this situation? A close friend of mine, Heather, is a single amputee below her left knee. We have had countless conversations on the phone where she has been sent amazon links from her consultants because the hospital no longer provides the medical equipment. However, I have had the same pieces of equipment funded by the NHS. I have realised how much I have taken for granted because I live in this postcode. Heather also has type 1 diabetes. She explained that early in 2021, the NHS announced funding worth £2 million for a pilot roll-out of hybrid closed-loop technology.

This means that 1,000 people who live with type 1 diabetes in England, who meet specific eligibility criteria, can access this life-changing technology on the NHS. The issue with this rollout scheme is that it's not available to everyone with type 1 diabetes. I am yet to hear anybody in my area who is on the trial. From what I have researched and with the information I have been given from different friends who have type 1 diabetes, it's not going to be available to everyone through the NHS. There will be some NHS services that will advise patients to pay privately for the looping system. This again shows how divided we all are due to the postcode lottery. I'm highlighting these scenarios wondering how we have gotten to this situation. How on earth have we managed to get into the mindset that it's acceptable, that The NHS Should be sending patients Amazon links while other NHS services are providing the equipment themselves? Now I could do a concise conclusion. That says We should get away from this postcode lottery and have access to every service, no matter where we live in the UK. Even though I agree with that statement, I don't think it's enough. We need to look at the broader topic of how we got into this mess Because, like most things, It's become.

So out of hand that there is no easy answer to this mess. A simple Comment about The wheelchair service providing all wheelchairs, no matter where you are, The idea, the way I would say that As if it's common sense, but The issue with common sense is at the moment, it's not very common. It's so easy for us to be able to judge first able to Point fingers, But We can't expect change overnight. I am very impatient. I don't want To spend months waiting for change. I wanted things to be done yesterday, but I have learned that change happens When democracy wins. Change happens when enough people communicate. I'm not talking about protesting with megaphones and seeing who can shout the loudest.

I'm talking about having conversations with your friends, family, and neighbours, booking an appointment to visit your local MP and asking them to raise the issues in parliament. Many questions need to be answered first to move forward. Many questions still need to be answered, But the issue I have found is that those questions that need to be answered are not being asked in the first place. MP's are not asking The Prime Minister or Ministers the questions that need to be asked, and If you're an MP, you need to ask questions that highlight everything the government has done. If you're an opposition party, you can ask questions that are easy jabs against the government. When questioning ministers and Shadow ministers, the media ask the questions that create headlines. I have yet to see a journalist, and TV presenters, ask ministers and shadow ministers about the postcode lottery.

It is because it's not being talked about in society. How do you think topics in the news get publicised? The media and politicians take notice of society talking about these topics. People say, and I've heard this a lot, That they are fed up with the fact that nothing ever changes. That the government never listens, That Doctors never listen. We just have to defend ourselves and people Reading this Chapter; we'll be forgiven if they presume that's what I'm saying. However, I genuinely believe change can happen. I truly believe that the fight is not over. I genuinely believe that we will be able to see The horrendous postcode lottery Being demolished once.

And for, I want to share That The postcode lottery system that we find ourselves in doesn't just affect us physically, But mentally and emotionally; the number of friends That Have become Depressed, Suicidal because That local authority that local hospitals are not able to provide them with the support that they need. This is not just become a minor issue anymore. It has got out of hand where people are not having their lives respected. The idea that this situation we find ourselves in is causing more people to commit suicide is heartbreaking. These lives could've been saved if we had better services, where people could get the services they need instead of working out if they can afford them.

In my next chapter, I will talk about employment scams and how difficult it is for people with disabilities to find work. Many people, including myself, have to live off universal credit and Personal independence payments. These payments go out as fast as they come in because of the medical equipment bills we have to pay. I am horrified that people in this country have to pay for a loan to pay for care because the local authority Changes The guidelines. I am horrified. The fact that some areas of the UK don't provide care is entirely unacceptable. People with physical disabilities are left not being able to toilet themselves, not able to cook for themselves, not able to do the washing themselves, and not able to dress because the local authority doesn't have care plans in place. The only option is to pay privately. If you're living off universal credit and personal independence payment, And you don't have any savings, Then you'll have to decide whether you pay for your care but then have no heating, or you pay for your heating but have no care. How have we gotten into this situation? We need to start talking about it because the more voices, the more we must be listened to. I want to set a challenge for all of us. The next time a consultant, a GP, a physio, or an OT Tells you they cannot provide the services you require, ask them Why; ask them If this is just a temporary decision And if this is new legislation that has come into place. I can guarantee the answer will be yes, even though, looking back at it, there were signs that this situation would unfold into the position we find ourselves in. Nobody, including myself, would have ever thought it would have developed as rapidly as it has.

Nobody, Especially I, would have thought that we would be in a situation where doctors, GPs, Occupational therapists, and Physios are sending Amazon links for pieces of equipment that are not luxury items. Amazon is for Luxury items, Items that, Yeah, would be great to have, but then not vital and in no way pieces of equipment that keep you alive. Next time you're on Amazon, go through your Last six months of orders. Are they luxury, or are they needed? Are they required for you to live? Because that would tell you the answer on if it's suitable for Amazon to be the point of call for medical supplies.

I'm trying to find a positive side to all of this, to end the chapter in a positive way. I think not every situation is positive. Not every situation Has the ability to be positive. How undignified do you have to get, To be able to get the services you require to live everyday life? How dignified do we have to get to Ways alarms that not all is well within the system? How undignified do we have to be before somebody stops and pays attention? If you are somebody who is privileged enough not to be In this situation that I'm describing, Imagine what it would be like not to be able to wash, Toilet yourself, Get dressed and cook for yourself. What would you expect? Would you expect the NHS to provide care so that you're all able to do these things? What would you expect? Would you expect the wheelchair service to provide the wheelchair that is needed for you to be able to get out into society? What would you expect? Would you expect your employer to create a setting that allows you to work from home? Of course, because you're human. You expect to be treated as a human. I go into schools talking about life with a disability. At the end of the talk, I say the following statement:

> "Disability or no disability, we all are human beings; we all communicate and participate in society. Our ability counts, and our voice matters."

Why do I say this? I have for a long time felt that I am just a case number for the social care sector. I am not Simeon but a number. All dignity is taken away, and that human interaction is replaced with paperwork and folders. A few years ago, I did a campaign called #WEAREHUMAN, a campaign to raise awareness about disability hate crime. The campaign is now a much more comprehensive campaign. The social media campaign shows that we are not a case number but human beings that deserve the dignity and respect that anyone with any common sense would want. I am Simeon Isaac Wakely, a son, brother, nephew and uncle. I am not a case number. At the beginning of this chapter, I asked why we got into this mess. The reason is that the system doesn't care if I am a son, a brother, a nephew or an uncle. The system doesn't care if I am an athlete.

They see me as damaged goods, Broken. The system that we as human beings have created is broken, not me! Above all of those things I am a child of god and I was made in gods image. We were all made in his image. Genesis 1:26-28 Then God said 'Let us make man in our image, according to our likeness, and let them rule over the fish of the sea and over the birds of the sky and over the cattle and over all the earth.'

CHAPTER 15

The Employment Scam

"The Employment scam is a scary spiders web that we are tangled in."

Imagine waking up in the morning, trying to work out if you have enough money to last the day let alone the month. How would you feel? Your electricity bill is due and so is your phone bill. You look at your bank balance; it's £0.00. You have 24 hours to find money; otherwise, your heating and phone will be cut off. How would you feel? You ask friends or family to bail you out but don't know how you will be able to pay them back. This is my life; This has been my life since I was 18. What I am about to share is my experience with finding work; this is not just my story but thousands of disabled people across the United Kingdom. We can have all the experience, skills, qualifications and volunteer hours in the world. We can create an outstanding CV that would wipe out the competition but none of this matters because we are disabled. I'm going to share my experiences with interviews, CVs and rejections.

It all starts with the application process. A simple and elegant form that gives you the chance to show off. This questionnaire looks innocent, and it is until the very last question. Most of you will never have noticed it, skipped past it like it's written in invisible ink. "If you have a disability, would you like to be interviewed automatically?" The question seems so innocent, making the company look so inclusive. I fell for that scam multiple times. I ticked the box because I thought it would give me an equal chance.

However, it makes the fall even more damaging when you get a phone call saying that you didn't get the job. Rejection is the most painful feeling for anyone. It's even more painful when it's to do with a disability that I had no choice about having. I don't wake up every day thinking, "I know I want to be in a wheelchair." I don't wake up enjoying the pain in my hips. I don't wake up wanting to be in a wheelchair. My disability is not under my control. In 2010 David Cameron, along with his coalition government, introduced the apprenticeship scheme. The scheme is to encourage young people to get into employment while earning a qualification. The scheme is for those 16+ who don't want to pursue higher education or want to work while getting a qualification.

The scheme works perfectly unless you have a disability. The database of companies would give anyone the confidence to find something they would enjoy doing. This comes to my second hurdle; none of the companies has to state if they are disability confident. Instead of just highlighting these hurdles, I will also provide changes that can be implemented without spending a penny. What does Disability Confident mean?

"The Disability Confident Scheme supports employers like you to make the most of the talents disabled people can bring to your workplace."

It is Disability Confident organisations that play a leading role in changing attitudes for the better by incorporating inclusive recruitment practices into their own businesses, networks, and communities changes behaviours and cultures. Employers benefit from the scheme by attracting and retaining great talent, securing qualified, loyal and hard-working employees, and demonstrating fair treatment of all employees to improve morale and commitment. The program can also help customers and other companies identify employers committed to workplace equality. Employers can take advantage of the scheme at three levels to support them on their journey to becoming Disability Confident, including:

Level 1: Disability Confident Committed

Level 2: Disability Confident Employer

Level 3: Disability Confident Leader

Level 1 (Disability Confident Committed) is an entry level for all employers, and they progress through the levels as their confidence increases. The scheme is voluntary, and guidance, good practice, and resources are available for free. The Apprenticeship scheme never asks the company if they were disability confident. Imagine you apply for a job and then get an interview; you think you have aced the interview. You walk or wheel out with your head held high, assuming you have it in the bag. You then get a phone call saying you never got the job because they don't have the resources to employ someone like you. Those hours you spent scrolling through the database, finding the best company to work for. The hours spent on filling out the form and creating a CV that shows your abilities to learn new skills. All waisted because the company wouldn't employ you in the first place.

Why have an option to allow people with disabilities to have an interview when you can't physically hire them? It just reminds us that we are different from the rest. Instead of feeling proud to be different, I feel segregated and left out. I believe employers are not discriminating against us on purpose. I believe they are good people in a discriminatory system. They are not all to blame for this situation. My views haven't always been this; I used to judge them and blame them for my financial situation. I needed to blame someone. If you apply for work and successfully get the interview, you need to ask them why. Why didn't they offer you an interview? Why didn't they offer you the job? However, because I ticked the box asking them to interview me no matter what, I never had that opportunity to ask what I needed to do to improve.

The ticking of the box is your way of saying, give me sympathy for being disabled. It is their way of patronising you without you feeling like a kid. It is their way of looking like a caring and charming organisation that helps and support disabled people to get employment. The truth is it's just as patronising as patting me on the head or talking to my friends rather than me. I know I need to find work; I know I need to earn a living. I can't live like I am at the moment for much longer. For the past five years, the government has said that electricity, gas and water will go up.

Now, I want to make it clear that not every single person with a disability can work. We shouldn't be forced to work if it puts our health at risk. Health comes before work. We need to stop branding those who are not able to work as lazy. I also have to state that I am guilty of being lazy and relying on the government to pay my bills. Until recently, I have been comfortable with that. I have got into the mindset that I do not need to find work as the government will bail me out. I need to find work, and I am able to work; I just have chosen to feel sorry for myself and not find work.

I have been lazy, so your following two questions will be why have I been lazy, and why should the government pay my bills if I am lazy? Here is a challenge for you, sit in a wheelchair all day for a week and try to carry on with your work and social life. Blindfold yourself for a week and continue your work and social life.

You will then be able to experience just how many hurdles millions of people with disabilities face. The truth is I am not lazy; it is society's perception that has become the reason I am not working. Companies do not want to make changes to their current structure just to allow one employee to work there. I'm not for one moment saying this is the case for every company. However, this scenario happens for often than not. I have just written a chapter on the postcode lottery; how does this affect my chances of getting employment? You can have all of the qualifications under your belt. You can have three years of experience in the field of work when volunteering for an organisation. You can have the most fantastic CV and ace the interview stage. None of this matters if the company is not accessible. None of this matters if the employer is going to judge you on your disability. And you can forget to take them to court because you don't have the evidence to prove there was any sign of discrimination.

I live in a beautiful Georgian city. It has the most amazing architecture. However, with impressive Georgian buildings, there is always a tax called "listed buildings." If you're not from the UK, you're probably wondering what on earth I'm talking about. If the building is listed, it means that it cannot be adapted, or if any building work is to be done, it must meet the criteria. That criteria, by the way, does not include accessibility needs. In 2010 the UK government announced that any new building had to be accessible. This sounds great, but most buildings in Bath were built in the 18th century when disability was probably not a priority! To be fair, if you had a disability back in the 1800s, the chances you would be able to get out of bed were probably very low. If you have ever been to Bath, you probably have been to all the tourist sites. If any of my friends come to visit Bath, I always suggest Roman Baths or Bath Abby. In Primary school, we would visit the Roman Baths every year, and I remember I used always to hate it. Why?

To see the Baths, I need to park core down three flights of stairs built in the 1800s. If I did park core two, probably three things would happen. Firstly, I would not be here to tell the story.

Secondly, If I did manage to live, I would go down in history as the one who destroyed one of the most iconic buildings in Bath and probably would end up in prison until 2030! What does any of this have to do with employment? In 2012 I had to attend a council event held at the Roman Baths. I was, of course, dreading it as I was under the impression I would not be able to access the majority of the evening. It got to the point where I almost turned the invitation down. After much convincing by my parents, I agreed to go.

Over the coming weeks leading up to the event, we heard rumours that the council had installed a lift into the building. A building that was built in roman times has now become fully accessible. This brought two significant problems for me; firstly, the event I was attending was recognising those in the Bath who was carrying the Olympic torch. Why was this a problem? I was more interested in looking around than socialising with people. The second problem was that I had a GCSE Exam the next day, so I needed an early night. I went home that night not buzzing because of the event but the fact I was able to access a building for the first time. I have recently been thinking that if an 18th-century building is now fully accessible, then why can't every building be redesigned to make it accessible?

There is a psychological and quite depressing snowball effect when a company decides to ignore people with different conditions. What the company is saying is, "We don't see you as a human being there for you're not part of society. If you're not part of society, why should we accommodate?" They might not say those exact words, but actions speak louder than words. Their actions lead to consequences that might not, in the short term, hurt their business but, in the long term, will see their company crumble. This is not me prophesying, but when companies crumble as their profits shatter, you need to stop and think, why? I am not for one moment saying it is all because they're not disability confident, but it is a significant factor.

Have they ever heard of the Purple Pound or Purple Tuesday? The Purple Pound refers to the spending power of disabled households. A disabled household is a household in which at least one of the members has a disability. Organisations are missing out on the business of disabled consumers due to poor accessibility and not being disability confident in their customer services approach. The stats I am about to share with you are scary and show how important it is to have an accessible society. The stats show that financially companies are loosing out.

1. More than 1 in 5 potential UK consumers have a disability.

2. Businesses lose approximately £2 billion a month by ignoring the needs of disabled people.

3. 73% of potential disabled customers experience barriers on more than a quarter of websites they visited

4. Taking averages per head, the online spending power of disabled people is estimated at over £16 billion.

5. Estimates show that the 4.3 million disabled online shoppers, who click away from inaccessible websites, have a combined spending power of £11.75 billion in the UK.

6. The number of disabled people is increasing: From 11.9 million (2014) to 13.3 million (2020).

7. 75% of disabled people and their families have walked away from a UK business because of poor accessibility or customer service.

8. Nearly 1 in 5 working adults have a disability.

9. The spending power of disabled people and their households continues to increase and is currently (2020) estimated to be worth £274 billion per year to UK business.

Most authors will want you to carry on reading and hope you will take in 10% of what is written. I want you to do something about these statistics. But Sim, how can I when I don't run a business? Take one of the 9 points and post it on social media. Write an email to your manager asking what they are going to make sure the company you work for is more accessible. Then carry on reading the book, knowing you have played a part in making society a more equal society. Sounds too easy, right? Yeah, it is because the more people post on social media, the more companies have to listen. The more emails a company gets, the more they have to listen.

Because companies are not pressured, they are getting away with this criminal offence. Companies are basically showing their middle finger to disabled people. Companies are able to register with companies house, create a business plan and buy offices without the obligation to make their company accessible. When setting up a company, there should be a requirement that they have to complete a course and become disability confident. If they don't complete the course, then they cannot become a registered companies. It is a shame that we have to get this far where we have to make it a legal requirement, but unfortunately, that is the world we live in now.

Companies need to have an Ofsted-style inspection every six months to ensure they comply with the regulations. Once we see this change, more people with disabilities will be able to access employment. We also have this stigma that if you're not earning money, you're not participating in today's society. We have become a culture where we easily judge people without asking why. We seem to hear the word benefits and instantly think about the documentary "Benefits Street". As I have said, this is not all down to society. As a person who uses a wheelchair, it is my responsibility to challenge the stigma. We need to challenge the stigma not in a complaining judgemental way but as a discussion.

I don't know about you, but I switch off if I feel like I am being lectured or judged. It can be frustrating when change is not happening but shouting and handcuffing ourselves to the gates of Westminster is not the answer. I am not for one moment condemning protesting; it is our human right to protest, and long may that continue. All I am saying is we need to con the media at its own game. The media thrive with sob stories, gossip and anything that makes headlines. Unfortunately, headlines about people with disabilities are either negative sob stories or, by some miracle, are informative and uplifting. They will be buried deep into the interweb, where nobody will ever be able to find them. However, I would say, and maybe I'm a bit biased at saying that "Businesses lose approximately £2 billion a month by ignoring the needs of disabled people" is a powerful headline that would create noise.

As a teenager, I was very much on the centre right-wing side of politics, believing business was the way forward and that all disabled people who can work should work. As I have gotten older, I have realised that even though I still believe in that statement, as a society, we also need to stop presuming that people with disabilities are incapable of working and lazy. The main reason for me, and I can only speak for myself, so do not dare take this as the same for everyone, is the idea of being rejected again. Mentally I don't think I could cope with any more rejection.

Physically I can work; mentally, I can work; I need to work. I do not want to work for society to accept me but because I want to work. I want to work in a team environment and be in a routine where my physical and mental health is looked after. Recently, I have seen social media posts mocking those on **PIP** (Personal Independence Payment). The shocking thing about this is that it's not just members of the general public but people in the public eye with millions of followers. I want to tell you what **PIP** is all about, how it helps me and how it is **NOT** my way to live an easy life having the state pay for everything. PIP is divided into two components, Mobility and Daily Living. Due to my condition, I get the Enhanced Rate which allows me to get an adapted car on the Motability Scheme.

PIP is not means tested and has nothing to do with how much I earn. Universal Credit is for those who are on a low income or who are trying to find work. This has been widely criticised and has become a controversial topic in Britain. It is a benefit that needs to be reformed to best serve those who need it most. Why are both important to me? First of all, I don't choose to be on PIP, and I don't choose to be on Universal credit. I don't enjoy taking money from the state and feel dirty because I have to rely on the state. I cannot, at this moment in time, live independently without universal credit.

It is how I get my rent and council tax. My plan is not to get comfortable with this situation and to come off Universal Credit as soon as I can. In the last seven years, I have visited seven schools talking to students about my journey and what I have learnt about my disability. I have mentored and coached kids of all ages. All of this has been paid work, but not none of it has been a reliable source of income. I have been blessed with the opportunities I have had and will never take them for granted. I have the qualifications, experience, and commitment; I just need the opportunity to show that I can. This is not me asking for sympathy, nor is I trying to prove myself for acceptance. All I am saying, and all I will be talking about in this book, is that we are all human beings. We all have the right to be financially stable. We all have a right to be a part of this world, so for goodness sake, let us!

CHAPTER 16

Actions Speak Louder Than Words

"What someone actually does means more than what they will do."

Actions speak louder than words. "We care about disabled people" while they refuse to add a lift. "We accept everyone" but choose to support minority groups that won't cost them a penny. Actions speak louder than words. This chapter could go two ways; I could write 17 pages complaining like everyone else or write a chapter about when companies and governments have carried out plans that make our world a more equal society. I will choose the latter as there is enough negativity in this world. Just so we are clear, the companies in this chapter have not paid me for advertising, and all the opinions are my own. Sainsbury's is the first food retailer in the UK to bring SignVideo to its customer service centres – revolutionising the way deaf British Sign Language (BSL) users can contact them. The year-long trial began in 2015, which enabled deaf customers using BSL to contact Sainsbury's call centres via a secure video interpreting service.

Sainsbury's is committed to ensuring the customer experience is as easy as possible. This service means that deaf customers using sign language can now call them instantly at no cost. The service allows customers to place a call to Sainsbury's care line and grocery online contact centres via a free link on the Help Centre. It instantly connects deaf customers to a BSL interpreter who phones the call centre and relays the conversation in real-time.

The service will be available at all times Monday-Friday, 8 am-6 pm and is free to use. Sainsbury's already offers Text Relay, which many deaf and hard of hearing people use. However, for the first time, deaf customers will have instant British Sign Language access when calling the supermarket. Previously, deaf BSL users had to rely on hearing friends or relatives make a call for them. With SignVideo, they can do it themselves from the comfort of their own home, with waiting times of less than 30 seconds. But it doesn't stop there! Sign language has been in severe limelight in the last 18 months. An Oscars acceptance speech; on the front bench of UK parliament; and it stole the show at Glastonbury, as one of Britain's few expert grime interpreters went viral during signing Stormzy's headline set.

Here in the United Kingdom, we have only seen BSL recognised as a language. I say just because it was only announced today as I am writing this chapter. To explain how significant this milestone is, we need to go back to Monday, 5th March 2018. A petition signed by over 35,203 signatures asked for British sign language to be a part of the national curriculum. The motion was supported by a majority of MPs across the house. However, unlike most debates in the house, the decision wasn't up to the MPs but to the government minister who was listening to the debate. The argument for the motion was that there are around 50,000 people in the UK using British Sign Language. Many children are born deaf, and we must give them a better chance at a more integrated future. This is why BSL needs to be taught in schools. In his closing remarks, he outlined the government's response to the motion.

It became clear that the government minister had made up his mind even before the debate started. The Rt Hon Nick Gibb stood up and prepared to give his response. He outlined several reasons why this was just not viable. He argued that the national curriculum was reformed in 2014, and the focus was on more of an academic core body of knowledge. As I stated earlier, I believe the education system needs reforming and focusing less on the academic core body of knowledge and more on work experience and life skills. His second argument was that it would not be worth making BSL a part of the national curriculum. He said, "Academies would not need to follow this anyway." This, again, isn't strictly true as schools have never been given the option, so there is no evidence to support his argument.

He said, "MPs want schools to have a period of stability where no new GCSEs and A-levels are introduced." At the time, this was not the view of all MPs across the house. Many MPs from both sides were calling for the government to change GCSEs. Also, if you look at what the government had introduced a few weeks prior to this debate, you would see that they were not stabilising education but introducing grammar schools. His last point was that although there was a pilot introduced by Signature, the process for accreditation is lengthy.

He felt it would be challenging for BSL to become a GCSE as it would require broad and deep subject content. Again this is untrue as BSL is already split into levels, so all teachers would need to do is teach levels 1 - 2 for GCSE and level 3 for A-Level. If students want to learn BSL at an even higher level, they should be able to study the subject at college and university, getting an NVQ. Let's now travel 374 miles east to Belgium. A country that is well known for its chocolate, waffles, beer, and its national football team, the Red Devils. Home to Nato HQ and European Parliament. Belgium is also one of the leading countries for accessible public transport. The word accessible transportation is alien to us here in the UK. It's like chalk and cheese; it doesn't exist. Just ask Frank Gardner, Baroness Tanni Grey-Thompson or Ade Adepitan.

In my counselling sessions, I am trying to work on not comparing myself to others. It is getting more and more challenging to do so. Comparison can be dangerous to our mental health. I can't help but compare our situation in the UK to the situation in Belgium. In Belgium, if you use a wheelchair and want to get the train, all you have to do is book tickets and wheel straight onto the train. At least 40% of Belgium train platforms are the SAME height as the train! The same height! To book a train ticket here in the UK, you have to book assistance. Despite booking assistance in advance, that doesn't always guarantee that you will be getting the assistance you require!

There is also a psychological issue with our current system, which is being eradicated across Belgium and other countries where platforms are the same height. If you have to book assistance and rely on staff members to help you on and off the train, it just reiterates that you are still seen as different and are not part of society. The issue isn't rocket science, it's being done worldwide, and the infrastructure is already in place. I was privileged to attend the first two days of the 2012 Paralympic Games. I was only concerned about public transportation.

What will happen if I get stuck on the train? Is there assistance at the station? The staff at Paddington and Stratford International Station were fantastic. Society can be inclusive and accessible without incurring additional costs when it wants to be! As a disabled person in the UK, spontaneity is nonexistent. It's not in my vocabulary! I am not being negative here; I am simply stating the truth. Situations like this have forced me to adapt. While accommodating is part of my life and nothing terrible, learning about other countries where people with disabilities can hop onto trains without any issues puts things into perspective on how far we still need to go. We now need to travel 4,691 miles west to The United States of America. Our friends across the pond have set the standard when it comes to disability rights.

Although they are not leaders in accessible public transport, they strive to ensure that people with different disabilities have a voice. I have seen situations arising throughout America that I am ashamed to say do not exist in this country. In a society where people are understood for who they are, they are seen for who they are, not for their imperfections. They are regarded as people who can contribute to society, not because of how much money they earn but because they are passionate about justice. In Congress, people with Down Syndrome have spoken. Currently, the unemployment rate for people with disabilities is 7.9%. In the UK, 28.8% are unemployed.

Our county isn't as business-minded as our allies. Taking a business-oriented perspective has both advantages and disadvantages. My primary anxiety is that we create a society that is already financially driven and even more financially occupied, and our core values will disappear altogether. As I will talk about in more detail later, money is not the key to true happiness. It's amazing how these companies in America have dealt with a problem like making their buildings accessible.

It has become second nature to them. Adjustments are not a hindrance to them. There is an emphasis on people's strengths. The reason we're here is that we're meant for something. We all were born for a purpose: to be loved and valued. I am not trying to be spiritual; I am just stating the truth. In our society, we have become very selfish. We will only make changes if it benefits us as individuals. We only give to Red Nose Day or Sport Relief or children in need because we feel good after, not because it will make a difference to many people. If we wanted to make a difference, we would make a monthly donation to a charity or volunteer to help those who need it most. In the US, they don't employ people with disabilities out of sympathy or because it makes them look good but because they see the strengths and qualities of these individuals. Everyone is treated the same and has the same expectation.

They are not scared to let someone go if they are not performing their best. There is no political correctness, yet there is still respect for other opinions. America is a place I would like to visit. If I had the money, I would travel there tomorrow with no hesitation. Why? So that I could learn more about what they are doing to support people with disabilities. As I mentioned earlier, public transport there isn't always accessible in America, so I'm not saying it's perfect. In order to make society more inclusive, we don't have to reinvent the wheel. We need to work together, come together, learn from each other and come with an open mind. If we fail to respond appropriately to a particular situation, we must admit that we were incorrect about how we handled it. Dialogue is critical; not constantly worrying about how much it will cost in the short run. Actions speak louder than words; not everything costs money. Most of the time, it's the simple things like customer service or having braille on signs and menus.

It could be just making sure that staff can talk in BLS. It is just asking someone if they are okay or need help. If you see someone struggling due to the lack of accessibility, ask if they need a hand. We have lost the sense of community in this country. I'm sorry to repeat myself, but we have become tribal, which is dangerous for so many reasons. If we do not radically change our mindset in the near future, this tribal attitude will only worsen. I think it is safe to say that when Zuckerberg creates the metaverse, and we all live in virtual reality, humanity will end as a result. Later in the book, I will discuss social media and how it destroys our lives. However, my main concern is that we have already got to the point where people are so glued to their phones that they do not see the world and society.

We will use the metaverse as an excuse not to change the culture. So for the rest of the chapter, I am going to talk about what needs to be done in the UK so that instead of trailing, we succeed in inclusion. This is for those in power, those who have a say in our laws and how this country is run. This is for the world leaders and those who are in charge of the economy; this is for those building their leadership campaigns to be the next prime minister or president. This is a cry for help, not because I am a victim but because I have seen with my own eyes where the system works and where it fails. The postcode lottery is the cause of this injustice; the postcode lottery is one of the leading causes of the economic crisis we find ourselves in. Without going political, we need our services back. We need our services to be taken back into public ownership. We cannot live in a country where it is one rule for Bath and another for Bristol. A country cannot exist where the fundamental human rights of exercising, going to the toilet, and eating are not respected. We understand that in 2016 you wanted us out of the EU to end freedom of movement. I never ever thought that would include British citizens.

And yet that is the case. People are imprisoned in their own homes because they are not able to access their local shops, cafes and schools. Children are forced to attend special needs schools because mainstream schools are not accessible. Prime minister, how have we got into a situation where 7000+ people are being attacked due to their disability? Actions speak louder than words; it is all well and good talking the talk but will you walk the walk? Will you have laws and policies that are not up to each constituency but that everyone has to follow? Are you going to wake up and smell the coffee?

We are not bargaining chips; we are not a department that can be cut from society. We are human beings trying to live a normal life. Hoping one day, we will be seen for our ability, not our disability. We need you to lead by example. We need you to show that we are all human beings; we all have a voice. People look up to you; they follow your lead. They develop their views on what you say. Care companies are deciding if the person in their care should have a DNR plan or not. I get that disability is not sexy or grabs headlines, but who cares? This is about people's lives. You say you want to save money, so why don't you save money by making every public building accessible?

Let us become the leading country in accessibility. Where people from all around the world want to visit because they can, because they are able to without anxiety. Please do not make us the victim that is hated, the victim with the tiny violin who should be muted from the world. Please stand up for us, talk to us, and show the world that we are all human beings. You need to ask us questions; let us show you what we go through. Our society would be shocked and appalled if we showed them the truth of what we go through. Being shocked and appalled is excellent, but actions speak louder than words. What are you going to do about these issues? We need to work together; as Jo Cox said, we have more in common than that which divides us. We need to get away from the left and right of politics; stop creating divisions and cults, and bring back community, support and honesty. There is no I in team. We need to build a society where we are all for one and one for all.

It starts in parliament, the home of law-making. How do we expect businesses and councils to be more accessible when the home of UK politics is not accessible for the public or MPs with a disability? Parliament needs to lead by example; I would love to watch PMQs and people with different disabilities sitting on the green benches, watching our first deaf mp deliver their maiden speech in BSL. That would genuinely put hope back into society and politics. Now I realise it is not all down to you and your government. Why change something that doesn't need to be changed? Because it 100% needs changing. We need to create a system that does not discriminate. That shows that ability counts and that our voice matters. Prime minister, we need a system that works for us all, not just in the constituencies that voted for you.

This is not us being woke, and not that it is a bad thing; this is us fighting for our life. A life that deserves to be treated the same as everyone else. Whether I use a wheelchair, catheter, or a hospital bed doesn't matter to me, and it shouldn't matter to other people. Who am I to judge someone for the way they talk, walk or dress? Who am I to judge someone who cycles or takes the bus instead of driving?

Who am I to judge people for believing in a different god to me? Yet, society judges me for just pushing out of the front door, answering the phone, ordering a coffee, and catching a bus. We are constantly judged, and yet we don't judge those who are deemed to be perfect. I promised not to make this chapter full of complaints, but the one question that keeps going through my head is, why? Why are we in the 21st century and yet feel like we were still in the 18th century? We need to work together. We know the infrastructure is there. We have seen it work; we just need to showcase where it has worked and expand it to all areas of the country.

We need to start marketing this, unlike any other disability component. In the eyes of the public, disability is not sexy; disability adaptions are not sexy; they don't always look aesthetically pleasing. We are in a world that cares about how buildings look and how aesthetically pleasing they look rather than how accessible they are. So what can we learn from other countries? Wishful thinking, some would say; I would call it saving the economy while creating a society that includes everyone. So here are my four steps to creating an equal culture.

Step 1

We must get society on board before investing in better infrastructure or anything practical. Our message needs to be communicated clearly and positively in the 21st century. Getting the media on our side will enable us to succeed - not portraying us as charity cases but as human beings. In order to show society that we aren't damaged goods, we need to show that we don't feel sorry for ourselves. Each person on earth faces challenges and hurdles they must overcome. Even though the challenges we face might seem intimidating to some people, we must remember that there are others who are in a far worse situation than we are. The disabled community must continue as if nothing is wrong and continue with their lives. I am not suggesting that we should hide our emotions or man up.

Instead, we should continue with what we're doing without the anxiety of being judged or rejected by others. I know how painful it is to be rejected. Throughout my life, I have been rejected for not being able to take a particular subject at school or being refused a job interview due to an inaccessible building. Having to deal with rejection has been the most challenging thing I have ever experienced.

Step 2

Once we have demonstrated to society that our ability counts and our voice matters, we can start to invest and build infrastructure that is accessible to everyone. By shifting our mindset, we can find the financial resources we need to develop a more inclusive society. No, it would be wishful thinking that we could change everything all at the same time. It is not practical and not physically possible. Of course, it will be fantastic to see every building, every public transport, every road, and every pavement all accessible at the same time. Still, it's just not going to be possible.

So once we as a disabled community, it has been a while to accept that it is impossible to do everything simultaneously. We then need to decide what we need the most. Is it better public transport? Should we start by ensuring every building has a lift, ramp and an accessible toilet? Or making sure pavements and roads are fully accessible? Is it ensuring that every building is dog friendly for those who have guide dogs? I suppose it's a bit like the question of what comes first, the chicken or the egg. Without the chicken, there is no egg. Without the egg, there's no chicken. It's difficult because everybody will have a different opinion on what should take priority as a person who uses a wheelchair to get from a to B to get around everywhere. I would love to say, let's start by putting lifts in every building or making sure that every building is accessible with a ramp. However, I know that that will not be practical for everybody.

Is there one single thing that we all need and all have used that can be at can be adapted that means that it will become inclusive for everybody, not just a tiny minority within the disability community? I would say public transport needs to be the first sector that gets transformed that gets a massive boost in funding. This would not only make going to places more accessible but would also help the economy.

Step 3

So, I have somewhat shot myself in the foot! What is the point of having fantastic accessible transport if the city isn't accessible? I did tell you guys that this is going to be challenging to decide on what comes first. The next priority is ensuring that roads and pavements are fully accessible. We get rid of the horrendous 10-second countdown on traffic lights. We need to use our brains and realise there is no point in putting a drop curb on one side of the pavement and leaving the opposite pavement. There is no point in making pedestrian-friendly roads when there are massive potholes every hundred yards. There is no point in having a row of shops and Cafes that are fully accessible when roads and pavements are the complete opposite.

It is not just about making roads and pavements fully accessible. It's about making sure that bus stops are fully accessible. When I lived with my parents, there was a bus stop, which, for some reason, was lower than the road. To access the road to get onto the bus, you'd have to walk up a steep ramp at an almost 25° angle. When the bus driver pulled down the ramp, I kid you not, the ramp was pretty much a 90° angle. So I wouldn't be able to push up onto the bus. The thing is that people presume that the bus stops are regulated and built by the bus companies, and for a long time, I presumed that was the case. However, I quickly realised that it was down to the council to ensure the bus stops were fully accessible.

We need to make sure parks and other public places have areas that can be accessed by everybody. As a kid, I dreamed about accessing a fully inclusive playground. The thing is, like everything that I'm talking about, the infrastructure is already available. We have seen on social media that communities in the UK and other parts of the world have funded parks that are fully accessible, save those who cannot transfer out of the wheelchair can still enjoy playing in the park and having the childhood they deserve.

Step 4

In the last step, You must realise it is painful for me to choose what needs to come first and what takes priority. This is painful. I have decided to create these steps, but it's still harrowing. I can just see the hate comments I'm going to be getting because, in an ideal world, we shouldn't need to be having this conversation. We shouldn't need to choose what takes priority, and more needs to be implemented first. As I said at the beginning of this chapter, we must be honest with each other and ourselves. We must be realistic and realise that not everything can be done simultaneously. I honestly believe that the next step should be making sure the building's public places, Cafes and businesses are all fully accessible. What do I mean by fully accessible?

Make sure that every building has a lift or a ramp. It's ensuring every café has an accessible toilet and that it isn't being used as a store cupboard. It's making sure that every theatre and every church has hearing groups. Theatre companies, concert organisers comedians, can cater to all disabilities. It's making sure that our one disability is not getting in the way of us being able to live a "normal" life. It's making sure that our disability is not becoming a burden. I have lost count of the number of times I have been made feel like a burden because the venue of the shop isn't fully accessible. It's making sure that counters are low enough for wheelchair users.

Now I want to make this a positive chapter, so I want to tell you a story of hope of acceptance of making me feel normal. This company is not paying me to advertise them. This is my experience with this company. This is my experience of feeling normal in a society that tries to make you feel anything but ordinary. Ten years ago, Bath city centre welcomed the first Apple store. At the time, I wasn't an Apple fan. There was no way that I would be able to afford any of their products, and therefore it was something that didn't interest me. However, over time I followed their progress with features that, to most people, look like a gimmick. Still, for many people with disabilities, they are vital to communicating with friends and family.

I became a fan of Apple. Just a side note, I am using one of their accessibility features to write this book! There was one defining moment when I thought, okay, this is just on a different level. My mum was getting her first Mac book. I went with her to collect this MacBook as we entered the store. We were greeted by friendly and welcoming staff. The atmosphere was warm and energetic, and I could see the passion for the technology they were selling. While we waited for a team member to Collect the laptop from the storage unit, we were told to wait by what is known as the Genius Bar. Now, the Genius Bar is the perfect height for standing and not for somebody who does not stand and sits in a wheelchair. It is not perfect.

Once a staff member walked towards that with my mum's new laptop, and they asked us if we wanted them to help us set the computer up. My mum agreed, and I thought I'd just have to sit there looking at this massive counter which was not the most beautiful thing ever, but this is where everything changed. They told us to come to the end of the counter. The guy who was serving us then pressed a button underneath the counter. As if by magic, a lower counter appeared from within the counter and, suddenly, without any hassle. I was able to see everything I was able to look at and talk to the member of staff without having to strain my neck.

For the first time, I felt like my ability counted my voice mattered that they didn't see me as a disabled person; they saw me for who I was as a human being. My friends tease me, saying I have been hypnotised to believe that Apple is the only company to go with when it comes to technology. I don't buy Apple products just because they are good quality but because the company treats people with respect like no other company does. As I said, I am not being paid by Apple to say any of this. This is my view, my opinion, and this is my experience. We won't all agree on what takes priority. We won't all agree on how to get to an equal society. Some will wonder why to bother; some argue it's too much hassle to fight. Many of us are tired of fighting for justice; we need to talk and listen and have a voice in how this country is run.

CHAPTER 17

Forgiveness, The Key To True Happiness

"To forgive is to set a prisoner free and discover that the prisoner was you." Lewis B Smedes

They say money is the key to true happiness, but that is false! 100% untrue! You can have all the money in the world, but you can still be depressed, feel alone and empty and lost. I genuinely believe the key to happiness is being able to forgive others and, most importantly, being able to forgive yourself. It's no secret that I have made a few mistakes in my life, and later in the book, I will be going into detail about some of those mistakes that I am still paying the price for today. The guilt I have is, at times, unbearable. If what I was saying earlier about believing in Jesus the Son of God dying on the cross to carry my sins, then why do I still feel guilty? The simple answer is that I have yet to forgive myself. It sounds stupid, but until we can forgive ourselves, then we will always carry that guilt with us until the day we die. Imagine taking all that guilt every day. That was me for five years. I kept fighting voices in my mind that said I'm not enough. Because of that guilt, I could not have a conversation with anyone.

Imagine going through life wondering if the people surrounding you are there to support you or just being patronising as they see the chair before they see you. None of this was true, but as I said, I was full of guilt, and it was difficult to forgive myself. It's not just myself whom I have had to forgive. It takes a lot of courage to say sorry; it takes even more courage to forgive someone who hasn't apologised and still thinks to this day that they are perfect and can't see the hurt and damage they have caused me for the past four years.

Forgiveness means that even if it still hurts and knocks your trust, you can move on and try to build bridges. As a kid, my parents taught me to forgive out loud. "I forgive you; you owe me nothing." That is the most powerful sentence I will ever say in my life. The idea of saying it out loud, even if you're on your own, means that you can go to sleep feeling at peace and knowing that the matter is therefore closed lifts a massive weight off my shoulders. I must stress that I don't forgive straight away. It can take days, weeks, months and even years before I am ready to forgive. I want to tell you three stories where I have had to forgive, even though I was hurt so much, to the point where I wanted to end my life.

By the way, nobody knows that I am writing this. For those who were involved in this situation, I want to say two things and something that I probably should've said at the time. Firstly, thank you, thank you for your support, your guidance for your friendship through everything. Secondly, I'm sorry that I dragged you into this messy situation. I'm sorry that I forced you into situations that were uncomfortable even for me. It's easy, especially working within a team, assigning tasks and roles that you know you don't want to do. If you can pass on the responsibility, you will because you do not want to experience the stress that comes with that responsibility.

So passing on the responsibility in the short term may look like the easy way out, which was me years later will come back and destroy you if you haven't resolved the issue. I haven't talked about this situation to too many people. My family knows most of the story, my counsellor knows most of it, and a few of my teammates know. Now I'm not going to name names or go into much detail on the situation; what I will say is that a 15-year friendship ended because of one question. I was 19 at the time, still learning and trying to get experience coaching basketball. My mentor and one of my closest friends were getting tired and emotionally exhausted at the time. He needed a break from work and coaching. He worked day in, day out, 24/7, to ensure that our basketball club was succeeding. Still, he was doing this on his own with his wife. No committee, just him and his wife running a wheelchair basketball team.

When he rang me up and asked me to take over the club because he and his wife were stepping down, I felt massive honour and a privilege to be able to take over the club. I've been with the club since day one, where I built friendships that I still keep. However, I could see that if I didn't take over the club, the kids that came to the club would not have had the same opportunity I had when I first started playing basketball. The kids were developing skills, not just on the court but also off the court, confidence in using the chairs and building friendships.

But I knew the club wouldn't succeed unless I created a committee dedicated to building and maintaining the club so that the next generation of Paralympic athletes could discover the sport. Over time, as I organised the committee, I asked them to liaise with the previous coach and team manager about the accounts about safeguarding policies about insurance. At the time, I didn't really understand how painful it was for the previous owners to let go of the club they had poured their life and soul into. My biggest regret of this whole situation was that I hadn't dealt with certain conditions myself and communicated with the previous owners myself. I was relying on my committee to do all of the communication. I am not for one moment saying that the committee communicated in the wrong way. They didn't know the previous owners as well as I did. You need to remember this was a 15-year friendship. They supported me through my darkest moments.

They came to my secondary school to coach basketball, And it's crazy to think that our friendship ended because of a miscommunication. Now, forgiveness is the key to true happiness. So much had been said over email, Facebook or the phone via text and not all of it was polite. Trying to communicate and resolve issues over email is not the way forward. Meeting up, having a coffee, chatting and talking face-to-face is and will always be the way to resolve any problem. Needless to say, my 15-year friendship ended and, even to this day, hasn't been fully resolved. There is not a day where I don't feel guilty for the things today did wrong, the mistakes that I made, for not taking their requests seriously enough. I have had to also learn to forgive someone who hasn't said sorry.

Now, this is not me being superior in saying all they never apologise, but I'm still going to forgive them. This is me learning to be able to let go and meet move on. I've got to forgive myself for what I've done wrong. In a few years, I would love to see that we are in a position where everyone involved could sit around the table and resolve the issues. I can't see that happening right now, but I can only hope. Before I tell you this next story, I need to warn you guys that everything you are about to read happened a few years ago. This is precisely how the situation occurred. Some of the language used in this story is expletive and will also trigger certain people.

However, I feel it is right to share the story because this happens daily for many people with disabilities. It's how we overcome the situation and move forward from the problem that we learn how to improve society's perception of disability. I am not for one moment saying this is the whole of humanity. This is a minority group within the community that think it is acceptable to treat those whom they deem to be damaged goods feel worthless. I felt powerless when this situation happened. I wanted to curl up and die. Just to give you a bit of context to the situation, at the time, I was volunteering at a local radio station, presenting a show with an old schoolmate. Our show was every Saturday between 1 and 3 pm.

Due to my parents having family over for lunch, I agreed to get the bus into town. As somebody who catches the bus almost daily, I was confident about the journey. It was a journey I knew very well, and there should never be any issues. I arrived at the station to set up. I quickly met with our producer to discuss the plan for the show, and the show was perfect as it always has been. Our segments ran on time to the beat, and everything was great. I left the studio feeling happy and confident and looking forward to getting home to see my family. This was where everything started to go downhill. I got onto the bus, and I hadn't even gotten to the wheelchair space when the problem started.

I'm used to people standing in the designated area for a wheelchair, especially if the bus is already overcrowded. It's the only place people can stand, and I'm used to asking people to move so politely so that I can access the designated space. This couple sat in the wheelchair space; usually, people will see me getting onto the bus before even asking one to move to another seat. However, despite seeing me getting onto the bus, this couple chose not to find another place to sit but confidently refused to move. The bus driver had to come and politely ask for the couple to move as it was not safe for me to just sit in the aisle after a little bit of complaining and sighing and swearing under their breath.

They reluctantly moved to the back of the bus. Before I go on, I need to set the scene for this. The bus was packed on this particular day. There were about five people, including the driver on the bus. There were plenty of seats available for this couple. As we set off from the bus station and started our route home, the couple kept staring at me and giving me evil looks. I tried my best to ignore to look out the window at what I could see in the corner of my eye, but they kept looking at me and pointing at me. The issue with buses is that the wheelchair space means you're looking towards the back of the bus, so you're looking at all the passengers. Hence, it's pretty difficult not to see who is staring at you and who isn't.

As we got closer to my destination, the couple that refused to give up their seat stood up and started to walk towards the front of the bus to get off at the next stop. The female bent down as if to tie her shoes as they walked past me. She said underneath her breath something I never ever thought I would hear from anyone, especially a stranger. "Your parents should have aborted you. You're a fucking waste of space." She whispered so that nobody else heard. I was left shocked and speechless at the fact that somebody I didn't even know had the confidence to say something like that. When I got home after that traumatic experience, I opened the front door and immediately burst into tears.

If I'm upset, I try not to show my emotions in front of my nephews and nieces. I don't want them upset or distressed just because I am upset. My dad took me to my bedroom, and we talked about the situation. He was appalled and completely understood why I was upset and hurt. I rang my counsellor. Again, her reaction was just a shock, and she was confused about why anybody would say something like that. At the end of the conversation, she said, "You know what you must do now." I paused and told her that I knew I had to forgive them, but at this moment in time, I couldn't. I didn't have the mental capacity to forgive somebody who had just hurt me.

It took me weeks and weeks to build up the courage to get on the bus again. To begin with, I had to do it with my mum to build up my confidence, not because I didn't know what I was doing but because I was still hurt by the experience that had just happened. I will never forget the day I had to get the bus on my own for the first time since the situation. The only reason, and I mean this, the only reason I could get the bus on my own was that I forgave this couple. I gave them without even knowing them, knowing that I would never see them again. Still, I had to forgive them to move on and live my life. I couldn't let that one situation define me for the rest of my life, but I knew I couldn't move on until I forgave them. The third story I've already told in a previous chapter. Some people might think, Why would I need to forgive myself?

Why would I need to apologise to myself? What could I have done to have caused myself home? My simple answer is that I didn't take my health seriously for many years, and I have been taking risks with my own health. I don't know how I hadn't driven my self-harm sooner. The sad thing is that it took me to self-harm four times before taking it seriously. The last time you already know when it comes to the pressure sore led me to be on bed rest for the whole of 2020. However, nothing compares to the time I cause myself to get sepsis, not once, not twice, three times. Because I did not look after my health, I did not take it seriously and did not carry on with the routine that I needed to do on time, which caused me great harm.

For those who don't know about sepsis, it is one of the most dangerous illnesses you can have. It could kill you if you're not careful with yourself and don't treat it urgently. It is an infection that could kill you if you're not careful. My heart rate was 140 my temperature was 42° C. I was on IV antibiotics. It took me three days to recover. Before having sepsis for the first time, I had never heard of it and didn't know how serious it was. It wasn't until I got home after recovering that I researched sepsis and realised I was close to dying. Most people would've seen this as a wake-up call to change, but I was young, stupid, and reckless. I relied too much on my medication and thought, well, why should I change my routine because the medication is the thing that's keeping me alive?

The issue with that mindset is that if you believe it for too long, it becomes a habit and a part of your life, and the mindset is difficult to change. It's not impossible to change over time, but it is a challenge at the time. My faith in God was weak. I didn't have a purpose in life, anything for me to strive toward save me; I didn't change. So a year later, I found myself in the exact same situation. I had sepsis for the second time. Again, my routine was shocking. I didn't look after myself; I didn't do my routine okay shut off now I've got an account has friends who have had a catalyst, and then countless reports of evidence to show that Hydrocephalus is an Executive Dysfunction Disorder, which means that my organisation skills my memory is shocking and my thoughts and my feelings on this issue have changed over time. At the time of having sepsis. My mindset was, "I have Hydrocephalus, so what's the point of trying to remember the routine? I've got friends who deny being in that mindset. However, if we're going, to be frank about this, they are in that mindset. I've got one friend in particular, whom I spoke about earlier they are younger than me by two years.

We have known each other for 16 years; we first met on the same basketball team before they gave up the sport after attending only three sessions. We both have Spina Bifida and Hydrocephalus. Despite being younger than me, I look up to them, which is a bizarre thing to be able to say that you look up to somebody more youthful than you. I look up to them because they seem to have overcome the challenges of organisation skills and built a routine that allows them to carry on with their day-to-day lives whilst managing their medical routines.

I have shifted my mindset from "I have Hydrocephalus, what is the point?" to "How do I overcome those challenges?" So that I can look after my life and my health so that I can be there for others. I have had to apologise and forgive myself for not looking after myself, for being selfish and self-centred and always looking for sympathy and feeling sorry for myself rather than thinking. Okay, how do I live my life to the fullest so that I can be there for others? I am not for one moment saying it is easy and those who make it look easy also have their challenges that they have to face. I've had so many obstacles they've had to overcome and years of practice.

Yes, it does look easy because they've had years and started practising the age say that now it's just become second nature And that is my goal. My view is that these situations can be avoided by setting up a routine that I can follow and that will become second nature to me. It's going to be difficult; it is difficult. I am learning and getting better. It's still not perfect, but it's a lot better than five years ago, so I have had to step back from the situation, apologise and forgive myself.

I've also had to apologise to my family for putting them through the situation and ask them for forgiveness. If we are going to move on and create an inclusive society, we also need to be able to not judge people for making mistakes to forgive them. We must learn not to be angry with society because we will all make mistakes. I think it's easy to judge society for making mistakes when trying their best. We need to understand as a disability community that people make mistakes, and if you don't forgive those who do, you make mistakes. We do more harm if we become very judgemental towards society and will put people off helping us. We're just going to be even more excluded within society. One question I get asked a lot when I talk to students is why are you so positive when there is so much discrimination? The simple answer is if I don't laugh and make a joke out of it then I'm going to get angry and there is enough anger and negativity in the world already.

There are enough people on social media getting angry on my behalf. It is also interesting that those who do look at life negatively are not really helping society change. A lot of my friends and family do not look at the news as much and if they do it is only gossip or local news. At the moment the headlines are about how many parties our current prime minister had whilst in lockdown. I cannot start to imagine how these headlines are affecting those who have lost loved ones during the pandemic. The families who could not say goodbye to their relatives who were dying in hospital. The anger they must be feeling is beyond belief. When you are full of anger and full of frustration, when you feel like nobody is listening to you and respecting you it is difficult to then let go and forgive. The longer this feeling goes on the more difficult it is to forgive. The more times it is brought up the longer it takes to move on. CS Lewis once said:

" Everyone says forgiveness is a lovely idea, until they have something to forgive, as we had during the war. "

The Lion, The Witch and The Wardrobe is one of the best stories I have read. For those who have not read the book or watched the films then firstly, why not? The book written by CS Lewis is part of a series of books call The Chronicles of Narnia. In this book four siblings are sent away from home during the blitz of WWII. They are sent to be watched over by an old Professor Kirke, who owns a mansion. Once there, they stumble upon an enormous wardrobe which transports them to the world of Narnia. Narnia itself was once a peaceful realm filled with talking animals, fauns, Giants and dwarves that is now under a cursed eternal winter by the villainous White Witch. With aid from the majestic lion Aslan, the four lead Narnia into an all out war as they fight to outwit the Witch and restore peace to the land.

There is a deeper and more important part of the book for me. Aslan represents Christ. Aslan's death to save Edmund's life and his subsequent resurrection are clear references to the life of Christ. The novel's depiction of Christ's death and resurrection is a clear allusion to the biblical story of the crucifixion and resurrection of Jesus. I believe that Jesus was crucified on the cross to take away our sins. For me this has been something that I have been struggling to get my head around for years. Why would someone die for my mistakes when I have not met them? The truth is I've seen miracles in my life. I have seen mountains tremble and walls come crashing to the ground. I believe he has forgiven me, that he loves me. I believe that he has ever Forsaken Me. For he is the same yesterday as he is today and forevermore. Just think for a moment a farther sending his one and only son.

In Matthew 3:17 it says as Jesus rose out of the water after he was baptised a voice from heaven proclaimed that, 'This is my Son, whom I love; with him I am well pleased.' God's love, even for His own Son, is central to who he is. It also adds heartbreak to the sacrifice God is making in offering the life of Jesus for the sins of humanity.

CHAPTER 18

Are We Completely Independent?

"There's no such thing as an independent person."

Peter Jennings

This one's for you, Sue! For the past six years, I have been having counselling sessions privately with someone whom I have known for over ten years. We have discussed many topics, from family and health to independence and being as independent as possible! I remember the first time I brought up the subject of wanting to be as independent as possible. We were discussing the idea of me moving out and living in the city centre. I was sharing with her my goals, and I said without much thought how I wanted to be completely independent. Sue paused for a moment. I could see she was thinking about what I had just said, and I could see that she disagreed with me. After a brief moment of silence, she asked two questions. What makes someone independent? And was she completely independent? To be honest with you, I was taken aback as I said my goals feeling confident as if that was the answer she wanted, and now I was questioning myself. Deflated is the wrong word, but I was all of a sudden confused.

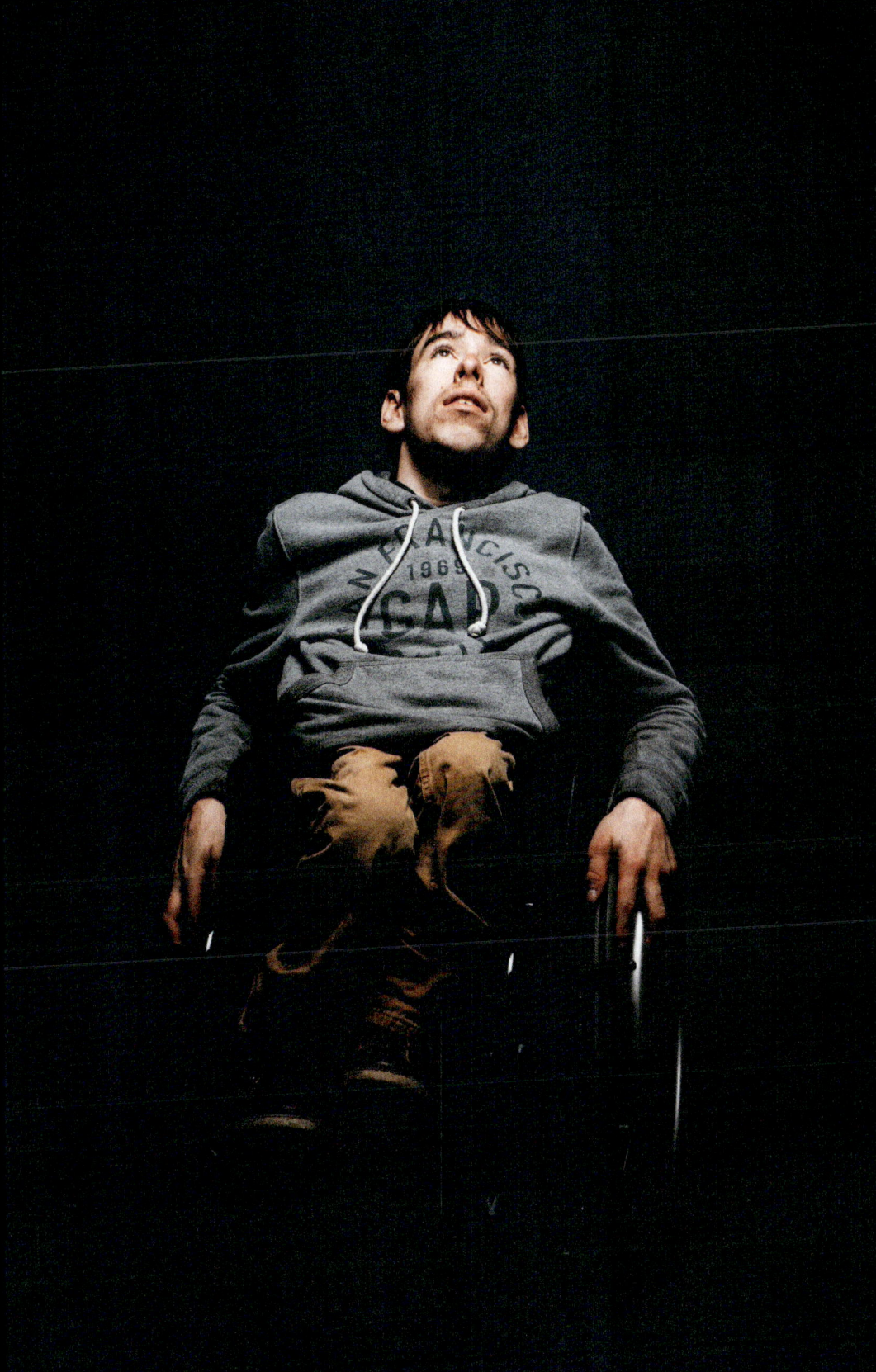

For my whole school life, I thought I needed to be completely independent; every time I asked for help, it was another mark against my name. Today, I sent her a voice note on WhatsApp asking for her opinions on the topic! Her reply, "One should never strive for independence, how lonely that would be." I promise myself that, when writing this book, I will be completely and utterly honest, however painful it would be. I have battled with the idea of independence. My whole life, I have felt like I have failed life because I wasn't entirely independent. I want to say that sense of disappointment gets more manageable. Still, for me personally, it only got worse because I was living with my parents, and we got into a very unhealthy routine.

It became hazardous, and it came to the point where I wanted independence, but I also liked to know that if I didn't do something, my parents would do it for me. I relied too much on my parents and became comfortable with relying on my parents to do pretty much everything that a 25-year-old should be doing him or herself. I was allowing my parents to treat me as a kid still. When it came to reminding me to catheterise or chivvying me along to ensure that I was ready for school or college or preparing for the bus, I remember that my parents and I used to argue and argue. They set an atmosphere in the house that was challenging. After all, I was putting pressure on my parents because I was late for school or college. All meetings and I would be putting pressure on them and depending on them to get me there if I was late for the bus.

There were obviously times when I did have to depend on my parents, especially when it came to cooking or laundry. Our kitchen at home was not accessible. Everything was at a height that I couldn't reach. It was unsafe for me to use the stove or oven without help. I could not get to the cupboards to grab coffee or tea unless my parents were home. To be able to wash the clothes, you'd have to go down a step into the garage. So there were things that I literally could not do alone without support.

I don't think I would be in my flat today if it weren't for eight people. I think I would still be in the same situation in Timsbury. The first person is Sue. Sue, you challenged me that day, making me question what independence looks like. You challenged me about what I could be doing already for myself. You challenged me on several things, and it pains me to say this, but you were right every time. We've known each other for over ten years, and you know how I hate to be proven wrong, but you seem to prove me wrong many times, and I am so grateful for that. You challenged our routine, our daily routine. You challenged both my parents and me on the way we handle situations. You brought my parents and me closer and encouraged us to discuss topics that needed to be addressed. We all had been holding back from talking about it for many years. So thank you for your ongoing support, your guidance and your wisdom. I wouldn't be able to handle life as I am without you.

The second person I want to thank is someone who has helped me over the past four years. They have helped me realise that there will be challenges regardless of our preparation. Everyone has hurdles and challenges. It's normal. Anybody who says that they haven't had a challenge in their life is lying. Alexander, thank you. Thank you for taking the time to hear my dreams for the future. Thank you for helping me articulate my wish to live independently. Thank you for your wisdom and guidance on how I should approach getting a property and getting myself on the housing list. Thank you for your guidance and wisdom in navigating social services and getting a care plan that works for me.

Your knowledge of the system is highly appreciated. I am so grateful for your time, talking to my dad and me and sitting around the table mapping out what life could look like if I lived independently. I still have the card you sent when I first moved into this flat. It reminded me that I could overcome any other challenges because I have network support from family and friends. You helped me overcome the embarrassment of needing support needing help, so thank you. You must come and visit the flat one day. I know it's something that we have been meaning to do for ages. Jonny, Ali, Pete and Fi, thank you for your time, patience and loving support over the last 25 years as I look back at the previous ten years and remember my time at school. Being able to call you despite either being halfway round the world or at work and just having a chat meant a lot. Words can't describe how much it means to me. You challenged and questioned my actions and responsibilities, but you understood my situation. You have a help me grow as a person and helped me develop my passions and values. You have helped me by not seeing me as a disabled person but as a human being. Words can't describe how grateful I am to have you as my siblings.

Mum and dad, I know we've had quite a few challenging moments over the past 25 years, and that's probably a bit of an understatement! Thank you for your patience, wisdom, and unconditional love and for showing me that I can put my mind to it. As I sit here writing in my bedroom in my flat, I can't say that any of us would have thought this would've happened 5 or 6 years ago. With the year that we just had in 2020, you not only made sure that everybody was safe and looked after, but you dealt with a situation that would've been a challenge in regular times. I don't think I ever appreciated how much support you provided during that year. Your patience and willingness to support me while I was on bedrest words can't describe what that meant for me.

I look back at times when, to be honest, I was creating an atmosphere in a house in your home that was everything against your values; for that, I'm sorry. Thank you for challenging me to become a more independent person. Challenging me to problem solve for myself and not rely on you guys to resolve the issues for me. You guys calmly explained what I needed to do. Yet, because I was panicking about being late, I didn't realise it was okay to make mistakes. It's okay to be late for things; how I deal with the situation matters. You helped me learn from the situation to ensure it doesn't happen again next time. I want to say that since moving out, I've gotten better in some areas.

I'm still learning, but you're always there to cheer me on and support me, especially when the system failed in this last year of living on my own. I've been so grateful that we can just hang out and talk rather than worry about medical routines or other stuff that we used to have to worry about daily. It feels like the carer role you had to adopt whilst I was living with you has now been taken away, and our relationship has strengthened. Thank you for everything, for encouraging me to carry on regardless of the hurdles society puts in front of me. An independent life has always been essential in our society.

It promotes confidence and self-esteem as well as motivation and perseverance in school. In addition, it fosters self-reliance, allowing your child to feel they have control over their life. Finally, it gives your child a sense of importance and belonging, essential for building social relationships and contributing to the world. This is a western trend. Personal blame, personal responsibility, and personal success. Freedom of independence, speech, religion, and isolation. Some societies are heavy on interdependence and constraint. It may even take a religious form. And those wishing to escape the interdependencies preventing them from fulfilling their dreams often relocate to America. What is needed is a balance. This balance can be achieved in many places, not just in the US.

But trends can be dangerous, and blindly striving to be independent is dangerous. That is how independence imprisons many people. It can also make the city a lonely place. So we should strive to be interdependent once again. I bet this time we can do better. Everyone would be treated more equal, The law would be more supportive, and few people would be criminalised. All human communities are interdependent, everyone with each other. People produce goods and services in an endlessly interwoven pattern of interdependence and cooperation. As a result, very few humans are capable of living entirely independent of other human beings. We have got it in our heads that interdependent is a swear word and is a sign of weakness rather than strength. As a kid, I loved the story "Jesus Feeds the 5000."

Known as 'The Miracle of the Loaves and Fishes', the miracle of Jesus feeding the 5000 is a famous Christian story. 'The Miracle of the Loaves and Fishes' tells the story of Jesus performing one of his miracles, as he feeds 5000 of his followers with only a few loaves and fishes. The story of Jesus feeding the 5000 is one of the few biblical stories to appear in all four Gospels. This story is famous for children as it teaches the importance of sharing, making the most of what you have, and that Christians must place their trust in God. Even if you don't believe in this story, we have lost the sense of community and sharing communion. We have lost our values and the longing to be together.

Maybe it's just the way I was brought up. Still, I believe we have as a society become so focused on being fully independent and making sure that we can look after ourselves that we forget about the wider community. We fail to make sure that Our friends and neighbours are okay. It's as if we are still stuck in the Victorian age, where we must be seen but not heard, and our emotions cannot be expressed because it makes us look weak. It makes us look as if we are a failure. I long for us to become one community again, alarm for us to be able to ask for help without embarrassment and shame. I long for us to be caring again, looking out for each other. I was naive in 2020, watching off neighbours all step outside and clap for the NHS. I thought; finally, we have decency, compassion and gratitude.

We recognise that people need care, people need help and need support. I've already spoken about my time in the hospital and being on bed rest. I was in a house with my parents, my sister, my nephew and one of my brothers. At that time, I realised that, despite not finding social events easy and challenging to deal with. I realised that I missed the interaction with other people. I missed going out for walks and talking to neighbours, and I missed the interaction. I missed going out for walks and talking to neighbours and interacting with the dog walkers telling me about where they've been. I missed going to the youth club and supporting use in my area.

When we talk about support and care for disabled people, it's not just about medical needs but friendship and interaction. On social media, I follow a couple called Squirmy and Grubs. I must thank my friend James for introducing me to their content on social media. For those who have not seen any of their videos, let me introduce you to them. Shane was born with spinal muscular atrophy, a genetic disorder that causes muscle weakness and wasting because of the loss of motor neurons, which control muscles.

Since he was 2, Shane has been in a wheelchair. Flying with a wheelchair often comes with a sense of apprehension. He met Hannah Aylward after she reached out to him online, and the pair have been in a relationship ever since. The couple even tied the knot in September 2020, but as their romance blossomed, they revealed the abuse and criticism they've received due to their "interabled" relationship. Recently I've been battling with the idea of having to be dependent on people. Now, Squirmy and Grubs recently did a light-hearted, very impactful, 30-second video showing that Shane was not a burden on Hannah and Hannah was not a saint just because she was married to somebody with a disability. Their attitude in life has really helped me over the past few months, remembering that it's okay to ask for help.

This video illustrated that Shane was not a burden on Hannah and that Hannah was not a saint just because she was married to somebody with a disability. Their attitude in life is something that has really helped me over the past few months, remembering that it's okay to ask for help. It's normal to ask for help. We need to get out of the mindset that if we ask for help, we are a burden; that is not true. As I said, I have battled with the idea of not being a burden when I ask for help. My first reaction when asking for help is to apologise, even before I ask for a favour. As Brits, we are great at apologising when we don't need to. My dad has always told me off for phoning him and instantly apologising for calling him.

I think one of the biggest reasons we feel like a burden, even though we are not a burden, is because we have had experiences where we have felt like a burden. Whether it's the bus driver moaning at the fact that he has to get the ramp down so that I can access the bus or the whether it's the bus driver sighing at the fact that he has to get the ramp down so that I can access the bus or the audience members who have to walk upstairs to the concert hall instead of taking the lift, but it's more than that it's those who are sat behind a computer writing comments on social media like "your parents should have aborted you" or " you should commit suicide" or the worst one "you do not participate in society, and you should therefore be dead". These are comments I see on my friends; Facebook pages every day.

No wonder we feel like a burden. The media's portrayal of disability does not help our case in showing that we are all human beings. We will carry that burden for the rest of our lives. We then slowly stop asking for help and struggle to find words when we do ask for help. Why is this dangerous? Let me tell you, in the past six months of my life, I have hardly gone out. I am exhausted from dealing with situations that make me feel worthless and a burden. I'm scared that those who write on Facebook will say these comments in the street. So I lock myself away and don't ask for help unless it is vital. Since moving into my place, I have become more independent. I had not relied on my parents as much as I did when I lived with them.

For example, if I need to attend a doctor's appointment, I will travel to the hospital alone, ensuring I catch the correct bus. I cook on my own, and I organise my food shopping. Yes, I get support cleaning the flat, ensuring that the clean clothes are put away and hanging up any washing in the washing machine. Julien, Thank you for your support, making me laugh so much that I can no longer breathe. I know you won't take this seriously, but I don't think I could manage without your help. The boy's a fool! It is okay to depend on people. We all depend on people, your employer paying your monthly wage, the mechanic fixing your car, the supermarket stocking up on food, and the list goes on and on. No one is independent, it is impossible to be, yet we strive to be and, more importantly, fail to be fully independent. So how do we build on our confidence to ask for help? First, it is being open with friends, colleagues and family where we might need help. Second, we need to build relationships that are real and true. Third, it's remembering that we have every right to live and to be a part of society. Fourth, remind yourself who you are, that you are loved, and that you are here for a purpose. You are not a burden.

You have never been a burden. By the way, I am saying this not just for you but for me. I get so caught up in what is happening online and in the news that I forget who I am, that I am loved and that I am here for a reason. I then feel like a burden relying on the state to provide me with finances. A few years ago, I went on an Independence Weekend away with a charity called Shine. I know what I am about to say will get much backlash from certain people, but this is my opinion. It was great to meet people my age who get me and understand what I am going through. It was great to get support and mentorship during the weekend, and I cannot thank Shine enough for their ongoing support. The one thing I struggled with while being there was some of the parent's attitudes to their situation.

They have been going through a lot of fighting for care, doctor appointments and PIP Assessments. Any parent will fight for their child and wants what is best for their child. My issue was not about fighting the system but complaining and thinking that you were the only person in the situation. A few parents dominated discussions and made the sessions around them rather than their son or daughter. Their language made it sound like the child was a burden because of their disability. It was a situation that upset me deeply and was something that we discussed on the way home. The idea that a parent would make their child feel like a burden is awful. It felt like the only reason they wanted to be there was to get sympathy from the other parents. It felt like the only reason they wanted to be there was to get sympathy from the other parents.

Parents were answering for their son or daughter despite them being over 18 and having a voice of their own. It went from a weekend for the adults with Spina Bifida to a weekend of moaning from some of the parents. I need to be careful not to include all the parents, as many of them were there to support their son or daughter and not interfere with their potential. Why did I go? Because I was not looking after myself, I relied on my parents for everything and did not take responsibility for my life. Let's try to normalise my situation. I am not trying to come up with excuses but to remember that we are all human beings. Most 18-year-olds still live with their parents. Most but not all 18-year-olds take drugs or drink an excessive amount of alcohol. Our brains are wired to take risks. What I was doing or not doing was just as damaging as taking drugs or drinking excessively.

I was not catheterising on time; There was always a smell of urine on my wheelchair and my clothes; I didn't look after my teeth and didn't care enough about my body. I never shaved or showered adequately. I didn't care if I had spots or if I didn't look presentable. I just had given up on my life and had no motivation to change. Why should I change my routine if I have no purpose in life? Once I changed my way, I found my purpose in life. Everything started to fall into place; I felt comfortable having friends and family over. I became organised and was not rushed to get to places. I was doing my medical routines on time and felt confident in myself. My relationships with my family changed. My counselling sessions changed.

We were not discussing the usual topics. I have started not to get so angry at society and realise that I can only control my actions and that I need to live my life without shame and anxiety, and I know who I am. I know what I am capable of and my weaknesses; this does not mean I am a failure. It is okay to ask for help; it does not mean you are a burden. For those who think that us being dependent permits you to talk to us in a patronising way, that is disrespectful and undermining. How would you feel if someone spoke to you in that way?

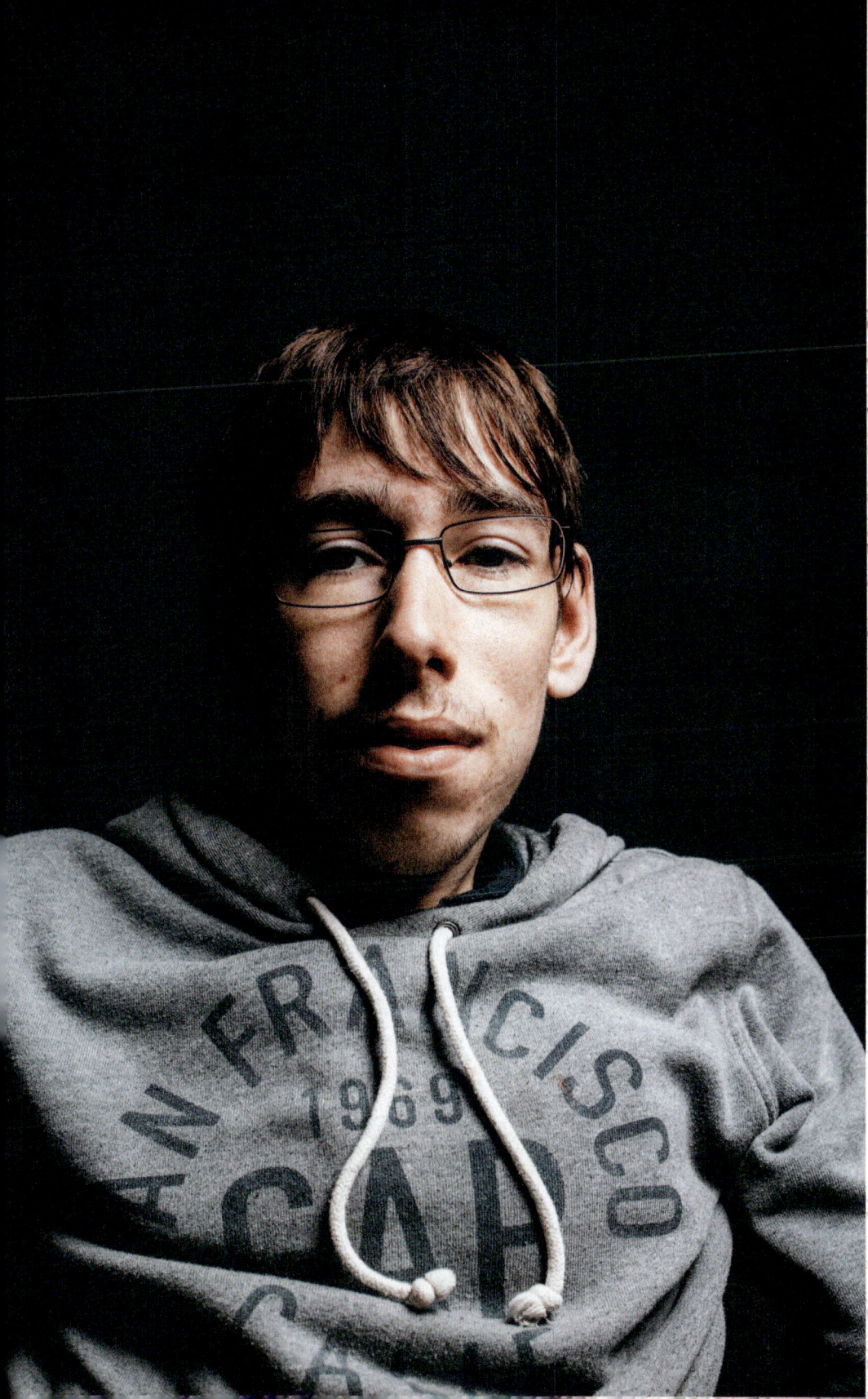

CHAPTER 19

Social Media, The Enemy Of Society

" We need to Social Distance from Social Media."

I am now 25; I am a part of the last generation that remembers life before the iPhone, where if you missed a program on TV, that was it; there was no way of getting it on catch up! The time when if you went out for a coffee with a friend, you actually had to socialise and hold a conversation. If you were using the internet and the landline went, or someone used the landline, then you could say goodbye to accessing anything on the interweb! The last generation that used VHS. Yeah, I'm now officially old! There was no TikTok or Snapchat. There was no WhatsApp, and the idea of video calling was bonkers. If you spoke to your phone, you would probably have many people staring at you. I'm going, to be honest with you I am worried about where society is heading. I don't mean to sound all doom and gloom; however, seven trends in our world now connect together to create a shocking vision of the next two to three years, starting with social media.

Social Media are the platforms that allow us to communicate with our friends and family across the world. The platforms let us share photos of us sunbathing on a beach in San Francisco. The platforms that help us share memories, the platforms that make us feel popular every birthday. What's not to love about social media? I want to talk about six key topics I have come across on social media that have led to me coming off all social media platforms.

A) How Social Media has affected my Physical Health

B) How Social Media has affected my Mental Health

C) The impact of Social Media on Violence online

D) The impact of Social Media on Hate Crimes

E) How Social Media affects Society

F) How You Can Help Prevent It

How does social media affect my physical health? I check social media from the moment I wake up until the moment I go to bed. I'm checking messages on Twitter, Facebook and Instagram. I'm not on TikTok or Snapchat, nor did I have Myspace or Bebo. I am glued to my phone or computer, and this affects my medical routine, my diet and my fitness. I choose to scroll instead of going to sleep or completing the tasks I need to do. I have had infection after infection because I have decided to see what Joe Blogs has done over the weekend or look at my friend's holiday snaps from their trip to Spain.

In pursuit to attract maximum user attention, app developers distort time by affecting the "flow" of content when scrolling. This distortion makes it difficult for users to recognise the amount they spend on social media. Principles similar to Skinner's variable ratio conditioning can be established with the irregular dispersal of rewarding reinforcements in an unforeseeable stream of "bad" content. This makes it challenging to eliminate behavioural training. Behavioural training is also carried out via the standard "autoplay" of streaming platforms. The more consumed the viewer is, the more time distortion occurs, making it challenging to stop watching.

This is combined with minimal time to cancel the next stream, which creates a false sense of urgency, followed by an absorbent relief. What I think is just 10 minutes on social media is actually 2 or 3 hours. I'm not looking at anything in particular and never post on my personal pages. Investing time in social media platforms creates an emotional connection with the virtual environment the user creates. The user values this above its actual value, which is called endowment effect. The more time a person spends curating their presence on social media, the more difficult it is for them to give up social media, as they have placed emotional value on this virtual existence above their actual value. Users are more likely to lose aversion to this fund. As a result, they are less willing to stop using social media.

This is also exacerbated by the mere exposure of the user to the respective platforms. This exposure effect suggests that repeated exposure by the user to a particular stimulus leads to an improved or unimproved attitude toward it. With social media, repetitive exposure to platforms improves the perspective of the user on them. The advertising industry has recognised this potential, but has rarely used it because of its belief in an inherent conflict between excessive exposure and familiarity. The more a user becomes exposed to a social media platform, the more he or she likes to use it. This makes the removal of social media problematic, and underscores the contribution of social media to the addictive nature of social media. Social media has developed expectations of immediate immediacy, which then generates social pressure.

A study of the social tensions created by WhatsApp's instant messaging platform showed that the "Last Seen" feature contributed to the expectation of a quick response. This feature serves as an "automatic approximation of availability," which refers to a time frame in which the sender is aware that the recipient will respond, and similarly a time frame in which the recipient must respond without causing tensions in his relationship. This is also evident in WhatsApp's "Read Receipt" (in the form of ticks).

The nudge of a double tick underscores the reception of the message; therefore, the sender is aware that the recipient probably has seen the message. The recipient would feel pressure to respond quickly, fearing to violate the sender's expectations. Since both sides know the working mechanics of the Last Seen and Read Receipt features, social pressure is generated on the speed of reaction. This effect is linked to the addictive nature of the features, as it provides a possible explanation for frequent checking for notifications. It was also proposed to undermine well-being.

Google is the first technology company to adopt the personalisation of user content. The company does this by tracking: "search history, click history, location on Google and other websites, language search query, choice of web browser and operating system, social connections, and time taken to make search decisions." Facebook similarly adopted this method in recording user endorsement through "Like" and reacted options. Facebook's personalisation mechanics are so precise that they can track the mood of its users. The overall effect is that it creates "exciting, personalised websites" tailored to each user, which leads to more time online and further increases the likelihood that the user develops addictive or problematic behaviour with social media.

The "Like" mechanism is another example of social media's problematic features. It is a social cue visually representing the user's social validation, either given or received. One study explored the quantifiable and qualitative effects of the "Like" button on the social endorsement.

The study asked 39 adolescents to submit their own Instagram photos alongside neutral and risky images, which were then reproduced into a testing app that controlled the number of likes the picture would initially receive before testing. The result found adolescents were likelier to endorse risky and neutral photo images if they had more likes. Furthermore, the study suggested that adolescents were more inclined to perceive a qualitative effect of the photos depending on the strength of peer endorsement. Whilst "quantifiable social endorsement is a relatively new phenomenon," this study suggests the effects of the "Like" option as a social cue on adolescents.

Another study, which examined different types, assessed three modalities (social interaction, simulation and search for relationships) and two genders (male and female) whether self-esteem contributed to Facebook use in the context of a social comparison variable. Men were found to have a less social comparison orientation between the tested contribution, but their self-esteem and time on Facebook were found to have a harmful link. For women, social comparison was the main factor in the relationship between self-esteem and Facebook use: women with low self-esteem seem to spend more time on Facebook to compare themselves to others and possibly increase their self-esteem, as social comparison serves the function of self-enhancement and self-improvement

In accordance with the individual characteristics tested, the study highlights the tendency to compare socially and its relationship with self-esteem and the length of Facebook use. The Zeigarnik effect suggests that the human brain will continue to pursue an unfinished task until a satisfactory end. The permanent nature of social media platforms influences this effect, as they prevent the user from "finishing" scrolling, thereby developing an unconscious desire to continue and "finish" the task. The Ovsiankina effect is similar to what it suggests, suggesting a tendency to take an unfinished or interrupted action.

The "brief, fast-moving give and take" of social media subverts the satisfying closure and creates the need to continue with the intention of producing a satisfying closure. Platforms consist of unfinished and interruptible mechanisms that influence these two effects. Whilst a tool of social media platforms, it is more clearly seen with Freemium games like Candy Crush Saga. Studies have shown differences in motivation and behavioural patterns between social media platforms, especially in terms of their problematic use. A survey of 1,479 people aged 14 to 24 in the UK compared the psychological benefits and deficits of the five most prominent social media platforms. The adverse effects of smartphone use include phubbing, which snubs someone by checking their smartphone in the middle of a real-life conversation.

The study was used to investigate the direct and indirect associations of neuroticism, trait anxiety and fear of missing out on phubbing through state fear of missing out on Instagram and problematic use of Instagram. A total of 423 adolescents and young adults aged 14 to 21 (53% female) participated in the study. The results showed that women had significantly higher levels of phubbing, fear of missing out, problematic Instagram use, trait anxiety, and neuroticism. Inappropriate use of social media (PSMU) presented in the study, which also invested in the influence of demographics and Big Five personality dimensions on social media use motives; demographics and use explanations on social media preferences; and demographics, personality, popular social media sites, and social media use motive explanations on PSMU.

The study consisted of 1008 undergraduate students between 17 and 32 years of age between 17 and 32 years of age. Participants who preferred Instagram, Snapchat, and Facebook reported higher problematic social media use rates. The study concluded that YouTube was the only platform with a net positive rating based on 14 health and well-being questions, followed by Twitter, Facebook, Snapchat, and Instagram. Instagram had the lowest rating: it was identified as having some positive effects, such as self-expression, self-identity and community, but ultimately outweighed by its negative effects on sleep, body image and "fear of missing out."

A three-week study on the limitation of social media use was conducted on 108 female and 35 male students at the University of Pennsylvania. Before the analysis, participants had to have Facebook, Instagram, and Snapchat accounts on an iPhone device. This study observed the well-being of the student by sending a questionnaire at the beginning of the experiment and at the end of each week. Students were asked questions about their well-being on the scale of: "social support," "fear of missing out," "loneliness," "anxiety," "depression," "self-esteem," and "autonomy and self-acceptance".

The study concluded that limiting social media use on a mobile phone to 10 minutes per platform per day significantly affected well-being. Loneliness and depressive symptoms decreased within the group with limited use of social media. Students with depressive symptoms had a much higher impact on social media restrictions when they started with higher depression.So why have I said that social media is the enemy of society? So why have I said that social media is the enemy of society? Despite everything I've just said, which should be enough to answer that question, it's how media has affected society and affected people with disabilities. I am all for free speech; I am all for having a voice throughout this book.

I have been telling you we need a voice. Every person on earth needs a voice in this world, and we will not change society unless we have a voice; we can talk and share our views, or we can listen to each other. If social media was all about connecting and keeping in touch with friends and family, and I'm on for that, like I said, I'm on WhatsApp. I'm on Twitter, Instagram and Facebook now because I care about what is happening, but to be able to connect and keep in touch with those who I don't get to see on a weekly basis.

If that was just a way to talk to family and friends, sign me up, but it's not just about connecting and staying in touch with family and friends. It's become a weapon of destruction. It's become a weapon to say what you like, without having to see the person you're directing that comment to. You do not see the reaction. There are feelings behind the post that you've just written. Social media is vicious and dangerous. The number of friends I have on Facebook who send me screenshots of random strangers, sending them messages on social media, telling them that their parents should have aborted them or that their life is worthless, that they should be locked up in their homes so that the rest of society can carry on with life as normal.

This is wrong; this is hate crime at its worst. This is why I do not enjoy social media. There is always and will always be a Dark side to search media, so this part of the chapter is dedicated to those who have the power to those who can change social media. This is a warning. This is not a prophecy, but the reality is already happening today and is far worse than anybody can imagine. I know the people who need to hear this will not be reading this book, but this is for those considering going into the industry. I was watching a video about social media by a YouTuber called Mrwhosetheboss.

I have to admit he was the guy who inspired me to write this chapter, because his views on the way society and social media are the same as mine. It is no secret that certain social media companies are exploring the idea of us entering a virtual reality world. This is wrong on so many levels. I know I've got friends who are excited about this whole virtual reality world concept, but I'm terrified. I am nervous for three main reasons. Firstly, this will give the big businesses the next excuse not to make their shops and buildings wheelchair accessible. I can see it now; companies like HMV and Costa will say we won't change anything, because you can visit us using virtual reality. If we get into that mindset even at this stage, the following argument will be that we can access everything that is easing virtual reality.

Then let's include the 6 pm curfew. The 6 pm curfew will be my following book guarantee because I could write not just one chapter on the 6 pm curfew for many chapters. Let me explain why the 6 pm curfew is so dangerous, and how it came about because it was one random stranger on social media, and it just exploded, and other people joined in with this one random tweet. The 6 pm curfew means those with physical, mental, and developmental disabilities will have to be in their homes by 6 pm in bed, tucked up with hot cocoa. This will allow everyone else in society to use disabled parking to be able to visit the shopping centres, cafes, bars and cinemas without the anxiety of socialising with somebody with a disability. It's a hard life having to talk to somebody with a disability, isn't it?!

It's a hard life having to walk an extra hundred metres to where you want to go, isn't it?! It's a hard life to walk up those stairs rather than using the lift, isn't it?! You poor guys are having to cater to every need. I am so sorry. The sad thing is that if these people read this part of the book, they would use it as ammunition to strengthen their argument for the 6 pm curfew. These pesky disabled people spend our taxes on wheelchairs. They get us to help pay their bills, using hard-working taxpayers' money. Why on earth would we want to help and support them? And these conversations happen on social media every day. When I talk about this to my friends and family, they are shocked and horrified at these posts.

They do not understand why people would be making these posts. They don't understand why these conversations are happening, and yet it's because of these conversations. It's because of these hate comments that we all get as people with disabilities that bring anxiety around us and prevent us from wanting to go out of the front door. For many years, I had anxiety about going out because I didn't want to approach anybody with that mindset. I have seen with my own two eyes what it does to people when they see posts that tell them that they should have been aborted, that they are not loved, but they are not accepted in today's society.

I'm guilty of believing his lies. It's difficult not to believe what somebody says about you. When you see it written down, it is difficult not to believe something. You know in the back of your mind that it's not true, that you are loved, and you are accepted for who you are, but that little voice is drowned out by the bigger voice of the lies that come from social media. When I originally planned to write this book, I didn't really know what I was going to say. My plan wasn't really to go down the spiritual route, which I feel like with every topic that I have spoken about, the one thing that has really helped me is my faith in God. Knowing that I am loved, knowing that I am here for a purpose, and whether you believe in God or not, we all know that we are here for a purpose.

Whether it's acting or whether it's being an artist, musician or comedian, we are all here for a reason for purpose. For many years I was looking for that purpose, that longing to belong to society. when you're in school when you're growing up in life it actually sort of matters to people how you look and then it matters to you because it matters to others. The fear that we have is that we are going to be alone. that we're not good enough and you know we have to change ourselves. Many individuals at school constantly belittled me, and I had peers approach me with hurtful comments like, "Hey Sim, you look so strange, and nobody really wants to be your friend. You can't do this, and you can't do that." I felt helpless, unable to change my circumstances.

It wasn't as simple as fixing my appearance one day to make everything right, nor could I suddenly wake up with functional legs. The weight of people's criticism took a toll on me, causing me to start believing that I was inadequate and a failure. I began to doubt whether I could ever be someone others would like or accept, and it was an incredibly difficult time. I questioned my purpose in life, unable to partake in activities like playing soccer, riding a bike, or skateboarding like everyone else. Depression crept in as I wondered if life had any meaning for me beyond living to die. I had so many unanswered questions, and I asked my parents and doctors why this had happened, but they couldn't provide a satisfactory answer.

Some things in life are beyond our control, and we must make a choice: give up or persevere. I want to ask you, without that sense of belonging, you may start believing the lies that you're worthless and that you don't deserve to live, as if you're unwelcome on this Earth. For many years, I believed I didn't have a reason to live. I thought I'd be better off not existing due to hurtful social media posts, even though they weren't directed at me personally but affected my friends and the wider disability community. It's perplexing why social media companies don't take this issue more seriously. I've considered leaving all social media platforms because they have a detrimental impact on my mental health and social life.

They also affect my job search since, if people on social media believe I should die, why would any company hire me? But then I remind myself that I am loved, and I have a purpose. Those individuals online who receive more attention than they deserve are just a minority. They are not the majority, the majority of society is loving, compassionate, and caring and fighting for change. So I beg to those who have the power to change social media, to help us become more accepted. Help us to feel loved, to feel like we have a voice. This is not me being woke or trying to cancel culture. This is me trying to be part of today's culture and today's society. This is me trying to build a voice for the many millions of voices that are not being heard today on social media.

CHAPTER 20

Are We Unreliable?

"Don't doubt your faith; doubt your doubts for they are unreliable."

T B Joshua

I have many weaknesses, and all of us have weaknesses that make us in some way unreliable. Our society tends to focus more on our weaknesses and inabilities than on our strengths and abilities as individuals. There is a tendency for us to see the inability in one area and automatically assume that they are not able to do anything else. It is difficult for me to stay organised, manage my time and deal with administration. There are two parts to this problem, one of which I have already discussed, but the other is my executive dysfunction disorder, which contributes to the problem.

Hydrocephalus, also known as Executive Disfunction Disorder (EDD), is a neurological disorder. Although I am aware of my hydrocephalus, my friends and colleagues have not always been aware of the side effects, as I have kept it secret from them. This has led me to take on responsibilities that I know are outside my skill set. My biggest downfall, even more than the lack of organisation, is my enthusiasm and optimism. Enthusiasm and optimism are great traits to have, as long as you can also be realistic and have an honest discussion with your friends and colleagues about what might be difficult for you. Now, I am only talking from experience, my struggles to come to terms with what my limitations are and how, as soon as I opened up about my struggles with certain tasks, it showed what my abilities were. I want to first of all talk about what goes through my head when I am asked to help with a project, organisation or charity. I get a real motivation boost and adrenaline rush.

I used to get these a lot when I was a child, even if my teacher asked me to take the register back or to take a message to the staffroom. It's the sense of feeling valued in a world where you are not meant to be valued if you are deemed to be damaged goods. As I got into my late teens, I didn't go out partying, I never took drugs (unless they were prescribed!), I have never gambled...Except for my health, I was pretty good. I did, however, have many "Projects" that I loved to do. These projects were all to raise awareness of various disability topics, such as hate crime, disability sports or lack of media representatives. I wanted to change society on my own, and building a team for these projects was out of the question. Why? Because I was selfish, and building a team meant sharing responsibility, but also sharing achievements, I didn't like that. I wanted to show that I was capable of everything and that my disability didn't affect my life.

The truth is that none of us can do everything. If we could do everything, then how boring and unsociable would that be? "There is no I in Team", Jen and Mike would always say to us at training. We all have our strengths and weaknesses, and we need to allow others to showcase their talents. It goes back to what I was talking about independence. How boring would it be if we were able to do everything? I can only talk about my own experience, so please do not presume this for everyone with a disability. I felt like I had to work harder and do more than most to counterbalance my disability.

I thought if I did everything myself, I could prove that I was just as capable as Joe Blogs down the road. The issue with that mindset is that Joe Blogs might be great at running a business, but might be rubbish at building a website or handling social media pages. I cared more about how society saw me than how God saw me. I wanted to break down the barriers that society has created. There is nothing wrong with breaking down barriers; it is a great quality to have. If you know something needs changing, but you don't have the drive to see change, then nothing will transform, and we will always be stuck in the same place. Inequality will increase, and this cancelled culture will take control of society.

You need to understand that I am not putting all the blame on society but on myself. I overpromise and under-deliver. I try to counterbalance my inabilities by over-exaggerating my abilities. I downplay the weaknesses and challenges that come with my conditions. It goes back to when I was talking about using the disability card. I am so scared to share about the challenges that come with my condition, just in case it comes across as an excuse and an easy way to get out of situations. My heart and my head would not communicate with each other at all. My heart would say stop, slow down, pause, get people on board, and my head would override these feelings. Before I knew it, I was in deep financial difficulties and owing people and organisations money that I clearly did not have. I quickly got out of sync with my standing orders and created new payment arrangements before considering if I could even afford to pay for them.

My heart was always in the right place, but my head was always five steps ahead of where it should be. So the question is, how do I become more reliable? Without sounding cliche, honesty is always the best policy. Being honest with people about what you can and cannot do will stop expectations from being raised, will stop you from feeling pressured and overwhelmed, and will allow you time to work on what you might find difficult. We also need to be honest about our strategies for completing tasks. For me, I need someone who can hold me accountable. I'm not talking about employment, but also my personal care. At the moment, I don't have anyone outside my family who can hold me accountable. Because I am not in employment at the moment, I do not have structure to my day. I don't go to an office, and I don't have deadlines. So when someone asks me to help them do a website or run their social media page, I don't have the confidence to share what I find difficult and what needs to be put in place to allow me to complete the work.

The fear is that they will label me unreliable and think it is too much trouble to provide support. The stereotypical disabled person is unreliable due to the number of times they visit the hospital, the hassle of organising support and is not flexible. The truth is that today's system contributes to us being less flexible. Throughout this book, I have highlighted changes that need to be made to allow us to become more involved in society, whether it's public transport, making roads and pavements more accessible or improving NHS Services. I said at the beginning of this book I have Hydrocephalus. Hydrocephalus is a disability that sometimes gets mistaken as a disability that comes with Spina Bifida. It doesn't! Hydrocephalus is when Cerebrospinal fluid (CSF) builds up and surrounds the brain. For someone without Hydrocephalus, the CSF can be absorbed into their bloodstream.

However, for someone with Hydrocephalus, the fluid needs to be transported using a shunt that helps the fluid flow into the stomach. This of course means that there are side effects that affect processing information and staying organised. This does not make me unreliable unless I don't talk about it and allow people to ask me to do things that stretch my ability to process and stay organised. This means I let people down because I have not been honest with what I find difficult. Honesty is the best policy, to be honest with others you first need to be honest with yourself. I think most professionals who have supported me over the years and even my family and closest friends would tell you I am very good a hiding things. It is not that I am lying but I am not providing all of the information. What I have learnt is that the truth, the whole truth always comes out in the end.

I am very good at hiding things, it is as one of my friends would say one of my most enduring qualities. If you put me in a room with any professional I can answer any question that will tick the box. The questions are so vague that I can just bend the truth. In a court of law, this would be misleading the court AKA lying! Okay, so I need to work out my defence because if you look at the facts and evidence I am guilty of lying and anything I say would be well increasing my sentence. The truth is I have no defence, I have no excuse and all I have are excuses that would not hold up in court. So for the rest of the chapter, I am going to tell you the truth about why I twist the stories in my favour. In Genesis 3:9 says

> "But the Lord God called to the man, Where are you?"

For a long time, I read that line and presumed it was some kind of hide-and-seek game. What I need to remember is if I truly believe in what the bible says then I also need to remember that god knows where we are. He is watching over us, so what did he mean when he asked Adam where they were? He knew they were hiding because they were feeling the guilt. You need to remember they have just eaten from the tree that they were told was cursed and forbidden. He was asking them the question to see if they knew where they were in their hearts. John Newton spent his childhood and his early adulthood at sea with his father after his mother died when he was only seven. During his time at sea, he was beaten with a whip for attempted desertion from the Royal Navy and captivity by a slave trader in West Africa. Once released he became a captain of a slave ship.

In 1754 he gave up the slave trade and worked with William Wilberforce to end the slave trade. After working in Liverpool as a tide-surveyor he started studying for the ministry. He was ordained in the Church of England. Whilst in the ministry he started to write hymns and contributed to 280 hymns including "Amazing Grace". The song is a proclamation of the promises god has made.

Newton wrote the words from personal experiences. Over the years the hymn has been used in other worship songs including Broken Vessels by Hillsong and Amazing Grace (My Chains Are Gone) by Chris Tomlin. The hymn grew in popularity when a revival broke out in America in the early 19th Century with people like Elvis Presley singing the hymn during his concerts. To this day the song is sung not just in churches but in secular settings. The hymn has become a song that inspires hope in the wake of tragedy.

In 2020 when we were all dealing with the pandemic I watched a video on YouTube of Andrea Bocelli singing this beautiful hymn. The video was titled Amazing Grace: Music For Hope. Bocelli is one of the most famous Tenor singers. He was born visually impaired and at the age of 12, he became completely blind. Here is a man in his 60s completely blind singing live From Duomo di Milano the lyrics "I once was lost, but now I'm found, Was blind but now I see." I was overwhelmed with emotions as I sat watching the video. Something started to happen, and my longing for change shifted. I no longer felt angry but excited as I was on a journey of discovery.

The mission was simple to find out who was Simeon Wakely. At that stage, it is clear Simeon is a disabled person, a basketball player but that is about it. For 20 years I thought his identity was clear but after looking at evidence it was clear Simeon was not who I thought he was. He was a lot more than that. He is a son, a brother, a nephew, a cousin and an uncle. I realised if I wanted to be like Ade or Tanni. If I wanted to have the confidence like Nick Vujicic I would need to firstly be honest with myself. However, because I had been living this fake version for so long I forgot who I truly was. This is when the journey of discovery started. I'm not sure about you but I will do anything I can to get out of awkward situations and conversations.

If I know I am in trouble I would try to misdirect so that they forget what they needed to talk to me about. I will prolong the conversation so that people then don't have the time to have the conversation. This is something I am trying to stop. I am trying to stop saying everything is fine when it isn't. I am trying to ask for help when I am struggling. The issue is and it is a big issue, my head wants to accept help but my mouth seems to say the complete opposite and decline help. I am known for being stubborn. A close friend of mine jokes that the only word I know is no. I am great at saying no, I feel safe when I say no. I feel in control of my life if I say no. I say no even if my head and heart are saying yes. If I accept help then I am even more disabled and have even less control of my life.

Before I carry on with this chapter I just need you to understand one thing. What I am about to say I have never ever discussed with anyone. I am going, to tell the truth however difficult it is to hear. It is going to be difficult for me to share as this has been bottled up inside for over a decade. I know I am not the only one who has felt like this, I hope and pray that if you are going through the same stuff then you can have the courage to share with your family and friends. I have had to learn this the hard way and trust me you don't want to go the path I have been down. I am so grateful to my parents and my family for not making me feel like a burden. I know I have not made it at all easy and the sacrifices that they have had to make to help and support me is indescribable. No words can explain how much it means to me.

I have in the past felt like a burden. My family has never made me feel like a burden but I have felt like a burden because of situations in which I have found myself. A few years ago my dad signed us up to go to a weekend away with a charity that supports people with Spina Bifida and Hydrocephalus. The conference was all about independence and how to become more independent while overcoming the challenges that come with having Spina Bifida and Hydrocephalus. I have already spoken at length about both those conditions and so I will not bore you anymore. Up to this point, I have looked back at this event as a waste of time. Up to this point, I thought I had not learnt anything from that weekend.

There were five points I learned that have shaped who I am today. It is because of these lessons that have shaped the past 3 years and why I am as stubborn as I am. It is the reason why I am so worried about what people think of me. It is the reason why I am so sharp and cautious with social care professionals. It does not excuse my behaviour when I get angry with them. I get angry because I see my friends and they don't need to have the extra support that I need. I know I should not compare myself with others but I do. I have a very high standard for myself and it is to show others what I am capable of. I don't want people thinking that I am either only able to be in the Paralympics or I am housebound with 24/7 care. I have lost count of the many times I have been asked if I play sports and if I was in the Paralympics. I'm not sure if that is a compliment on my skill level or a complete disrespect and insult to the many Paralympic athletes who train day in and day out.

I am thinking the latter. I do not have the skill, strength or discipline to ever represent the UK in the Paralympics. I enjoy playing for my local basketball team Bath Romans. As a child, I dreamt of being in the Paralympics but now I am in my mid-20s I am less interested in playing and more about showcasing the heartfelt stories of the athletes. I have, as always gone way off topic and I have managed to wander on to a different path. As I mentioned there have been five main takeaways from that weekend away. There is so much I want to say about each point. As always I am only sharing my opinions and experiences.

1) Parents
2) Social Care
3) The Spectrum
4) Unsung Heroes
5) The Cotton Wool Syndrome

I have been staring at the screen now for about 30 seconds with my hands hovering over the keyboard. When I am nervous about saying things that I know will offend people I try to go around the subject and find ways to get out of a conversation. I can't do that with the book. There is no hiding or getting around this. I am, however, going to stress that this is not about all parents. I have met some amazing parents who do not wrap their kids in cotton wool, and they will do everything in their power to help their sons or daughters achieve their dreams, no matter what their abilities are.

They do this without complaining. They do this without making their child feel like a burden. I need to stop here for a second and I need to talk to you about a couple who did exactly this. They brought up two boys with disabilities without making them feel like a burden. They dealt with challenges that I will never ever understand with grace and patience. They encouraged their sons to be themselves and to strive to be their best.

They have spent hours sometimes days and weeks in hospital looking after their youngest son. They have done all of this while raising three other children., looking after seven grandkids and working relentless hours building relationships with churches across the city. I am of course talking about my parents. They have never seen my wheelchair before me. They have always challenged me to be as independent as possible. They have been my inspiration (Not that I have ever told them that). We have had our arguments like any kids with their parents. I would not be where I am today without them. I have never ever seen them complain or moan at a situation. They are the most gracious and understanding. They have had to take on an extra role as my carers. This is a role most parents don't take on and nothing ever will prepare you for that role.

There is no handbook for raising a child with a disability. If there is then I am sorry but it should be shredded and burned. These support groups for parents are great and parents can share their experiences and talk about the challenges. These support groups are a great way to meet others and to get advice when it comes to wheelchairs and medical equipment. I want to share with you about three groups of parents. All have their merits and flaws. The first group of parents are those who will do anything to support their child. They will make sure that their child is in the best education and will not be scared to say when something is not working. They will get carers to help with personal care.

There is nothing wrong with this approach and if it is done properly then it can sometimes be the best solution. It prevents the parent from becoming a carer and allows them to just be a parent. Unfortunately, I have yet to see it work. I have seen situations when the carers know the child better than the parent. I have seen situations where there is no relationship between the parent and the child. The carer is there to wake the child, get the child ready for school, meet the child after school, prepare their meal and get them ready for bed. When it comes to the weekend the carer is always with the child so there is no quality time with the parents.

I have no issue with getting a care agency involved to help with personal care. I do have an issue with parents using it as a get-out clause to spend time with their children. I have seen families fall out and prodigal sons and daughters leave because they feel abandoned and unloved. As I write this I am now wondering if this is the reason I have been rejecting extra support. I don't want to be one of those kids who has an unhealthy relationship with their parents, because I have seen the drastic version I wanted to go the complete opposite. This then presents a situation that is even more dangerous and life-threatening. If I am going to be completely honest I have abused myself both physically and mentally for over a decade and I should not be here. God hasn't finished writing my story.

We hear every day that the system is broken, we hear every day that we are in a society that is broken. We hear every day that our beloved NHS is falling apart. During the weekend away these statements were being said left, right and centre. These statements were not being said by those with disabilities but by their parents. Scrap all of that, it was not said by every parent but only a couple of parents. They have obviously been hurt by the system, and they have had to fight for their child. The problem was that they were in their own bubble and thought they were the only person dealing with these issues. They dominated the discussions and kept interrupting the sessions. Put aside the fact that they were dominating the discussions and trying to base the sessions on their situation. How do you think the child feels when all they hear is their parents complaining?

They become so fixated on their disability and their limitations that they start to think that they are a burden, that they are a waste of space. They will lack confidence and will have no ambitions. They will become shy and will not speak for themselves. They will allow their parent to be their voice. I have seen this happen way too many times and I have never seen it end well. Parents feel alone because their friends fade away due to the constant negativity. I am by the way not saying that it is easy for the parents. Raising a child with a disability opens up a wide range of challenges that no parent should encounter. All I am saying is there is a way to express how you are feeling and that the situation you are dealing with is not just unique to you. There are others who are in the same boat, dealing with the exact same stuff as you.

You do not need to go on Facebook and post about how awful your life is because your child is not "acting" like other kids or that you have to spend your boxing day helping them build their Lego set. When parents tell me stories and try to get the sympathy card I turn it around and tell them it is amazing that they can do stuff with their kids when most teenagers don't want to engage with their child. I am off social media as I said earlier. A lot of the parents I had as friends on Facebook had children with disabilities. I got fed up seeing them complain that their child was clingy or was wanting to watch the same movie night after night.

I understand it is stressful for parents when they are tired and they have to tread carefully just in case their child has a massive tantrum and starts shouting to get everyone to shut up. Sorry mum and dad! I am not a parent but imagine if your child heard what you say about them behind their back about things that they cannot help. Imagine how they would feel. On the same subject, I need to mention another point that I did not list. The general public. The majority are great and see the person before they see the disability. There are some members however that I need to single out. The members praise the person for doing a mundane task like ordering a coffee or just wheeling up the street. You know who you are.

I am talking about members who think it is appropriate to praise others for being friends with someone with a disability. It is as if it is a brave thing to do. I suppose my friends are brave to hang out with me as I have one of the worst disabilities that cannot be controlled. It is called **BDJ** Syndrome and the main symptom is that at any time I can send friends really really bad dad jokes. The worse the better. When I find something funny I will laugh until I cannot breathe. If I need cheering up I call a close friend who is an encyclopaedia of bad jokes. His favourite one is what do you call a sick bird? Illegal! I told you it was bad. He has the ability to make the conversation sound serious and then hit you with a joke and for some reason, I always end up being the punchline.

Right swiftly moving on, with your permission I want to answer points two, three, four and five together as they all interlink. I have already talked a bit about social care but I want to talk more about the fantastic work they do and what I have seen over the past few years. As always I need to stress that each person will have a different experience and every county in the UK has a different system just to make things more interesting. I was about to write that I am going to be putting some myths to bed once and for all but that is a bit too ambitious even for me. Just because I have a social worker or a direct payment PA it does not mean I cannot talk for myself. Just because I sometimes have district nurses coming in a couple of times a week it does not and will never mean I am housebound. Just because I have an adapted flat it does not mean I need a carer with me 24/7. Is that clear enough?! I want to talk about social services, the district nurses, the Occupational therapists, the Physios and the tissue viability nurses who have supported me over the last few years. No words can describe how grateful I am for your support. Coming to my flat every week and helping me with pressure sores, continence issues and making sure I have the correct care package. I know I have never made it easy for you, and I can only apologise. You never ever get the credit that you deserve. You are always short-staffed and working overtime. I can honestly say without you guys I would not be here today to tell the story!

Okay, so now that I have said all of those nice things, let me get into why, despite all of the great and wonderful people who spend every hour of their day looking after sick and vulnerable people, the system that is currently in place is detrimental to my work, social, and family life. When I talk about the system in this context I am talking about the protocols and guidelines. It is about the rules and regulations that have been put into place to safeguard both the health professionals and the patients. These protocols may seem pretentious but looking back at my own life these protocols have saved my life multiple times.

The system, the foundation of our social care sector was fit for purpose in the 1990s. The advancement of medical equipment has evolved over time but the protocols and the structure of the sector have not. Now I am talking from a patient's point of view. I am in my mid-20s, and I am mentally able to work. Work for me is not about the salary but playing my part in society. I do not feel comfortable with the state paying my bills. My ethos is and always has been if you can work you should be looking for work. I am not saying for one moment that every disabled person should be in work and if it is going to be detrimental to their health then they should not be forced into work. This might feel like I am going off-topic here again but hear me out. It feels like there are a group of people who see wealth as a swear word.

They see people who are earning millions of pounds as negative and demonic. We have rightly associated money with greed and while there is truth to that statement I also believe that if you have a good work ethic and you have worked up the ladder then you should be recognised for that. I say all of this while only having £0.01 in my bank account. Thanks a lot, Jeff Bezos! It feels like the system is still in the era where if you're disabled then the only option is for the state to pay for everything. Again, I say all of this knowing that I am going to be shot tomorrow because that is a very controversial statement.

The system sees the disability and decides ah this needs a case number. Case numbers are more crippling than the disability. The truth is we all have case numbers even if we do not realise it. In fact, we have many case numbers. Case numbers are a great way to categorise people and to put society into the boxes according to their case numbers. The majority of case numbers are harmless and give us the freedom to drive cars, access free healthcare, and gain access to certain venues like bars and clubs. Case numbers are just another way to identify you. The current social care system uses this to work out what care package you require. It allows all of the professionals who are a part of your care plan to keep up to date with what is happening. This system can be accessed by most health professionals. As a patient, you have every right to access these notes as they are of course about you.

Growing up I have always been told by many consultants, GPs and healthcare professionals that I am a complicated, unique and sometimes difficult case. I am never sure if I should take that as a compliment or not. I am 100% unique but so is everyone. We can share DNA and we can share some of the same interests but everyone in the world is unique. Our lives are unique, nobody has the same life. We can share experiences but nobody is going to experience the exact same thing in the exact same way at the exact same time. Our lives can all be complicated. Messy relationships, unemployed, being forced to relocate.

Everyone has their own challenge and if you say you have no challenges either at work or in your personal life then congrats on digging a deep enough grave to hide everything. We are all humans, we all go through challenges and we all have hurdles to jump over. My challenges are no greater than what Joe Bloggs is dealing with down the road. I have in the past thought my challenges were the most important and that nobody else was dealing with a greater challenge. The truth is what I have to deal with daily is nowhere near as important or as difficult as a parent who has lost their child or who has been told that they have a few days left to live. So what has this all got to do with being reliable? My current challenges are of course all to do with my health. These are all repercussions of my actions. I am in this position because of my actions and my actions alone. There is nobody else to blame for the challenges I have faced over the years.

Some will say the system is to blame but just saying the system is being too vague. Are we talking about the nurses who spend every day keeping us alive? Are we talking about the social workers who have miles and miles of cases to get through in a short period of time? Are we talking about the physios and occupational therapists that travel around the city dealing with complex issues whilst trying to complete the piles of admin on their desks? Oh, and they also argue in front of countless panels trying to get funding to help their patients become more independent. The thing is I do not accept that they are the system. They are employees that work for an organisation that is within the system but they are not to be blamed for the system being the way it is. These members of staff are our unsung heroes. They never get the credit they deserve but they get all of the abuse.

To understand why the current system is out of date and out of touch we need to talk about the spectrum. This is now turning into one of my school sessions! Back when I started talking in schools I knew absolutely nothing. I mean how I managed to get into the schools is still remarkable. I thought I knew everything but ha that soon changed when I spent the majority of the time reading from a piece of paper and I never gave the students eye contact. I did not think my life was enough so I tried to educate them on the different disabilities. I had a slide that categorised the different types of disabilities. I listed a handful of disabilities within each category praying that a hand didn't go up asking me to explain more about each one. Yeah, that slide no longer exists.

We love order, we love categorising people and objects. I remember once I saw a picture of a tin of tomato soup with the caption saying 'Labels are for food not people.' I agree with this statement and I have come to realise how reliant society is on labelling people. The issue with categorising people with disabilities is that each person with a disability is different. Take my friend, Jack, we both have Spina Bifida. So we should have the same challenges right?! No, there are three types of Spina Bifida. When I first met Jack I did not know he had Spina Bifida. He never used a day chair and it wasn't until 5 years later that I found out that he had Spina Bifida.

I saw Jack for a coffee a few weeks ago and we were discussing everything from work to basketball. We got onto the topic of health and It became clear despite having the same disability we both had completely different challenges. I was born with Hydrocephalus and he was not. I have scoliosis and he doesn't. His type of spina bifida is progressive whereas I have a type where it is at its worst already. I have used a wheelchair since I was four. His classification in basketball is higher than mine but that surely is a mistake BWB?! Jack is definitely a 0.5, he falls out of his chair all the time on the court. Get my point? No disability is the same and everyone has different abilities.

The system sees that you have scoliosis therefore you need x y z. I am living proof that using the x y z system does not work. The x y z system is a narrow-minded way of dealing with situations. This system is based on a few factors. The main factor is always down to funding and I know it will always be a factor. The chances are that most of the specialist seating if not all types of seating is going to be made in a different country. So, not only will there be material and labour costs, but you will also need to factor in shipping the piece of equipment overseas. For years the wheelchair service provided me with seating that unfortunately caused my spine to curve even more. Of course, they are not entirely responsible for this but because I had scoliosis they were adamant that this type of seating was the only way to support my back.

In the midst of all of this, I was also talking with my consultant about the possibility of having a metal rod in my back to help straighten my spine. This is a major operation that has massive risks as well as major rewards. Now, I have to be honest with you about the main reason I wanted the operation. It was not to make my breathing easier. It was not because it would make it easier to digest food. It was not because it would improve my seating position. I was because I was ashamed of the way I looked. I was ashamed of my body. I am going to do a whole chapter on my health but because I saw my spine the way it was it made me want to give up looking after myself. I stopped doing other things like cleaning my teeth, I didn't care if my hair was greasy, I didn't care if I didn't shave.

I didn't care about my personal care routine. I would have days when my blinds would be down all day and I would be staring at screens watching absolute crap on YouTube. My image became more important to me than anything else and because I could not fix my spine I didn't want to look after myself. The truth is I used my hydrocephalus as a great excuse to not look after myself properly. Yes, I was using the disability card. Just quickly before I carry on I have never spoken about any of this before to anyone. It is funny how I can be so open when I am writing and yet I can talk about this when I am having a conversation. Anyway, before my mind wanders onto a different path. According to a 2009 study published in the European Journal of Social Psychology., it takes 18 to 254 days for a person to form a new habit.

The study also concluded that, on average, it takes 66 days for a new behaviour to become automatic. While I would never want to question and disagree with the European Journal of Social Psychology, I would suggest that the main factor for anyone who wants to change their habits is to start with the question Why? Why do you want to change the habit? Is it peer pressure? Is it because you feel society is pressuring you? Or is it because you genuinely want to change? I can tell you from experience only the latter works. If you change because you feel it is the best thing to do to please others then you won't keep the routine. If you start comparing yourself to others and you try to be like them and act like them then you are going to fail. You cannot just copy a routine off the internet and expect it to work.

I don't want to sound like a life coach but it is all to do with your mindset. The most difficult part of the weekend away for me was that I felt some of the parents wanted their son or daughter to act a different way. They thought the weekend was an antidote for people with hydrocephalus and that after the weekend the child would be cured from having hydrocephalus. I saw adults older than me who felt ashamed and disempowered due to their parent's or carer's attitudes towards them. They seemed to have no hope or ambition because their parents had no hope for them. They were stuck and needed to have the cotton wool taken away.

They didn't have the ambition for change because their parents did not believe in them and encouraged them. It was heartbreaking to witness. This is where this gets interesting and I promise I am nearly finished with the chapter. I am not here to judge anyone and everyone has the right to parent their child in any way they think is best. I am not here to say what style is best, I am not a parent and I do not know what it is like to be a parent to a child with a disability. As a child, I would physically and verbally abuse my mum. As I write this I am trying to hold back from any tears because I am ashamed. My mum is the most caring, loving and gentle person you will meet. The sacrifices she made to look after me I will never understand. Like every parent and child, we had our arguments over really stupid things that neither of us can remember. One of my many flaws is that if I am angry and I mean very angry and can become aggressive and manipulative. If something got me angry I would get way out of control and I would go into this state where I would kind of lose my conscience. It would take a long time and I mean hours to get me to calm down. My actions towards my mum are unforgivable and there is nothing I can do to mend the past. The arguments would always be around routines. I was always late for the bus and would argue and argue with my mum until I got my own way and made her take me to where I needed to go.

I was controlling and aggressive and it always ended with my mum in tears and exhaustion. I made her feel worthless just so I could have my own way. It is strange reading this back and it feels like I am reading about another person. It feels like I am reading about someone else. I don't recognise this person and I don't really want to come to terms that the person I am describing is actually me. I am no longer like this and I hope those around me will agree with that. I have over the years worked with counsellors and mental health teams to control my anger and frustration. I used to go from zero to ten in 0.2 seconds. I sometimes still go from zero to ten in 0.2 seconds but it is very rare.

If I feel like I am not in control or feel like I am backed into a corner and do not feel like I am being listened to then I do get angry. I cannot just walk out and slam the door I use my words to try and gain authority. Why do people, men in particular, think that if they raise their voice or get aggressive then it makes them look more authoritarian? In reality it does the complete opposite and drives people away. I have learnt this the hard way. I have had members of my own family scared of me. They have been scared of saying anything just in case I get angry. Scared to the point that I have made the atmosphere hostile for the rest of the afternoon. Im better now I think? I have learnt how to control my anger and frustration.

Before I get too emotional and start bawling my eyes out, I have said a lot in this chapter. As you are probably aware this is the longest chapter so far but I feel this is one of the most important chapters. Before I end this chapter I want to talk briefly (I hope) about having a voice. As I have said I have in the past used my voice aggressively. I have used my voice to gain authority when feeling weak and small. This has never resolved any issues. The only thing that makes me reliable is using my voice wisely. In this chapter I have spoken at great length about the challenges I have faced. I have spoken about how I lied to people to get them to respect me and to look up to me. What I have realised is that it is okay to ask for help.

The one thing I struggle with to this day is asking for help or accepting help. In my head I see it as being weak when it is 100% not. It is okay to ask for help if you need help understanding the assignment. A note to pretty much every person with a disability if a random stranger asks you in the street if you need help because they see you struggling putting your wheelchair in the car or trying to push and carry your McDonalds at the same time. It is not them trying to interfere, they genuinely want to help. They do not see the disability before you. They do not see you as an invalid. They are genuinely wanting to help. Please stop taking it so personally because it is doing more damage than good. I have friends without disabilities come to me and ask how do they know when to offer and when not to.

The short answer is there is no way of knowing without asking. I encourage them to keep asking but in a way that is friendly and not patronising. The way we become more reliable is recognising where we struggle and finding ways to combat those struggles even if we need someone to give us a helping hand. I am reminded of a conversation I had with one of my close friends, Chris Young. Our first conversation on the phone was around the same time as the 2016 Paralympic Games. Channel 4 had just released the slogan and advert for the games.

Now, I am not going to go into the catastrophic organisation of the games, mainly because I said I wanted to keep this point brief. I am on my fourth paragraph since saying that. The reason I bring this conversation up is because my views on the Channel 4 advert was and still to this day is very cynical. The slogan was "We Are SuperHuman". The main reason I disagree with the slogans is that it patronises us. In a way it is using the disability card but using fancy and artistic shots to misdirect us. We are not superhuman because we have a disability. We are not superior over everyone else. We all have an equal voice. It is how we use it that makes a difference. How we relate to others is how we make a difference. When we open up and share about what we struggle with is when we make a difference.

What I have learnt over the past few months is that when I am able to ask for help and to keep my personal care routine in place then I can be there for my friends and family. I am the most reliable when I take my routines seriously and get the right support. I don't need it to be complex and I 100% do not need it to be 24/7. I need the support so that I can showcase my abilities and to be more employable. I don't want it to be a control plan where my voice is not heard. I don't want it to interfere with my life. Once the system see's us as humans and not case numbers we will see a greater inclusive society. We will not be seen as super human who deserves a medal for bravery. What we shouldn't do is open up about our struggles and look for sympathy. We need to stop using the disability card to get sympathy.

I've totally been there! It's like, I've caught myself doing this thing where I just keep talking about my problems, but then I realised it's not doing me any favours in the personal growth department. Instead of brainstorming ways to tackle these challenges, I've been stuck in the endless loop of talking about them. It's not just me, though – it's like a whole societal problem. We've sort of accepted that life dishes out these hurdles, and we're all like, "Okay, fine, we'll just deal with it," but somewhere along the way, we forgot to be proactive problem-solvers.

We need to flip the script and start figuring out how to conquer these challenges rather than just going along for the ride. It's time to roll up our sleeves and tackle those obstacles head-on.

End of chapter!

Well…let me just unpack that last bit for a second. As a society I feel like we have got used to big government that deals with everything. It is so easy to blame Westminster for everything. For a long time I also blamed Westminster for everything. I blamed them for not fixing the roads and pavements. I blamed them for the lack of accessible public transport. I blamed them for the lack of employment opportunities. Can you see a pattern? If something was not working in my life then it had to be the governments fault and not mine. We need to as a society stop accepting that life is the way it is and try to work out a way out without conflict. We need to come together with new ideas, we need to take responsibility for making the changes that need to be made.

We have forgotten our identity, we have become custom to the idea that we cannot take control of our own lives. We have become blind to our abilities. I am worried that we will forget who we are. We have become custom to conflict. Conflict with Westminster, conflict with our NHS, conflict with our police, conflict with society. What has this got to do with how being reliable? Our attitude to life determines how reliable we are.

If we are always in conflict with the world we will see people leaving our lives and not wanting to connect with us. I see this on a daily basis, parents shouting and swearing at NHS Staff which then puts the staff off wanting to help the patient. Our attitude to life is what makes us reliable. I just want to leave you with this, in the chapter about politics I quote a speech written by Aaron Sorkin for the TV series The Newsroom. I missed out the last part of the speech, mainly because of my OCD and wanting to fit the speech onto one page! The end of his long dialog where the main protagonist Will McAvoy is asked why is America great is how I am feeling about society at the moment. This is not to see society as doom and gloom but to show that things can change. We can change if we want, the question is how bad do we want to change?

We used to stand up for what was right; we fought for moral reasons. We passed laws, struck down laws for moral reasons, and we waged wars on poverty, not poor people. We sacrificed, we cared about our neighbours, and we put our money where our mouths were.

And we never beat our chest; we built great, big things, made ungodly technological advances, explored the universe, cured diseases, and cultivated the world's greatest artists and the world's greatest economy.

We reached for the stars, acted like men, and aspired to intelligence; we didn't belittle it. It didn't make us feel inferior, and we didn't identify ourselves solely by who we voted for in the last election. We didn't scare so easily. We were able to be all these things and do all these things because we were informed by great men, men who were revered.
The first step in solving any problem is recognising there is one. America is not the greatest country in the world anymore.

Amazing grace how sweet the sound
That saved a wretch like me
I once was lost, but now I'm found
Was blind but now I see

'Twas grace that taught my heart to fear
And grace my fears relieved
How precious did that grace appear
The hour I first believed

Through many dangers, toils, and snares
I have already come
This grace that brought me safe thus far
And grace will lead me home

The Lord has promised good to me,
His Word my hope secures;
He will my shield and portion be,
As long as life endures.

When we've been here ten thousand years
Bright, shining as the sun
We've no less days to sing God's praise
Than when we first begun

CHAPTER 21
Health Comes First

"Ah, Your Health is your wealth now don't you forget it" Mike Denver

The transition from adolescence to adulthood is a pivotal period in one's life. For most young individuals, this transition involves higher education, aspirations of employment, and the pursuit of independence. At the age of 16, I embarked on this journey, enrolling in a Computer B-TEc Level 3 program at Bath College. Little did I know that this endeavour, meant to set me up for employment, would be riddled with challenges and teach me profound lessons about the importance of self-care. This chapter is going to be different for many reasons. For anyone who knows me, I hate admitting when I am wrong. After realising my mistake and acknowledging that I've dug myself into a hole, I attempt to justify my previous statements by playing the opinion card, but I fail miserably.

As I said this chapter is going to be a bit different. I want to make sure that as I talk about this subject is that those in my life understand the lessons I have learnt along the way. There are a number of ways I could write this chapter and there are a number of different paths I could go down but I won't. Why? Because it would be too easy and I would not take any responsibility for my actions. Putting all the responsibility onto others is the cop-out version. There are always three versions of a story, my version, the other person's version and then the truth. The truth is probably a mixture of the first two versions put together with added detail. If I am completely honest with myself I am not happy with how I have looked after myself in the past. I don't like to talk about it and every time the topic of the past comes up all I want to do is curl up into a ball and hide. This is when I wish the invisibility cloak was actually real. A popular image is St. Peter standing outside "the pearly gates," deciding whether or not a particular person is to be allowed into heaven. If this is true I am dreading the long list of things I have done wrong in my life. The chapter that you have just read was the most difficult chapter to write.

It was that difficult that I had to stop and start writing this chapter. I wish Angie had told me how challenging this project would be! I needed to write the chapter to close that chapter in my life but nonetheless, it was a difficult chapter to write. When I had this strange idea to write a book I thought it would be easy, all I needed to do was point fingers at everyone and pass on the responsibility! When I wrote the first draft of this chapter I had not learnt the lessons that I needed to have learned. I thought I had but evidently not. I could go on another tangent about education and how the education system is in need of a complete change but I am conscious that would take us down a completely different path to the one we are currently on.

The path we are currently on is one with many potholes and uneven paving stones. The path we are on has dark, hidden steps that if you are not careful can trip you up. The skill is to try and navigate the different potholes and hidden steps without breaking a sweat. Once that path has been completed it is right and proper to look back at what has just been accomplished and take a deep sigh of relief. The penny will then drop when the clouds disappear and that leg of the journey that was just completed was in fact only 1%

of the entire journey. Right, so I now need to unpack that mysterious piece of writing. Reflection is always good, I don't think as a society we reflect enough. We are now so used to always being active and on the go that we don't take the time to stop, breathe and reflect.

Sunday in the Christian faith is the day of rest otherwise known as the Sabbath. Jews believe the Sabbath is the Saturday and that Sunday is the beginning of the new week. The Bible says God took the seventh day to rest. Rest is important, I have had friends take a year out to go travelling and explore the world before they start the next chapter of their lives. I think those who travel around the world exploring different cultures and traditions have a different view of life. I love hearing stories from friends who have travelled to Asia and hearing about the culture and the food they had whilst travelling. Just a side note is it just me or is British food so boring compared to other countries? It feels like countries like South Korea and the Philippines have more respect for the food they eat. Food is meant to be shared and eaten with friends and family. Why have we lost that tradition? We instead eat in front of the TV whilst scrolling on social media wondering why our food has got cold.

Anyway back to the main subject. In the grand narrative of my life, it was just three short years ago when I embarked on a path that would irrevocably change the course of my existence. At that time, I prioritised work above all else, willingly neglecting both my physical and mental well-being. It was a period marked by attending various events that catered to my interests, often overshadowing the fundamental needs that should have taken precedence. I even defied the warnings of health professionals, determined to stay off my wheelchair, driven by an unwavering desire to prove to society that I was not just capable of working but could also attain the highest levels of independence. This mindset, while admirable, came at a hefty cost, setting me on a journey of recovery that continues to this very day. In retrospect, it's clear that I allowed the perceptions of society to hold a stranglehold on my life.

I lived with a constant fear that others would label me as lazy if I dared to take a step back from my relentless dedication to employment. My sole mission in life was to validate my worth through work, an ambition that, in hindsight, blinded me to the vital stepping stones scattered along my path to success. These stepping stones, I now understand, should have been seen not as obstacles but as essential markers guiding me towards my ultimate destination. They should have been my companions, my allies, not something to be cast aside in pursuit of an elusive goal. Looking back, I see clearly the areas I should have been nurturing:

1. Cultivating Wellness: A Symphony of Self Care

A pivotal stepping stone that, in my fervent pursuit of ambitious goals, I regrettably overlooked, was the establishment of a steadfast and unwavering personal care routine. This routine, as I now comprehend with the clarity of hindsight, should have been the very cornerstone of my journey, the bedrock upon which I could build a resilient and thriving existence.

It ought to have been the unshakable foundation upon which I could ensure the perpetual well-being of both my physical and mental faculties. In the throes of my relentless ambitions, I unwittingly turned a blind eye to this fundamental aspect of self-preservation. Like an architect constructing a magnificent skyscraper, I was so engrossed in raising the towering edifice of my career that I failed to lay the groundwork, to fortify the structure with the essential elements that would ensure its enduring strength. A consistent personal care routine, I now realise, is akin to the vigilant caretaker of a prized garden, tending to the delicate blooms of physical health and nurturing the resilient roots of mental well-being. It is the ritual of self-care that rejuvenates the body and replenishes the spirit, creating a harmonious synergy between the corporeal and emotional facets of our existence.

Had I not bypassed this essential stepping stone, I might have reveled in a daily regimen that incorporated nutritious meals, invigorating exercise, and rejuvenating rest, all working in tandem to maintain my physical vitality. In the realm of mental well-being, I could have practiced mindfulness, embraced meditation, and sought out the solace of self-reflection, ensuring the equilibrium of my emotional state. In essence, this overlooked stepping stone would have acted as a sentinel, guarding against the erosion of my health and well-being that resulted from my single-minded dedication to professional success.

Instead of compromising my physical and mental fortitude, a consistent personal care routine would have fortified them, enabling me to not only achieve my ambitions but to do so with vitality, resilience, and a deep sense of equilibrium. The lesson learned, albeit belatedly, is that the pursuit of one's dreams need not come at the cost of personal well-being. Rather, it should be a harmonious journey where each step, including the establishment of a robust personal care routine, contributes to the fulfilment of one's aspirations. For it is in nurturing ourselves that we find the strength and stamina to surmount the obstacles that invariably lie along the path of our ambitions.

2. An Adequate Care Plan in Place:

Yet another pivotal stepping stone that remained elusive to me throughout my journey was the concept of a meticulously crafted care plan. This missing piece of the puzzle, I now recognise, could have been the compass guiding me through the labyrinth of my ambitions, offering the support and accountability I so fervently yearned for. Alas, it remained an uncharted territory in the landscape of my life, leaving me adrift in a vast void, where the absence of guidance and structure allowed my vulnerabilities to persist unchecked. A well-structured care plan, had I embraced it, would have been the guardian angel of my aspirations, a blueprint for ensuring my success while safeguarding my physical and mental well-being.

It would have been a comprehensive roadmap, meticulously tailored to my unique needs, addressing both the intricacies of my professional journey and the nuances of my personal growth. Within the comforting embrace of such a plan, I would have discovered a support system that extended beyond the boundaries of self-reliance. It would have been a network of resources, a safety net of guidance and assistance, designed to catch me when I stumbled, and to bolster me when my determination faltered. This support would not merely be a luxury but a necessity, for every ambitious endeavour is fraught with challenges, and it is through the collective wisdom of a well-structured care plan that one can navigate these obstacles with resilience.

Accountability, too, would have found its rightful place within the framework of this care plan. It would have been the guardian of my commitments, the mirror reflecting my progress, or lack thereof. Such accountability is not a burden but a beacon, illuminating the path towards self-improvement and professional growth. It is the gentle nudge reminding us of our obligations and encouraging us to stay true to our goals. However, the void in which I found myself was a stark contrast to this ideal. In the absence of a structured care plan, I was left to my own devices, adrift in the vast sea of ambition without a navigational tool to guide me. The vulnerabilities that lay dormant within me remained unchecked, festering beneath the surface, and occasionally rearing their heads to undermine my pursuits.

My journey became a tightrope walk without a safety net, a high-stakes gamble where the odds were stacked against me. It was a precarious balance between ambition and self-preservation, and all too often, the former overshadowed the latter. In hindsight, I am acutely aware of the opportunities that slipped through my fingers in the absence of a well-structured care plan. It was a lesson learned the hard way, but its significance cannot be overstated. It serves as a testament to the importance of seeking guidance, embracing accountability, and creating a support system that champions both personal well-being and professional achievement.

The absence of a care plan may have been a regrettable oversight, but it is a mistake from which I have gleaned invaluable wisdom. As I move forward on my journey, I do so with the understanding that success is not solely defined by the destination but by the manner in which we navigate the path. A well-structured care plan is not a crutch but a compass, and it is in its embrace that we find the strength to navigate life's challenges with grace and determination.

3. Active involvement in My Care Plan:

Perhaps one of the most vital stepping stones I missed was the realisation that I could be an active participant in my own care plan. I should have recognised my voice, my ability to have a say in my care, and the importance of being heard. This involvement would have empowered me to take ownership of my well-being and allowed me to tailor my care to my unique needs. When I moved into my current residence, a new flat that marked a fresh chapter in my life, I was faced with a stark reality. There was no care plan in place to guide me. No one took the responsibility of ensuring my well-being, and my vulnerable areas remained unattended. This circumstance forced me to step out of my comfort zone and actively engage in designing a care plan that aligned with my specific needs.

The absence of this stepping stone had left me in a state of profound unhealthiness, even though I had convinced myself that I was perfectly fine and capable of sustaining employment.In truth, my inability to maintain gainful employment stemmed directly from the deterioration of my physical and mental health. I had, for far too long, allowed these vital aspects of my life to wither away in the shadow of my relentless pursuit of professional success. If I could rewrite those pivotal years, there are several key changes I would make.

I would no longer view medical advice as a barrier but as a source of invaluable insights to be embraced and considered. Rather than shying away from the challenges posed by my physical and mental health, I would confront them directly, understanding that they were opportunities for personal growth. In the grand tapestry of existence, my journey from those pivotal formative years to the present day has unfurled as a narrative far from the ordinary. It is a chronicle of unmet needs, an absence of support, and an unwavering fixation on the pursuit of work. As I reflect upon this winding odyssey, I find that it has, with the wisdom of hindsight, unveiled profound lessons, each as valuable as the last. These lessons centre around the art of self-care and the unequivocal significance of recognising and embracing the subtle stepping stones that quietly guide us through life's labyrinthine paths.

In the annals of my life, the journey I embarked upon was anything but conventional. It was marked by a series of unmet needs, a relentless thirst for validation, and a relentless dedication to the world of work. Throughout these formative years, my journey was far from a walk in the park, more akin to an expedition through uncharted territory. It was a path laden with pitfalls and hidden caverns, devoid of the sturdy support beams that one often seeks in times of uncertainty.

The spotlight was invariably fixed on the pursuit of professional success, casting a shadow over the essentials of self-care that should have held precedence. However, as I trace the intricate lines of this narrative, I find that it is not merely a tale of trials and tribulations. It is a story enriched with the profound wisdom of hindsight, the kind that is only acquired through life's rugged experiences. These experiences have gifted me invaluable lessons, and at the heart of it all lies the paramount importance of self-care. The stepping stones that I once overlooked, scattered inconspicuously along my path, have since revealed their true significance. These modest markers, often camouflaged by the grandeur of my overarching goals, have proven to be the bedrock upon which my journey was built.

They have illuminated the importance of nurturing oneself, both physically and mentally, in the relentless pursuit of dreams. They are the guides that help us traverse the treacherous terrain of life with grace and resilience. By baring my own experiences to the world, I aim to kindle a spark within others, to inspire them to embark on their unique journeys with a heightened awareness of the profound importance of the journey itself. It is not solely the destination that defines us, but the moments and experiences woven into the fabric of the journey that truly sculpt our characters.

My hope is that, through sharing my story, I can illuminate the often unnoticed stepping stones that beckon to us in our own narratives. These stones may be unassuming, but they are the ones that pave the way to self-discovery and the attainment of true success. Success, in its most profound sense, is not measured solely by societal accolades or material gains; it is the culmination of a life well-lived, a journey that has been embraced, and a spirit that has been nurtured. As we stand at the crossroads of our own lives, may we be mindful of these stepping stones, these subtle beacons of wisdom.

May we heed their call and recognise that in nurturing ourselves, we nurture the very essence of our being. And in doing so, we find not just success but a deeper, more fulfilling journey towards self-discovery and the realisation of our true potential. The path may be unconventional, but it is uniquely ours, and it is in its twists and turns that we uncover the true essence of our existence. So the big question is what have I learnt from this? As I sit here contemplating what I have learnt I am reminded of a book that I read during 2020. I say read what I mean is flick through the beautiful illustrations whilst reading the quotes that went with each illustration. I loved the book so much that I got prints of the some of the illustrations commissioned so I could put them up around my flat.

Charlie Mackesy's beautifully illustrated book, "The Boy, the Mole, the Fox, and the Horse," has provided me with a profound source of solace and reflection during the recent months. Its pages carry a message that resonates deeply within me, emphasising the transformative power of asking for help. The book beautifully underscores that seeking assistance is far from a sign of weakness; in fact, it's quite the opposite. It reminds us that many individuals harbour the fear of judgment when considering asking for help.

We often expect ourselves to be capable of handling whatever life throws our way and perceive our vulnerability as a form of failure. This self-perception can be coloured by the belief that we are somehow less capable because things are not going as smoothly as we'd like. We assume that others will judge us in the same harsh light. Yet, the wisdom within these pages gently encourages us to reconsider this perspective. It reminds us that our self-doubt, our hesitancy to ask for help, is a reflection of our own judgment upon ourselves. In truth, most people we encounter genuinely want to help, and their intentions are rooted in empathy, not judgment.

Moreover, they are often more understanding than we give them credit for. What might surprise us is how many of these individuals have walked a similar path, facing comparable struggles and challenges. Understanding that asking for help is not a manifestation of failure but rather an act of courage and self-awareness can provide immense comfort and support when life presents its inevitable obstacles. "The Boy, the Mole, the Fox, and the Horse" is a testament to the fact that, even in our most vulnerable moments, there is strength to be found in reaching out for assistance.

It is a reminder that, through seeking help, we invite compassion, empathy, and understanding into our lives, ultimately helping us navigate the complexities of the human experience with greater resilience and grace. I'm writing this as a reminder to myself more than anything else. As I mentioned earlier, I often find it easier to offer advice to others than to take my own advice.

In my mind, I have this ideal vision of a perfect life: a meticulously crafted care plan, daily exercise, and a balanced diet. The reality of my life, however, is quite far from that idyllic picture. We live in a world where we're bombarded with messages about our bodies. Society and certain media outlets often promote a specific, idealised body shape as the standard of beauty. We are constantly exposed to these images and narratives, and it's easy to start believing in them. But the question we must ask ourselves is: why do we take everything we read in magazines or see on certain news websites as gospel truth?

It's essential to maintain a healthy level of skepticism, especially in today's digital age. One piece of advice I'd offer is to be cautious of the sources of information we rely on. If a website is inundated with a thousand pop-ups and advertisements, it's a clear sign that it might not be a reliable or credible source. It's important to differentiate between sensationalised and misleading content and the work of genuine, hardworking journalists who strive to deliver accurate news.

Putting these two categories in the same box is simply unfair. For instance, comparing such sensationalised websites to the reputable BBC is a disservice to the dedicated journalists who work tirelessly to provide us with well-researched and reliable information. This note is not only a reminder to myself but also a call to anyone who stumbles across it. Let's be more critical of the information we consume, especially when it comes to our own well-being. Let's be kinder to ourselves and not let unrealistic ideals overshadow the unique and beautiful lives we lead. Instead of chasing perfection, let's strive for balance and self-acceptance, recognising that life, with all its imperfections, is a beautiful journey worth cherishing. Can I suggest we become childlike? We need to regain our childlike thinking, our childlike curiosity, and our childlike imagination.

Can I suggest we need to regain that childlike faith, the faith in believing in each other no matter their ability? That childlike faith that believes in something far greater than humanity. That childlike faith that believes in someone that is invisible to the naked eye and yet is real in their heart and mind. Can I suggest we need to become childlike in our conversations and in our meetings? Instead of having narrow minded conversations where everything is discussed and yet nothing is accomplished, can we not start asking questions and exploring different options. Instead of trying to be the adult we think we should be can we not be childlike in asking for help without the anxiety of what others will think? Can we get to a stage when our pride will not become a barrier for us to evolve? Self pride is the root of all evil.

Pride stops you from realising your true identity. Pride is a mask, a mask that I unfortunately know all too well. I am still serving my sentence for the crime that I have committed. The punishment for Pride is one that I would hate anyone to go through. Now, can you be proud of what you have just painted? Absolutely! Can you be proud of scoring your first basket in a Wheelchair basketball match? Yes, unless you scored in your own basket then you should be ashamed of yourself. I am not proud of some of my actions, I am not proud of how I have treated those I love the most.

To quote my friend and poet Joshua Luke Smith "I'm Proud of all my friends". My friends have shown me that life with a disability is a life with ability. If you become too proud and do not accept help the cogs that keep everything running will start to move in the same direction and therefore will jam. Life will suddenly come to a halt and what you thought you had under control becomes out of control. My friends have shown me that when you're humble and willing then everyone is willing to partner and help out. Asking for help is not a sign of weakness but a sign of strength. You will achieve more with help than on your own. You are reliable no matter your weakness. You can be there for your friends no matter what you're currently going through.

You might not think you have the strength and sometimes you may not but even a text asking how they are doing helps. For a long time I thought I had to have a perfect life for me to be able to support others. I thought because I had a disability I was unable to be there for others. The truth is that everyone has the capability of helping others in their time of need. Everyone has the capability of lending a hand, maybe it will seem to be small to you but I guarantee it will be major for the person you have just helped. We have to leave our tribal, wealth and our strive to be popular. How does this all have to do with health? Good question and to be honest I may have gone down a completely different path that is miles away from the original destination of this chapter.

My pride, my longing to be popular, my eagerness to follow a crowd that was more tribal than I ever thought lead me to become increasingly unhealthy both physically and mentally. My closest friend says to me that I dig myself holes and can never seem to get out of them. Sometimes that is true. I sometimes have got myself in to situations that I have struggled to get out of on my own. I want to end this chapter with a last thought, for most of you this will be meaningless and strange. For most of you it might take a while for this to sink in. Our health is in our control. Our health is out of our control. We need to learn to look after ourselves so that when our health is out of our control we can emotionally process what is happening. I have been influenced to think, feel and act a certain way to prove I do not fit a certain community.

I have followed certain people so that I do not identify with certain communities. I was wrong to follow and become influenced by those people. I was wrong and now I am paying the price. The lesson I have learnt is that I need to look after spiritual and physical and my mental health in that order.

CHAPTER 22

I Messed Up Big Time

"As long as you've done your best, making mistakes doesn't matter. You and I are human; we will mess up. What counts is learning from your mistakes and getting back up when life has knocked you down."

— Shawn Johnson

How on earth are we meant to learn unless we have made mistakes? I feel like this is my confession, instead of saying it to a priest in church I'm writing it for all to see. I am not perfect I think that is already clear, I have made many mistakes and I have hurt too many friends and family and for that I am sorry. In this chapter, I want to tell you five stories of when I have messed up, Why? I want to show you that we are all human beings we all make mistakes we all hurt those who we love the most. When I do any talk or interview I always end by saying "We are all human, We all feel, We all make mistakes and we all participate in today's society."

It is easy to forget that we are all human and that we make mistakes and do the wrong things from time to time. No greater example of this is with those who we deem to be higher up the food chain than us peasants. It is easy to judge someone who is in the public eye. Now, I am not going to go political as I have already talked enough politics in this book but we also need to remember that even our politicians are allowed to make errors of judgement. It is how we deal with the situation that will define us not the mistake itself. Now, I mentioned to you that I have been guilty of many mistakes. Hang on no I can't call them mistakes. Mistakes are actions that you intentionally make. It was not my intention to hurt those close to me or put myself into debt with my actions.

Instead, I wanted to be there for my friends, to support them and to get their problems sorted. I was trying to be god. I was and to a degree, I still am unable to say no. The word "No" sounds negative and rude. It feels selfish and as if I don't care about the other person. In my head, it feels like I would be highlighting my limitations if I said no. The truth is it does not highlight limitations but heightens your ability to understand your strengths and weaknesses. How do you develop your ability to understand your strengths and weaknesses? By making mistakes and being ready to learn from them. We will then develop trust and become more reliable. I regret my actions, I regret the consequences that came with my actions. I truly feel remorse for the hurt I caused to those whom I love the most. I am sorry for the stress and anxiety it caused to my family. I regret the financial strain it caused to all those involved.

I regret how I handled certain situations. I am glad though that I experienced what I have. Why? It sounds odd I know but if I did not go through those situations I would not have learnt some very valuable lessons. I feel like we have taken our friends and family for granted and it isn't until they have gone that we realise how instrumental they were in our lives. I have learned this many times in my life. A friend once reminded me that I cannot control what happened yesterday.

I cannot control the future, but I can and I must control what I am doing right this second. If I worry about the past or the future then I am wasting all my energy on things I cannot do anything about. Instead of building relationships and making sure I am growing as a person and in my faith, I was and to a degree still am worrying about my actions from five or six years ago. It is no longer 2015, I am not Marty, I don't have a retrofitted DMC DeLorean vehicle with a flux capacitor. I am now stalling if you have not yet realised. When I was thinking about rewriting this book I started to work out what had shaped my views and my life. Our weaknesses should never be something to be ashamed of but something we should be proud of.

My dad has always told me when I mess up that the mess is not as significant as how I handle and clean up the mess. If you leave it until it has spiralled out of control, it is most likely to take longer to clear it all up. In every mess I've been in, I've swept it under the rug and left it there so nobody would find it. What are the consequences of that? People will start to not trust you, you will start to not trust yourself and your confidence and motivation to carry out the simplest of tasks will disappear. Your true identity will be overshadowed by guilt, self neglect and self judgement. The five stories I am going to tell are the reason I have guilt. The five stories I am going to tell are stories that I have hinted throughout the book but I have yet to talk in detail. Taking risks with my health and not putting my health first is probably the biggest mess I have been in and one that I am still unfortunately paying the consequences with.

Having a £15k debt is quite a big mess to be in at the age of 17. It is a moment of my life where it caused strain and great stress on not only me but my parents and those involved at the time. I have already talked about how when I have a project in my head that I sometimes get ahead of myself and do not lay the groundwork first to make sure that the end goal is achieved. As I was once told Rome was not built in a day. We have got into a stage in society that because information is so easily accessed via our phones that we expect everything to happen with the click of our fingers.

The truth is unfortunately not everything happens as quickly as we would like. We all have dreams about our future and if we are honest with ourselves we are very impatient and want to be living those dreams now. What has contributed to this false sense of hope? Well reread my chapter on social media and there is your answer! We have seen influencers such as Steven Bartlett and Gary Vaynerchuk who have built a strong and stable following on social media. They have understood what makes a brand succeed and to be honest I have not. They did not wake up one morning with millions of pounds in their bank accounts. They did not one day wake up and start speaking in front of billions of people on stage. They did not wake up one day with contacts with people like Simon Cowell and Peter Jones. They worked hard day in day out.

They had a vision but they also had five very key attributes that is almost always forgotten about. Those attributes are:

1) Building a foundation
2) Being a team player
3) Knowing your strengths
4) Knowing your weaknesses
5) Willing to say no when you don't feel ready

Having a dream is pretty easy if you allow yourself to dream. Forget for a second if money was not a barrier, if access was not a barrier what is your dream?

_____

_____

Now for me my dream was to be like Nick Vujicic, traveling the world and talking about my experiences as a disabled person. I saw him talking to millions of people. I saw him talking about hope and love in a society that has lost hope and love.

I saw him talking to Oprah Winfrey and presidents. I saw him travelling the world and I wanted to do the same. The problem for me was I was just a 17 year old boy living at home in the middle of nowhere in England. I did not have a social media following, I had not spoken in front of anyone let alone a stadium full of people. These people who are achieving their calling are not thinking about the next payment or how many followers they have. They understand that the big dream is achievable with the correct foundation. It is like building a house. You need the foundations to be correct otherwise the rest of the house will just crumble. So what was stopping me from creating those foundations? My big fat ego was in the way.

I wanted everything including the kitchen sink but I wanted to also take all of the credit. I wanted to prove that my ability counts and that my voice matters. The problem was that I was going about it all wrong. I was forgetting what Jen taught me at training. There is no I in Team. You do not get anywhere if you try and do everything. I feel like I am basically repeating myself here but nobody is completely independent and if they say they are that is completely untrue. I feel like this book is about three main topics; Identity, Independence and Society. At the age of 17 I didn't know my identity, I didn't understand about independence and my view on society was cynical. However, that did not matter I thought I was an expert in all three areas. The thing that separates me with the others is I was not willing to learn and I thought I had everything in place.

Education is important, experiences are the best education. Growing up I didn't really understand that just because I had Spina Bifida, Hydrocephalus and Scoliosis I was automatically going to be an expert in those conditions. I am still learning and experiencing new things when it comes to my disability. The biggest lesson I have learnt is how cynical I am towards others. It is all to do with anger that I have not dealt with. I was angry because I was not finding life easy. I was not where I wanted to be. I was seeing friends and family traveling across the world doing amazing things and there was me sat in my bedroom not doing anything. I did not have the same drive to try different options. I just wanted the ending where everything was perfect and I was earning a decent wage. I didn't understand that nobody starts at the end. There are steppingstones and there are always ups and downs. The main thing that separated me from the others is that I crumbled at every hurdle and gave up. I didn't pick myself up and learn from the mistakes.

I didn't pull the emergency cord to stop myself from going into debt. I didn't want to look like I failed. I was blind. Blind from the truth, my adrenaline was pumping and I was loving every second of it. I didn't share my dream and kept it to myself. Why? Because I didn't want people laughing and saying no. I didn't understand constructive criticism I just saw it as criticism. I saw any feedback as a red mark against my disability. I wanted to prove that I am capable despite my disability. I wanted to prove that the labels I was born with didn't bother me when they did. I wanted to be known as the champion for disability rights and looking back that makes me want to be sick. They say that too many chefs spoil the broth. There are enough people campaigning and speaking up for better access. This is not the time for pretexts but a time for conversation.

My biggest mistake was following the crowd. I joined multiple tribes trying to fit in but all it achieved was me becoming more angry and cynical. I joined tribes hoping my voice would be heard and there was no chance of that ever happening. When you enter the tribes I entered they build anger and desperation. These tribes scam you into thinking you will gain a voice and will be able to shape society. These tribes have one agenda and only one agenda. If you for some reason speak out and disagree with a policy within that tribe then you will be shamed and forgotten about. You will no longer be apart of the tribe and none of the other members will contact you ever again. They will distance themselves from you because you are the enemy. They will steal your identity and will try to force a new one onto you. I was young, dumb and careless.

I accepted the new identity and all my core values were thrown out of the window. I didn't understand what I had let myself in for. I didn't care because for a moment I felt like I was accepted. I didn't care if their views were the complete opposite to mine. I didn't care if my core values that I grew up on were buried because I felt accepted. I was accepted until 2020. Covid struck and reality kicked in. The tribe that I was meant to be against was having to make decision that nobody would want to make. The tribe I was meant to hate was trying to win a war and the enemy was invisible. The casualties were in the billions. Loved ones were killed and families were left to grieve on their own. The tribe I had been fighting against were making decisions I agreed with.

Maybe they were slow and making those decisions and maybe they were not always clear. They made mistakes and who knows if it was intentional mistakes or not. The tribe I was in didn't care about the challenges that the world faced. All they cared about was seeing the other tribe slip up and they were ready with the accusations. The tribe thrives when their enemy makes a mistake. The tribe will never ever accept when their enemy makes a good decision or will declare it as their own idea that was stolen.

The tribe I was in was not willing to accept that it was a cult. They were in their element when they were angry. They were in their element when they had been arrested for breaking the law. They were in their element when they were shouting at their enemy. It is not unless you are in the inner circle that you realise how dangerous the tribe is. The tribe was built on a foundation of great values but then started talking about identity crisis without facts. They didn't go down to the root of the identity crisis. They just made a lot of noise and fuss. My mistake in all of this was I was trying to share my views on a subject that was close to my heart and they brainwashed me to believe that the only way to change was to be angry and protest. That hole that I was trying to fill just got bigger and bigger. That feeling of excitement and the rush of adrenaline turned into stress and anxiety. All of a sudden reality caught up with me and I was in a lot of financial trouble.

The feeling that the truth was out and that I was no longer needed to hide anything was a massive weight off my shoulders. Just because the truth was out and I was talking to my Dad about the mess I was in did not mean I was out of the woods. I still needed to build bridges with people I hurt, I still needed to pay back my debt. I still needed to forgive myself. As I am writing this part of the chapter I am listening to one of my favourite worship songs at the moment by a band, We the Kingdom. The song is called Holy Water and it is a prayer asking for forgiveness and asking for gods grace. The part of the song that hits me the most is when they sing:

> I don't wanna abuse Your grace God,
> I need it every day
> It's the only thing that ever really
> Makes me wanna change

> Your forgiveness
> is like sweet, sweet honey
> On my lips
> Like the sound of a symphony
> To my ears
> Like Holy water on my skin

At that moment in time with the mess I was in there I felt like Adam after he ate the apple. I wanted to hide, I did not want to face the music. I was ashamed and rightly so. Just like Adam my hiding spot was useless and God found me again. I have found that when I am at my lowest moments he shows up the most. The problem is I am slow at realising that God is there, it is not until years later that I realise God was there for me and still is here for me. This brings me to my biggest mess, bigger than a £15k debt! For some this will seem minor or not even a mess. For me and for my faith this was the biggest mess. I lost my identity.

I forgot who I was. I allowed society to define me. I allowed peoples views define me. I allowed my appearance to define me. My confidence, my trust, my passions, my dreams were trampled on. I kept my views to myself so that I was not embarrassed if I was wrong. I stopped putting my hand up in class just in case I was wrong. I stopped asking questions just incase it was a stupid question. I kept apologising when there was no need. It is only now that I am starting to slowly building my confidence, my trust and my passions. It has only been in recent months that I have started to forgive myself and exploring who I am. Maybe if I ever write another book it will be about finding my true identity. I am so used to being Simeon, Disabled, Physically impaired and wheelchair bound that I could not see past that.

I wanted to share this chapter because I wanted to show that we are human, we all make mistakes, we all dig ourselves holes then wonder how on earth we are going to climb back out. Despite our flaws and weaknesses we all have strengths that allows us to participate in society. I could end this chapter in three ways, I could end by just listing the things I have learnt from my epic messes. I could write an apology to everyone I hurt or I could end by quoting my favourite movie scenes about getting control of life after a messy situation. Let's do all three! Being deadly serious, there are no words to describe how sorry I am for the stress, anger and anxiety I have caused to those I love the most. I am not going to name them but they know who they are. I am sorry for the lack of transparency and keeping the truth hidden away. I am sorry for the financial strain it caused and the sleepless nights.

Trust me I also have had sleepless nights because of the stress. I am sorry for the position I put you in and for breaking your trust. I am sorry for not being honest about the challenges I face. I am sorry for becoming unreliable when you relied on my most. I am sorry for not putting my health first and for causing stress and anxiety when I should have put my health first. I know that no words can fix the pain I have caused and that actions speak louder than words. I know I need to accept help and to allow others to help me.

I know that there is no such thing as being completely independent. I know I messed up big time. I am sorry for getting caught up with trying to make everyone happy when it is categorically not possible.

I have learnt my lessons maybe not as fast as you would like but I have. I understand the importance of over-promising and under-delivering. I am learning to ask for help and to say no if I am unable to achieve what is required. I am still stubborn and say no even when I need help but I am overcoming that. I know the importance of education and that it is okay not to know everything. I now know the my ego can get the better of me if I am not careful. I know I am still a long way to go before we can put everything behind us but I hope one day we can. I hope that one day we can build our friendships back to how it used to be before I messed up. I know trust was broken and that I need to fix that. I know that my communication isn't always the best and I am working on that.

I know I need to be more honest with myself because I can see if I am not then things can quickly snowball out of control. I call you my family and how I have treated you is not the way anyone should treat their family. I know things will take time to heal but one day in the near future I hope we will meet again and be friends once again. I am reminded of a scene in West Wing where Josh is required to see a Dr. Stanley Keyworth of the American Trauma Victims Association. When Josh goes back to the office he is greeted by the Chief of Staff Leo McGarry. Leo tells Josh the following story. It is a reminder that it is okay to ask for help. I can promise you that you're not the only one who has been stuck down the hole and there are people around you who know the way out. I promise asking for help is not being weak.

This guy's walking down the street when he falls in a hole. The walls are so steep he can't get out. A doctor passes by and the guy shouts up, 'Hey you. Can you help me out?' The doctor writes a prescription, throws it down in the hole and moves on.

Then a priest comes along and the guy shouts up, 'Father, I'm down in this hole can you help me out?' The priest writes out a prayer, throws it down in the hole and moves on.

Then a friend walks by, 'Hey, Joe, it's me can you help me out?' And the friend jumps in the hole. Our guy says, 'Are you stupid? Now we're both down here.' The friend says, 'Yeah, but I've been down here before and I know the way out.'

CHAPTER 23

The Comments

"You should get a horn on that!"

"Or people should look where they're going instead of glued to their phones."

"How long do you have to be in that?"

"There is not an expiry date on a disability."

"You're so brave!"

"Nah, mate, I am just catching a bus!"

"You must be a good driver!"

"I haven't passed my test yet, but thanks for the vote of confidence!"

"Are you in the Paralympics?"

"Just because I have a disability doesn't mean I instantly qualify for the Paralympics."

Isn't it funny what we say when we feel awkward? Isn't it funny what comes out of our mouth when we feel like we should say something but we don't know exactly what to say? Over the last 25 years I've had every single comment and question you can think of. The truth is these questions that I am being asked, they are harmless and if they were worded better it could be a great discussion into the world of disability. At the beginning of this chapter, I take the mock out of all these comments that I have had and I could just leave it, but I'm fascinated at the psychological aspect of why people have the tendency to ask or make comments when they don't need to. At the beginning of this book, I talked about the question why me. I talked about how children are not scared about asking questions.

There is no political correctness and I love it. What I love more is seeing adults try to ask questions but stumble with not knowing what terminology they should use. Adults seem so scared about offending that Stan, not knowing how to approach someone with a disability and they're not sure if they should. The truth is nobody knows how you should've approach the subjects I don't know how to approach subjects is going to approach the subject differently for me. I'm very honest and will always talk about my disability to help educate society.

I have become very good at reading peoples body language I can now tell if they are asking these questions in a genuine way of if they feel awkward and try to create small talk. Isn't small talk so awkward! Brits love to start conversations with small talk where people across the pond seem to want to go straight into the main conversation. Brits love to start any conversation with the following topics in this order:

1) The weather (especially in the winter)

2) The Traffic

3) The family

Sometimes they will add what they have watched on TV or Netflix but that is becoming more and more rare. People reading this in the UK will be laughing about how accurate this is. I am sat here by my computer on FaceTime with a close friend of mine who I have spoken enough of in this book! After calling Basketball training "A mental institution" they don't even deserve 0.2 seconds of my time. Anyway they're kindly helping me find quotes and funny awkward situations. She has visited me in my flat many times in the past few months. When she is sat outside in what I like to call my front garden, which is basically just an open space with a beautiful green area. Anyway while she waits for me to leave my flat a number of random strangers see her just sitting in her wheelchair listening to music and go up to her asking if she needs help.

Truth is she does need help if she thinks basketball training is a mental institution. In all seriousness why is it that we see someone who is physically impaired and instantly think we need help? If someone is just sitting there minding their own business why is there an urgent need to find out if they're needing help? I would understand it if she had fallen out of her chair or was struggling to control her wheelchair but even then people feel awkward and panic. They suddenly become disabled themselves. They suddenly lose the ability to talk. Their brain sees a problem and they act before thinking. Imagine you fall and a stranger comes up behind you and grabs hold of you without any warning or without saying a word. What would you do? Probably freak out and punch them.

I have lost count the amount of times random strangers have grabbed hold of my wheelchair thinking they're helping me. I truly appreciate the help, we all do but please ask us first before acting. I can see what is in front of me, I can see the potholes and the uneven surfaces. I can see when I need to do a wheelie. People who come up and start pushing cannot see those barriers. When I am pushing my chair I have control, I can stop myself from tipping out of my chair. I can balance myself. When someone comes up and starts pushing all of that goes out of the window. I lose balance, I lose control, I lose my safety net. I truly appreciate people trying to help and being kind. Im not wanting this to be a rant at all. I am trying to learn not to get angry if it happens. I am trying to still thank people because at the end of the day they have the best intension. A few years ago Scope Charity did a very clever campaign called HIDE. It was a campaign to end the awkwardness between "Able-Bodied" and "Disabled" people. It was a campaign that was perfect for the season we were in at the time. HIDE was an acronym for

Hello

Introduce Yourself

Don't Panic

End the Awkward

Over the years society has evolved and language has evolved for better or for worse. I am probably already in a lot of trouble with the woke community so why not dig an even bigger whole. I agree some words in society need to be as Piers Morgan would say "Canceled" but I do think we are getting too sensitive with our language. People are now so scared at what to say it is just easier for them not to say anything just incase it offends them. So let me be clear here right now just incase I have not been clear in my previous chapters. I am Simeon Isaac Wakely, I am 25 Years old. I am the youngest of 5 and I have 7 nephews and nieces. I use a wheelchair to get from A to B, I do not need 24/7 care. I do not have milk or sugar in my coffee. I love wheelchair baseball but that does not mean I want to be in the paralympics. "That thing" is called a wheelchair and it is not a curse word and I am proud to be using it. If I say I am in pain please don't mother me because I will just break your arm. If I cause you distress by sitting quietly at a table listening to music I am truly sorry. If you hear someone say something a bit rude look at my reaction before you act. Not everything is intended seriously.

The amount of people who get offended on behalf is quite funny. It does make me laugh when people are trying to ask genuine questions but then get shouted at by random strangers because they apparently said it in the wrong way. I am capable of deciding if something is offensive to me. I think we use the word offensive way too much. Comedians are being canceled because people are getting confused with being offended and not finding them funny. I am guilty of that, in fact I think we all are if we are being honest with ourselves. I like it when people recognise an issue with the pavement or road and then ask my opinion. How are things going to change unless we ask questions?

So I am going to do something a bit risky, I may be really stupid here but there is nobody here to stop me and once my family find out its too late as it is printed and published! I am going to give you my mobile number. It is not my personal number but it is a number that can text me on. Why am I doing this? To end the awkward. If I want people to ask questions and to learn then I need to be open to people asking questions. But I have two rules:

1) Remember HIDE, do not just ask the question.

2) Only text or what's app message me

So here is my actual number:

07396772094

Well either I am an idiot or just way too confident in society. I will only reply in working hours. I will try to respond the same day but if not it will be the next day. Okay just to give you a bit of behind the scenes into writing this book. It is now the next day and I am sat at my desk with a strong black coffee. I have opened the document to finish this chapter and hopefully the book. I thought last night that I had dreamt that I had written my number in the book and that I am about to wake up. Turns out it was not a dream and I have actually written my number in the book! The boys a fool! By the way if you have been trying to work out the references that I have been referring to then wait until the end and I will do a list of all the references. Some only people close to me will understand.

The whole point of this book was to rant, but it has become more than that for me. It has helped me articulate my thoughts and opinions that have shaped my outlook on life. There are four main groups of people within the disability community. Whenever I talk to students I explain about each group and get them to guess which group I am in right now. The answer might shock you. The first type is the group that is the group that takes everything so sensitively. They will take everything personally and will take offence at every comment. I have been in this group and I get why people are in this group. I did not want anyone to judge me because of my disability. I was against being called Disabled. They also hate being called disabled but unlike the first group they will use the terminology if needed.

They pretend that they are less sensitive to comments but they are just as sensitive. They will become comfortable within their own bubble and over the years their bubble will shrink and their social life vanishes into thin air. They will come up with reasons not to go out because to them it is too much effort. They become alone and will be comfortable being alone. They lose all hope and passion. They do not see their ability, they see the mess but they do not have the energy to change their circumstances. They have lost all hope in society, in the government and in life. They have gone past the point of caring and would rather stay at home than making a difference. The third group are the group I like to call the reactionists. These are the people that like to make a noise, they like to shout on the rooftops making their voice heard. These are the people that are not ashamed at being angry and are more than happy to show how angry and frustrated they are at society and the government. These are the people that know how to control the narrative and how to get the media's attention.

These are the people that will always see the glass half empty. They will only see one side of the story and that is it. They will always complain about the government even when they are empowering disability issues. If you disagree with this group on anything then you become their enemy. These three groups will make up around 50% of disabled people in the UK. I now want to talk about the fourth group. The group that wwantsant to make a difference. The group that just wants to fit in and not make a fuss. The group that just wants to work and socialise like everyone else. As long as the buildings are accessible they are willing to give anything a go. They don't care about politics and the negative press.

They have kept the passions at the front of their minds. I am honoured to have so many of them as friends. They have helped me and they have challenged me. Their disability is 1% of their life. The rest of their life is about work, family, friends, traveling and sport. They understand there is more to life. They look after their health so that they can carry on with their passions. They don't care about the social media comments and the looks they get in town. They don't care if they get asked a question from a random stranger. They embrace the challenges and will not allow the hurdles to shake them. I think if we are all honest with ourselves we can find ourselves in all four groups at some stage of our lives even if we don't want to admit it. I certainly do not want to admit it! I have been in all three groups. All the groups have pro's and con's. Some have bigger con's than others. For a long time especially at school I was in a mix of the first two groups. I kept myself to myself. I was not open to making news friends. I concentrated too much on the problems which led me to getting low and my social well-being went out of the window. I took everything personally and didn't understand the difference between a joke and a mean comment.

I was unable to differentiate between a joke and someone bullying. I just instantly thought they were bullying so played the victim card. I became the person I tried not to be. I became the person that was always complaining about society. I saw the glass half empty, I did not see hope. I came to the conclusion that the only way to see change was to become one of the angry members of society. Deep down I was comfortable with how I was living because I was safe in my bedroom where nothing was going to harm me. I was happy in front of my computer. When I did go out I was a completely different person. I was engaging and I became motivated. During the last two or so years of living with my parents I was going out less and less. This had nothing to do with Covid but just my motivation.

I would not open any blinds in my bedroom and I was happy just staying in my bedroom. I did not see the point of looking after myself. I relied on my parents for pretty much everything. I became comfortable yet I was not happy. Deep down I was not comfortable the way I was living but I did not have the motivation to change. In my mind there was no need to change. Those comments I wrote at the beginning I took personally and I am not sure why. Perhaps it was because I saw them as patronising. I now have a filter where I allow those comments to go into one ear and out the other. I have now taught myself to not get so sensitive about the tone of voice. I have allowed myself to embrace society. I just need that motivation to explore, to try new things.

I want to show I don't care about society's opinion of me. I want to get out of my comfort zone. I want my ability to count. I want to be seen as Simeon Wakely not as the disabled person. I don't want to be known as the guy who relies on people all of the time. I have friends who have told me to stop caring on what people think, not necessarily in those exact words but I want this to be a book without too much bad words. I know my parents will be reading this so I want to keep this book clean! How am I doing mum and dad? The truth is as I bring this chapter to a close the comments I get are less and less and that makes me sad. I want those people to come up to me and to have these conversations with me.

I want the comments to carry on because it ends the awkwardness. It shows that we are all apart of society. I have spoken a lot about society, let me be clear we are all part of society. I am partly responsible of how society sees people with disabilities. We all play a part in shaping society. We are all responsible for how the government runs this country. We are all responsible for our actions. It is how we treat each other that matters. It is how we love each other that matters. It is how we respect each other that matters. Am I asking that question because I care or because I feel I need to? Am I making this comment because I want to empower this person or belittle them?

I want us to have honest conversations. I want us to have conversations that are not leaving anybody behind. I want us to have conversations that don't leave us having to tread on eggshells. I don't want us to be panicking about how we act just incase it offends someone. We are not going to make everyone happy. We cannot become a cancel culture where it is just easier to stay indoors. I do not want this to get to the point where employers feel scared to employ people with disabilities because of the mental strain it will cause. I want us to be able to let our guard down and be ourselves. I want us to be able to act the way we want without getting judged. I want us to be able to go out with friends and not get sympathy comments. That world I speak of is now. The society I speak of is already here. We just need that push to go and explore.

Those comments you're scared of will not be as frequent as you may think. Those people that want to treat you like you're worthless are not as many as you might think. Those trips away are not as difficult as you might think. Those people that are out there to diminish your many abilities are not as loud as you expect. Some of us have become tired and bored of being seen as damaged goods. We need to stop seeing the world being against us. I know that is easier said than done. I still see the world from time to time against me. It is easier for me to talk than to act on what I am saying. I know the challenges that come with trying to fit into a system that seems to be against us.

What you need to understand is that those "things" that prevent you from going out, achieving your dreams are smaller than you think. The system wants you to think that it is safer to be indoors with a blanket watching deal or no deal with a hot cup of milky tea. The system wants you to believe that it is safer for you to be indoors by 6pm because it is too dark and cold. The system wants you to think that you are unreliable due to your imperfections. Those comments at the start are harmless compared to the other challenges we face. Those comments are funny and should not be taken seriously. Are we going to let those comments stop us from being us? I say no! I want to conclude with this story I was told recently.

I tell this story because I just want to highlight how ludicrous some people are. They are the minority not the majority. They do not represent the rest of society. A guy gets a parking ticket for parking in a disabled bay without a blue badge. He appealed it and went to court. He was asked to take the stand by the judge. He was asked why he was parked in a space that was dedicated to those with a blue badge. He was asked if he had a blue badge, he shook his head confidently saying "No, I do not have a blue badge." When asked again why he thought it was okay to park in a disabled space without a blue badge, his reply was "Welll, it was past 6pm". The judge looked confused and asked him to explain what he meant. "Well, disabled people don't come out after 6pm". True story!

CHAPTER 24

A letter

Dear Uncle James,

It's been 14 years since you left us. A lot has happened, and a lot has changed. I was in year 5 when we last saw each other. I came to visit you in the hospital with Mum. You were, of course, sitting in front of the television watching England prepare for the Rugby World Cup! I'm sorry to say we didn't win the cup after losing to South Africa in the finals. I would love to know what your thoughts are on our current team and coach! Remember when we raced to your living room? I had only just got my first wheelchair, bright yellow, and you were in your electric wheelchair, which I think gave you a slight advantage. You were the first person I saw in a wheelchair. You taught me that despite the label and all the issues that come with the label, I can do anything. It is a value I still hold today. I think you will agree we are never disabled, that society disables us, not the condition!

I spent three years at college and was able to spend time with your dear friend Maz. He had a lot of stories to tell! He told me stories and campaigns you created to raise awareness of disability issues. My favourite story is when you stuck posters on cars that were parked on the pavement or in disabled bays that had no blue badge! I love it! I want to say things have changed, but that would be a complete and utter lie! People are still using public accessible toilets without a disability, parking in disabled bays when they don't have a blue badge, and wheelie bins are still left in the middle of the pavement. I swear they just want me to show off my skills doing slaloms and seeing how many I will hit! Pavements don't all have dropped curbs; shops don't all have lifts or ramps.

And to top it all off, over 8,500 disabled people last year were attacked because of the label they carry! That's not including the cases that were not reported. I wish you could see me now; I'm living in a one-bedroom flat in the city centre and trying not to give myself food poisoning! My neighbours are amazing and are always there for me. The local cafe is a 30-second push, so it's easy to meet up with friends and family. A few years ago, I had the privilege of speaking at St. Greg's Catholic School. The teacher organising the event remembered you and shared fond memories of when you taught there. He gave me a frame with photos of you when you were teaching.

It is strange to be writing this letter, in my head I was thinking that this book would be 90,000 words max but I have somehow managed to exceed that target. Why could I not have done this with my course work and exams?! I would have loved to have spent more time with you and to try and get your guidance on what I should have expected as a wheelchair user. I don't know about you but I hate that term! I am still believing that we will see a more tolerant and peaceful society. I was too young to understand what it meant to be paralysed. I thought it was normal to be attending doctor's appointments every week. I thought it was normal to have no feeling in my legs. I wish you had warned me I was different to everyone else!

I wish we could have spent more time together, you seemed to have had so much strength and wisdom to draw on. As I look back at the memories we did make one thing that will always stay with me is your ability to keep your passions despite everything you went through. You never let the condition define you. In front of me on my desk is a photo of all of us for uncle Andrew's birthday. We had just spent the day on a narrow boat and the band that had been playing invited Peter to play the tambourine. He was in his element! He wouldn't even stop playing it when we tried to get a whole family photo. For a long time I wanted to be treated equally, but I have come to realise the longing to be treated equally is just a cover up. I don't want to be treated equally anymore, I don't agree with the way society is going with the topic of equality and diversity. I think you would agree that everyone is unique and has different strengths and weaknesses. Everyone has a different way of studying.

Everyone has a different way of working, some like to work from home while others thrive in an office environment. Some people are introverts and others are extroverts. Some enjoy stepping out of their comfort zone and others don't. I think you get my point! We need to recognise that we are all different rather than just a select few. Statistics show that the current education system is not fit for the 21st century. We are not allowing the next generation to be creative and to express themselves. We are bowing down to the tech giants and they are rapidly using AI to take our employment opportunities. For many years now people have said that we will get to the point where it is not necessary to work as AI will be able to perform the tasks at a faster rate.

I realise that this book is going to make me sound old fashioned and to be honest I probably am to some degree. In a few years I will be turning 30 and that is a scary thought but I am also excited about what is coming. I am excited at the opportunities that are out there fore people with disabilities. My worry is not that there is a lack of opportunity but a lack of motivation and a lack of ambition from some members of society. We have allowed ourselves to become tired and wary. We have allowed ourselves to take on the world's problems in a way that has made us fractured and divided and we are now physically and emotionally tired.

We have forgotten the basics of being human. We have allowed ourselves to forget our true identity. We have listened to the negativity and taken everything as gospel. We have allowed ourselves to become so sensitive in the way we act, in the way we view others. I say all of this while also being guilty of this. I have for the past decade allowed society to define me and to tell me what I can and can't achieve.

I have created my own bubble and have become comfortable and refuse to step out and to socialise and to try new things. I have used the disability card to get out of situations that are out of my comfort zone. Things need to change to save humanity, things can change and will change to save humanity. We are talking more about enemies than we used to. We are talking about conflict more than we used to. We have allowed ourselves to hate those who we disagree with. We have given ourselves permission to send hateful and sometime threatening messages to those who we have not even met. We can no longer be bothered to listen to other peoples view and to walk in others shoes. We have forgotten how to strive to be better.

We have forgotten to be live in the moment, to take a breath and to step out of our comfort zone. We have forgotten what our passions are because we are so tied up with life. I have friends who say to me I wish I could learn an instrument or learn a language. I have friends who say they wish they had time to read a book or study. When I ask them what is stopping them, they reply with one simple word "Time". We have become blind to the fact that everyone has the same amount of hours per day. We have convinced ourselves that we do not have a lot of time in the day to complete what we need to do. We have all used the disability card without realising. It has become second nature. I can't wake up early because I need my beauty sleep. We have become so impatient with services and we have become demanding that we have forgotten that things are not just going to happen when we snap our fingers. We want everything done yesterday and if we are told no it is not possible then the world is about to blow up.

We have become custom to the idea that everything is free. I am not going to start a debate about the people on the left…yeah I am! I would say I am more centrist in my views in politics. For the past few years we have had the far left leading the labour party. The party is no longer recognisable. Under Corbyn the party has become a protest, campaign party. The left has raised a number of key issues that need to be resolved but they have come up with solutions that are Disney answers. At the moment there is no credible centrist party. A party that showcases societies abilities. A party that encourages community. A party that funds youth centres and gives more powers to local governments. A party that encourages growth and investment. We need a party that is clear on policies and is not scared of admitting when they are wrong. We need a party that is not blind to the key issues.

Starmer may be the future this country wants. For all the partisan noise made on the margin we are a country of centrists. History proves that! When was the last time a far left Prime Minister was elected? The key issue that Starmer needs to overcome is that the Liberals in his party are going to force him left while the moderates are going sit on the fence for as long as possible. I think I have said quite enough about politics in this book. What happened to the days when we knew our local post office. That is what I miss the most of Timsbury. Everyone knew everyone. We had summer fairs with great music, great food and local charities were able to share what they do in the community. I miss going to the local cafe on a Saturday morning. It's not until it is gone that you realise how much you have taken it for granted. It is not until you have left that you realised how much you took the community for granted.

I love the area I live in now but there is no sense of community. I love my neighbours and I love how close I am to town. I love how wheelchair accessible the area is which as you know is a big deal! As you are aware Bath is a beautiful Georgian city, it has a history that excites film directors and producers. Bath is a safe city where nothing really happens, unless you live in Foxhill, Snowhill or Twerton. It is not until you move out of bath that you realise the beauty of the city. As you look over the city in Victoria park and see the landscape that goes on for miles. I forget sometimes how close I am to Victoria Park and how close I am to the most spectacular view of the city.

A city that is evolving and trying to keep up with the modern world. Im not sure if I am overselling Bath or not. Whilst this beautiful city is trying to modernise and keep up with the world it feels like the cogs in our brain jam when we explore accessibility and keeping Bath's heritage. Accessibility and beautiful architecture is like oil and water. However many times you try to combine the two elements they split in blink of an eye. The truth is we can keep the beautiful architecture whilst making it accessible for everyone. Bath is famous for many things, the location is perfect for any period drama. Students from all around the world travel here every year to study.

Every time a friend comes to Bath and asks what they should do I always recommend The Roman Baths. Before you passed away the Baths were nowhere near as accessible as they are now. Back in 2012 I was about to carry the olympic torch in Bitton. A few days before I was meant to carry the torch there was an evening celebration. It was a beautiful evening, I got to meet the other people carrying the torch. The evening should have been all about carrying the torch but for me it was all about access. It was about accessing a building that has a lot of history. A true icon for Bath. It is literally where it city gets its name from. I thought I would do some research into the city I call home while I write this chapter.

As soon as I started I was overcome with acute nostalgia from my days at primary school. At school we had four teams that competed. We competed each week to get house points. We competed every year for sports day. We had different coloured T-shirts depending want house we were in. We had a chant that I have been trying to remember. Each team was named after a famous person that lived in Bath, Ralph Allen, Richard Beau Nash, John Palmer and John Wood.

The education system has not evolved as fast as one might expect. We still have the basic core subjects that are taught in the exact same way. Students still read the same books at school and learn at least one if not two Shakespeare plays. I am not great at reading or writing which is ironic as I am writing this book. At school I struggled to read at the same pace and process the information. There are only two books that I studied that I still remember.

The first book "Of Mice and Men" is the classic American dream style book written by John Steinbeck. The second book is An Inspector Calls. Both books I presume you would have taught over and over again. I would have loved to have been in your English lessons. While I don't think the education system has changed I think the style students learn has changed and evolved. Tech has shaped and formed how students learn, revise and complete their homework. It is probably no secrete that most students copy and paste from Wikipedia and other websites. As a year 7 student I thought I could get away with it by changing the layout of the paragraphs. I'm not sure how many teachers I fooled doing so. I couldn't have been the only one?! Instead of reading books all you need to do is ask Siri or Alexa to get information. The tech that is being built means the brain does not need to retain any information.

I have just looked up the specs for a nonfiction book, apparently Non-fiction books are best between 100 to 250 pages. Im now on my 300th page. What is going on? Also they recommend a book like this should be around 20,000-60,000 word. I am now well over the 97,000 mark! What is going on? Why could I not do this at school? I have learnt of big lessons but I am sure I am yet to have bigger lessons to learn. Is it bad I do not recognise the society that I grew up in? The last generation to remember life before catch up TV. The last generation to remember the floppy disk. The last generation to remember life before smart phones. The idea that the phone is basically a mini computer would have been a crazy idea back in the early 2000's.

I wish you were still here so that I could pick up the phone and talk about everything that's going on at the moment. I know I should be looking after myself better. I know I could be doing a lot for my self. I wish you were still here to tell me to snap out of it. I wish you were here to remind me what it is I am fighting for. I wish you were here to show me that no matter what our disabilities are that we can achieve our goals. I wish you were still here so that we can share stories of our experiences. I wish you were still here to see me in my own flat. I wish you were still here to watch the rugby together. I wish you were still here putting posters onto peoples cars who are parking as if they're blind. I wish you were here so I could hear stories of when you were a teacher. I wish you were still here so that we could go to the pub and talk politics.

I don't know if I can ever live up to your reputation, I don't have the confidence to go round town with posters. That is still to this day my favourite story. Uncle James, thank you for showing me life is not about the disability but about our many abilities. Thank you for showing me that we can still have a smile on our faces and have a laugh. Thank you for showing me that we should never let go of our passions. Thank you for showing that we are all on a different path.

References

Before I talk about the references from the book let me end this whole book by saying thank you. Thank you to everyone in my life who has supported me through some of the most toughest times. Thank you to those who have put up with my messy life. Thank you to those who have inspired me, encouraged me and guided me. Thank you to my family for always putting up with me. Thank you to my family for your love and support. No words can describe how much you all mean to me. I would

Thank you to Angie for inspiring me all those years ago in our English lessons. We had a laugh Drawing cartoons on note books rather than listening to the teacher! Thank you for your encouragement and guidance. Thank you to Sue for always supporting me from day one of secondary school. Thank you for being there, for listening to me and for allowing me to share how I am feeling. Thank you Richard Handly, Paul Davis and Steve Paisley, for always being there for me and for encouraging me. Thank you for empowering me and for reminding me that we were all called here for a reason.

Thank you to Richard Horlock, without you I would not have made it through GCSE's. My fondest memory is when we went to IZB finals and you got to be there as I scored my first basket in the competition. I still have photos from that day. Thank you for not only cheering me on but also challenging me. Thank you for not seeing the wheelchair before you saw me. Thank you for respecting me as a person. It is because of your confidence in me that I am able to do what I love the most. I know you are now traveling the world coaching and playing futsal.

Thank you **Neil Oliver** for helping and guiding me through school. Thank you for allowing me to spend my lunch times in your classrooms. Thank you for including me in everything at school and always being there for me and supporting me through school.

Thank you for seeing me as a person first before my disability! Thank you for introducing me to YellowCard. Thank you for being there to listen to all my crap!

To Romans, thank you for just being you. Thank you for the great sessions. Thank you for pushing me without actually pushing me! Thank you for the laughs. Here is to next season where we will prove ourselves once more. Thank you to AJ and Jenny, you guys have put all of your time and energy into Nova and I know that you do not get the thanks and recognition you deserve! So from me thank you for everything you do! I know you will push me to be the best I can. I know I am a better person because of you and romans.

Jonathan Horsfall, words cannot describe how much your friendship means to me. Thank you for encouraging me to keep going. Thank you for your support through college. Thank you for believing in me! Thank you for encouraging me in my faith. Thank you for reminding me who I am. Thank you for reminding me that my disability is only 1% of my life. Thank you for reminding me that I have a heavenly father who does not see the disability. Thank you for including me!

Jules, I would not be living in my flat if it was not for you! I could do a very serious, heartfelt appreciation but we both know we will just end up laughing. We have a joke that we cannot be sat next to each other at a wedding or a funeral. We always misbehave! When my dad suggested that you supported me, we both burst out laughing. Being serious for one moment if I can, thank you for always going above and beyond. You have dedicated your life to supporting others and putting others first and I am truly grateful. We have had some laughs overt the years and I am sure there will be plenty more times! As our favourite comedian said The Boy's A Fool!

Which leads me on nicely to the point of this chapter, As promised here are all the references in the book. Some will be obvious but others are not clear until pointed out but even then unless you are a certain age or like certain comedy you might not get them!

The Boy's A Fool! - I am a massive fan of old comedy. My favourite comedy duo is Morecambe and Wise. If you live in the UK, you have provably heard of them, you may have seen a couple of their most famous sketches like the breakfast scene. One of Eric Morecambe's favourite lines is "The boy's a fool!". A very close friend of mine who's an even bigger fan says it every time I see him. We could be about to do some DIY around the flat and he will question me and finally finish by saying the famous catchphrase. "The Boy's a fool!" We end up laughing and talking about our favourite sketches.

BDU - Ever been in a tech shop to get a phone or computer fixed and the technician says to you "It is all fixed! It was the BDU"? Sounds technical doesn't it? BDU is not a microchip, It is not a computer virus. It is not a component of the computer. BDU stands for Brain Dead User. Basically the guy is calling you and idiot. The phone or computer was not broken you just have no clue on how to use it. You have just paid the company £100 for a 0.2 second job. Thanks Lyall for teaching me that!

0.2 Seconds - This reference will only make sense to one person. We can have the worst days and yet after talking to each other we can be laughing and everything is okay. We have joke between us where if we go from one place to another in a blink of an eye we say 0.2 seconds. We always get each other and can work out what the other person is thinking before they say a word. That is what true friendship is. When you can make someone smile by just being yourself that is true friendship. When you can be a listening ear, that is true friendship. Just for you I have ended on an even page, but I have ended on the 99,363rd word, Sorry!

Printed in Great Britain
by Amazon